P9-CKZ-934

SOME ASPECTS OF MODERN POETRY

WORKS BY
ALFRED NOYES

THE HIDDEN PLAYER
SOME ASPECTS OF MODERN POETRY

HODDER AND STOUGHTON LTD.
PUBLISHERS LONDON, E.C. 4

TALES OF THE MERMAID TAVERN
THE ELFIN ARTIST
THE FOREST OF WILD THYME
DRAKE
THE TORCH BEARERS
SONGS OF SHADOW-OF-A-LEAF
SELECTED VERSE
COLLECTED POEMS (14*th Impression*)

BLACKWOOD AND SONS

SOME ASPECTS OF MODERN POETRY

BY

ALFRED NOYES

enthusiastic - dogmatic - unreliable

HODDER AND STOUGHTON
LIMITED LONDON

First Edition Printed . . .	*September 1924*
Second Edition Printed . .	*December 1924*
Third Edition Printed . . .	*June 1925*

Made and Printed in Great Britain.
T. and A. CONSTABLE LTD., Printers, Edinburgh.

NOTE

Two of the essays in this volume are, in substance, addresses which were given to the Royal Institution. Those on Shelley, Wordsworth, Tennyson, and *Shakespeare and the Sea*, embody six Lowell lectures which were delivered in America. The last essay in the book was given to the Royal Society of Literature; and my acknowledgments are due to the Editors of the *Fortnightly Review*, *Contemporary Review*, and *Bookman*, for essays that appeared in those periodicals.

A. N.

THE LAST OF THE BOOKS

Is it too strange to think
  That, when all life at last from earth is gone,
And round the sun's pale blink
  Our desolate planet wheels its ice and stone,
Housed among storm-proof walls there yet may abide,
  Defying long the venoms of decay,
One still dark throng of books, dumb books of song
  And tenderest fancies born of youth and may;

A quiet remembering host,
  Out-living the poor dust that gave them birth,
Unvisited by even a wandering ghost,
  But treasuring still the music of our earth,
In little fading hieroglyphs that still bear,
  Through death and night, the legend of our spring,
And how the lilac scented the bright air
  When hearts throbbed warm, and lips could kiss and sing?

And, ere that record fail,
  Strange voyagers from a far-off world may come
On wingéd ships, that through the void can sail,
  And gently alight upon our ancient home;
Strange voices echo, and strange flares explore,
  Strange hands, with curious weapons, burst these bars,
Lift the brown volumes to the light once more,
  And bear their stranger secrets to the stars.

CONTENTS

ALICE MEYNELL

By those whose love of poetry claims them wholly—making demands on the intellect as well as on the heart, on their spiritual being as well as on the senses—it has long been recognized that Alice Meynell, with her hundred poems, is among the imperishable names. But her stature is not yet realized.

Others have written sparely. Others have been reticent—so reticent, sometimes, that they never expressed themselves to any real purpose. Others have refrained from publishing anything but their best, and their best was by no means equal to that of the superabundant poets, Browning or Wordsworth, or a dozen others of the first rank. Limitation has often been praised for its evasion of difficulties. But in Alice Meynell the restraint was not merely negative. It was sacrificial. Her silences were a part of her music.

> Oh, not more subtly silence strays
> Amongst the winds, between the voices,
> Mingling alike with pensive lays,
> And with the music that rejoices,
> Than thou art present in my days.

They were vital silences, to which life returned "in all the pauses of her breath," and they gave her music its form and its strength. They held "the ecstasy of prayers," and were not lightly to be broken. The result is that she has given to English literature now, and to the literature of the world in centuries to come, what no other poet has been able to give—

a volume of little more than a hundred pages containing only masterpieces.

Her instrument is not to be confounded with the slighter reeds of poetry, no matter with what delicate art these may be blown. She moves in the higher realms of the creative imagination, and her note is always that of great poetry. There is nothing with which her volume can be compared among the merely "frugal" poets. Nor has her austerity anything in common with that loosely sentimental negation, that easy reduction of the world to dust and ashes, which is too often confused with high thinking, and wildly praised for it, at the present day. In intellectual and spiritual stature she towers above the deniers of the hour; and to find a comparison for her, one has to imagine a Wordsworth who would give the world nothing but his best—the greatest of his sonnets and lyrical poems, "the flower of the mind." She has an intellectual kinship with that great poet that has hardly been recognized by the quick-witted, but far too hurried criticism of to-day. She herself has praised Wordsworth for busying himself "neither with imitation nor with revolt." He was the "natural heir of the language and the literature as it was in his own appointed day—the equal of the few very greatest masters." And when she calls his sonnets "great works," she is not using the word "great" in the common sense of the advertisements. There were more than two hundred "great" books announced in a recent issue of the *New York Times*. She was confirming the thought of a brief poem which begins:

> Nuns fret not at their narrow convent-room,

—a poem that might almost have been written by herself, in its restraint, its amplitude, and its demonstration that the narrow room may yet enfold the heaven of heavens.

—is the awakener of the mind and soul to the eternal Beauty.

With what an ethereal touch again it is suggested in that other landscape—*Spring on the Alban Hills*.

> With wild Spring meanings hill and plain together
> Grow pale, or just flush with a dust of flowers.
> Rome in the ages, dimmed with all her towers,
> Floats in the midst, a little cloud at tether.

Her eye for nature is as true as that of Tennyson or Wordsworth. In her poems one feels this through the truth of their atmosphere and their lucid accord with natural law rather than through any particularity of detail. But in the essays there are a thousand instances of the observation and insight which have made the poems possible. Her essay on the "tethered constellations," a marvellous picture of the stars reflected in deep water, is one of the incomparable masterpieces of English prose; and her *Rhythm of Life* shows us the whole universe obeying the "metrical rule of the interior heart." It contains some of the noblest sentences—with some of the profoundest philosophical implications—ever penned in our tongue. To ears rightly attuned it makes audible something of that universal music in which all men, with their tidal joys and sorrows, must play their part, "*knowing that they are ruled by the law that commands all things—a sun's revolution and the rhythmic pangs of maternity.*"

And this cosmic range of the intellect is implicit in the simplest of the poems. They outsoar the modern philosopher, even in the darker skies of to-day. They include his "evolutions" and carry his own thought up to the loftier kingdom of eternal light again :

> Thou art the way.
> Hadst Thou been nothing but the goal,
> I cannot say
> If Thou hadst ever met my soul.

I cannot see—
I, child of process—if there lies
An end for me,
Full of repose, full of replies.

I 'll not reproach
The way that goes, my feet that stir.
Access, approach,
Art Thou, time, way, and wayfarer!

Throughout her work she never fails to fulfil the highest function of the poet—to use the visible world, whether by *schema* or by symbol, as a means of shadowing forth the invisible. It is the power to do this, the power to seize the celestial meaning (this power alone, and not any of those lesser and sometimes base gifts which are so constantly mistaken for it to-day), that constitutes "genius."

Rossetti's tribute to her sonnet—*Renunciation*—has often been quoted; but it falls short of the truth, though it was not even her greatest poem. The three greatest sonnets ever written by a woman are *Renunciation*, *Thoughts in Separation*, and *The Neophyte*, and they are all by Alice Meynell. More than this, the last two are greater than the first, and ascend to heights that have been touched very rarely in the history of literature. The vast spiritual landscape of *Thoughts in Separation*, the love, the passion, the devotion, the grief, the two life-histories, the exquisite celestial vision, world-embracing and expressed with complete and effortless lucidity in fourteen lines, make it a poem without parallel in our language.

We never meet; yet we meet day by day
Upon those hills of life, dim and immense:
The good we love, and sleep—our innocence.
O hills of life, high hills! And higher than they,

Our guardian spirits meet at prayer and play.
Beyond pain, joy and hope and long suspense,
Above the summits of our souls, far hence
An angel meets an angel on the way.

Beyond all good I ever believed of thee,
Or thou of me, these always love and live.
And though I fail of thy ideal of me,

My angel falls not short. They greet each other.
Who knows, they may exchange the kiss we give,
Thou to thy crucifix, I to my mother.

In *The Neophyte*, as in several other poems of her youth, she saw her whole life in perspective; saw that the dedication of her youth then was the dedication of her age also. It transcends the illusion of time, seeing that the one vow was eternal, and that death could only seal it, for a warfare accomplished and a certain victory. No poem in any tongue has so completely foretold and symbolized its author's own life, or been so deliberately and serenely fulfilled in life and death.

Who knows what days I answer for to-day:
Giving the bud I give the flower. I bow
This yet unfaded and a fading brow;
Bending these knees and feeble knees, I pray.

Thoughts yet unripe in me I bend one way,
Give one repose to pain I know not now,
One check to joy that comes, I guess not how.
I dedicate my fields when Spring is grey.

Oh, rash! (I smile) to pledge my hidden wheat.
I fold to-day, at altars far apart
Hands trembling with what toils? In their retreat
I seal my love to be, my folded art.
I light the tapers at my head and feet,
And lay the crucifix on this silent heart.

These poems—though they are caught up into the universal voice of great poetry—are like no others. They have taken their own way to the heights and to the summits—comparisons are impossible in that region; but the judgments of literature are not arbitrary; and when it is affirmed that Alice Meynell is of the immortal company, the judgment is based on eternal realities. Her work belongs to the order of poetry in which Matthew Arnold said that, "as time goes on, our race will come to find an ever surer and surer stay." It is something utterly beyond the notorieties and fashions of this hour or this generation, when "greatness" is affirmed of every May-fly. There was a woman, a poet, thousands of years ago, of whose work only a few fragments remain, but they are enough to make her memory immortal, though she sang of an earthly passion only. We are touching here, with our living hands, the hardly less brief poems of another woman. Twenty-eight lines of these outsoar everything bequeathed to us by the earlier; and when other thousands of years have gone by, they may surely still be treasured, for they embody a divine passion.

In her own lifetime she was a tower of intellectual and spiritual strength, lifting through the mists of the age one of the very few steadfast lights; but there was another sign of her greatness that was quite unmistakable—her humility. That noble intellect, that incomparable artist, never once stooped to the pride that is so common to-day among lesser minds.

Those who were honoured with her friendship find it difficult to imagine the future without that sustaining power. The memory is not one that can fade; and, through her work, the living voice will still speak. But they will be forced, often, and hardly without tears, to wrest her own words from their sacred intention and turn them against herself:

Home, home from the horizon, far and clear,
    Hither the soft wings sweep.
Flocks of the memories of the day draw near
    The dovecote doors of sleep . . .

Oh, which are they that come through sweetest light,
    Of all these homing birds ;
Which with the straightest and the swiftest flight ?
    Your words to me, your words.

THE POET OF LIGHT

In the strange history of literature it is not exceptionally strange that the greatest artists and poets have often been praised for qualities in which they were conspicuously lacking, and that equally often they have been condemned for the lack of what was afterwards discovered to be their chief contribution to literature. The victims themselves have sometimes been responsible for a large part of the confusion. It was not altogether the fault of the academic authorities that the young poet who was sent down from Oxford for "atheism" should have concealed his wings and their celestial nature so successfully. But English criticism has concealed, or obscured, their nature from the larger world also for more than a hundred years. The twaddle about the atheism of Shelley has lost its meaning at the present day. But, unfortunately, it is now the custom to take it more or less for granted that Shelley is somehow detached from the world where things are believed or disbelieved; that he is a "poet's poet," an Ariel, greatly to be admired for the delicate quality of his moonshine. That is what even the praise of Shelley has meant, in most recent criticism, and it is partly due to the charm of a phrase in a usually faultless critic, Matthew Arnold. It has not been fully grasped that the legend of Shelley's atheism was a bewildered inversion of a very real fact. Shelley was guilty of something that might very well be called "atheism" by those strange persons who are able to subscribe to their creeds because they have no living belief in anything at all. He annunciated the most vital belief in God that had been held by any of the masters of our literature with the sole exception, perhaps, of Milton; and in that burning annunciation rites and forms "melted like snow." It was disturbing to the placid conventionalists to be confronted by a man who not only swept away their flimsy make-believe, but profoundly did believe in the reality of that Eternal Power to which he poured out his prophetic music:

> That Light whose smile kindles the Universe,
> That Beauty in which all things work and move.

And in their passionate vitality the lines are comparable only with some of the supreme passages in the Prophets or the Gospel of St. John. In one of his earliest poems Shelley wrote:

> Throughout this varied and eternal world
> Soul is the only element.

He was more burningly possessed by this belief than almost any poet in history; and because he found his "substance" in the soul, criticism has too often declared that his poetry lacked "substance."

If one considers, for a moment, some of the most representative criticisms of Shelley, two curious facts emerge. The first is that almost every critic has used adjectives that suggest "radiance," and no attempt has been made to discover the exact reason for this. The second is that nearly every critic suggests that this radiant poetry had something of the disembodied spirit about it. Carlyle combines both ideas in a characteristically lantern-jawed fashion by calling Shelley "a ghost." In almost all cases, these two ideas appear to convey a condemnation. Sometimes it is a mild condemnation, saying the best that can be said for a spirit so misguided as to be "radiant."

Sometimes it is exceedingly severe, and suggests that all efficient spirits have their feet solidly planted on the earth, are quite opaque, and would be better occupied in translating the classics than in writing odes to skylarks.

Nothing is more dangerous to literature than the growing habit, in our chaotic literary criticism, of suggesting praise or condemnation—according to the personal predilections of the critic—by a vague reference to a single characteristic, which remains unexamined in all its relations; or by question-begging assumptions presented without any evidence whatsoever; or even by the twist given to a single word or phrase chosen at random from the author in question. A very beautiful book of poems was once dismissed by the contemptuous ejaculation of the single word, "fairies!" And the critic seemed to be unaware that, whether the book deserved it or not, the grounds of the dismissal were utterly wrong and would have permitted him to dismiss *A Midsummer Night's Dream* with equal speed. This, of course, is an extreme case; but, in slightly more elaborate form, it is the most common method of pronouncing judgment on literature at the present day. "Keats, with his perpetual nightingale," is the tone; and it destroys. Swinburne can be dismissed by the ejaculation of "great sea-mother!" or "forsaken gardens!" or the mocking use of these phrases in a paragraph. A bilious critic, with a grudge against things in general, can muddy half the wells in English literature by this method. Only too often it imposes on a careless and hasty public, and delays true criticism (which is, in the strictest sense, appreciation) for a decade.

Carlyle, whose judgment was too often at the mercy of his health, cannot be held guiltless in this matter. There have been far too many "temperamental" divagations from the truth in modern criticism since Carlyle mistook scorpions for meat. Shelley, he said, was always mistaking spasmodic violence for strength. "It is like the writing of a ghost, uttering infinite wail into the night, unable to help itself or any one else." Great writer as Carlyle, at his best, undoubtedly is, it may fairly be replied that he has uttered nothing so memorable, nothing that will visit the minds of men so often with healing in its wings, as the passage in *Adonais* beginning

> That Light whose smile kindles the Universe,
> That Beauty in which all things work and move.

It has the passionate serenity of one who has attained to the Light itself; a Light which Carlyle was always struggling to reach, but never even saw clearly.

Moreover, there is nothing more fruitful of critical error, nothing that confuses values more disastrously, than the statement or implication of general truths in a personal judgment on a particular case. It is perfectly true that spasmodic violence is often mistaken for strength. Carlyle made that mistake very often; and, as most men impute their own characteristics to others (another common source of critical error), he imputes his own mistake to Shelley, and imputes also his own personal habit of uttering infinite wail into the night. That is simply Carlyle, not Shelley. Shelley was sometimes too violent for strength, and in those cases he is to be condemned; but the condemnation must not be extended to his most characteristic work. Delicacy, ecstasy, light, and colour (not violence and infinite wail into the gloom) are everywhere the prevailing characteristics of this poet when he is most himself. If the *Ode to the Skylark*, the happiest poem in literature, be set by the side of Carlyle's criticism, it is obvious that the real personality of Shelley shines through the poem, while Carlyle has merely been drawing his own gloomy portrait and criticizing it.

Matthew Arnold, too, with his "beautiful ineffectual angel beating in the void his luminous wings in vain," is imputing more than a little of his own "hovering between two worlds, one dead, the other powerless to be born." But his criticism at least recognizes the glory of the wings. Lowell, echoing Arnold's criticism, said that Shelley's genius was "an ineffectual fire, beating about the luminous points of his thought." It is one of the most curious echoes in literature, from a critic of so fine a quality. Tennyson said that, for him, Shelley was "too much in the clouds," a perfectly just phrase, proceeding from that more scientific vision of the universe which set the later poet nearer to Goethe than to the author of *Epipsychidion.* Browning, in his youth, hailed Shelley as the "Sun-treader." Francis Thompson sees him "as a child making bright mischief with the moon," and in many other radiant disguises. Mr. George Moore speaks of his "crystalline poetry"; of the "dazzling stanzas of the 'Sensitive Plant'"; of his "atheism" (Mr. Moore still clings to that!); and of his craft, "fashioned of mother o' pearl, with starlight at the helm and moonbeams for sails."

Almost every criticism, in short, that has been made of Shelley plays similarly with the idea of light, and flutters in a confused moth-like way around it without knowing or attempting to discover why. For Carlyle it is merely a phantasmal phosphorescence, but for the others there are luminous wings, points of fire, clouds, and a foot upon the sun. And in Browning's phrase—"Sun-treader"—there is more insight into the nature of Shelley's poetry than in all the other criticism put together. Most of the adverse criticism of Shelley seems to take it for granted that the light around which it plays is a vain illusion, and would like to say with Jonson's criticaster:

> Light, I salute thee, but with wounded nerves,
> Wishing the golden splendour pitchy darkness.

Browning, almost alone, in the virile and conquering phrase, "Sun-treader," reveals the poet, in his greatest work, with the universe under his feet.

> Sun-treader, I believe in God and truth.

One of the most elementary laws of sound criticism is that we must discover, before we begin to praise or blame, exactly what the artist is consciously or unconsciously trying to do. We must not criticize a landscape adversely because it is not a portrait; or a romantic novel because it is not a realistic description of a slum; or an ode on a nightingale because it is not an indictment of modern society. If this elementary rule had been observed in the past, some of our greatest artists in literature might have enriched the world with even finer work than we sometimes allowed them to bequeath to us; and some of the lines that Shelley wrote on the death of Keats might have been unnecessary. "Luminous wings" and "ineffectual angel" are pretty phrases, and they concentrate attention on the delightful manner of their maker; but they give us not the slightest indication of the meaning of all this devotion to effects of light and air. They merely suggest that Shelley's interest in them was in itself a fault. In the same way one finds modern critics expatiating on the very characteristics which differentiate a new writer as if, in themselves, they must necessarily be faults. This man uses long lines. This other uses short lines. This man loves colour. This other loves the music of language. This man writes harshly and with difficulty. This other appears to write easily. Every one of these statements could be made, and has been made, the basis of condemnation and praise, with a complete evasion of the real task of criticism. In the case of Shelley, part of this task was certainly to discover the significance of his preoccupation with effects of light, not merely to borrow them for our own picture of his "ineffectual wings."

Criticism is continually forgetting that poetry is an art, and that poets are to be judged as artists. It has been well said that light, with its infinite variety of tints and shades, is the most spiritual element of nature. Shelley—whether he theorized about it or not—was an artist, using effects of light for symbolical and spiritual purposes. On this side of his poetry he anticipated Turner in painting. He is the supreme poet of light. Nobody else has ever obtained comparable effects; and most certainly it has not been recognized by criticism that there is hardly a single poem of Shelley in which he does not give some new effect of light and shadow that has never before been translated into words.

> Wrap thy form in a mantle grey,
> Star-inwrought!
> Blind with thine hair the eyes of day.

It is quite beside the point to talk about wings beating in the void when we are considering work of this kind and quality. One might as well describe Turner, after a glimpse of his "Rain, Steam, and Speed," as a beautiful ineffectual mechanism, whirling through a mist his luminous wheels in vain! The beauty created by the artist is not ineffectual, and it completely justifies the artist's own intention. There is no lovelier twilight in all literature than is breathed upon the page in that line from the poem to the Night:

> Blind with thine hair the eyes of day.

The first four words of it, dimmed with the most exquisite of all shadows, and the last four glowing with the softest and most beautiful light in all nature, the light of the eye—it is a perfect picture of the mingling of night and day.

And, in that hour when the Spirit of Night had answered the prayer of the poet; when the cruder lights that blind us had vanished, with all the discords and dusty tumults of the day; when the granite mass of things had dissolved into the music of the one pure element—the boon that he craved was granted to him; but it was transfigured, and he expressed it in terms of a light beyond our world:

> The golden gates of sleep unbar
> Where Strength and Beauty met together
> Kindle their image like a star
> In a sea of glassy weather.

Swinburne owed much to Shelley, but when he tried to reproduce effects of this kind he failed. It was obviously the line

> Blind with thine hair the eyes of day

that suggested the later poet's more elaborate picture of the "scornful day" as he represses

> Night's void and vain caresses
> And from her cloudier tresses
> Unwinds the gold of his.

But the touch is heavier here, and the quality of the work cruder and harder. The depths of the shadow, the softness of the light, the trembling and exquisite life have vanished. There were some things that Swinburne could do better than any one, but this was not one of them. The sea with its tidal pulses was his own kingdom, but in the realms of light Shelley reigned supreme. Both Byron and

Swinburne found in the sea an image of the Eternal; and this, in the case of Swinburne especially, lent a peculiar significance, a peculiar emotional depth, to the rendering of any of its momentary aspects—a flight of spray, a distant sail like a blown white flower, a foam-bow on a breaking wave, or that exquisite farewell to his slightest book of poems:

> Fly, white butterflies, out to sea.

In exactly the same way, but with more subtlety, Shelley uses the light; and everywhere, because it is for him an image of "that Light whose smile kindles the universe," his slightest picture of any of its momentary aspects has a peculiar significance.

> It seemed as if the hour were one
> Sent from beyond the skies,
> Which scattered from above the sun
> A light of Paradise.

And again and again through that spiritual element his poetry achieves the consummate miracle, rises to those heights of vision from which the poets have seen, as clearly as Thomas à Kempis, "all things in one."

> When the night is left behind
> In the deep east, dim and blind,
> And the blue noon is over us,
> And the multitudinous
> Billows murmur at our feet
> Where the earth and ocean meet,
> And all things seem only one
> In the universal sun.

The light of common day merges into that larger light and derives its beauty and mystery from it. He describes this process in his poetry again and again. The description of the poet in *Prometheus Unbound* is a typical instance:

He will watch from dawn to gloom
The lake-reflected sun illume
The yellow bees in the ivy-bloom,
Nor heed, nor see what things they be;
But from these create he can
Forms more real than living man,
Nurslings of immortality!

When he speaks of forms "more real" it is not good criticism to ignore this affirmation, and to take it for granted that there is no reality at all in his realms of light. If there be none, then there is certainly none in Plato and none in the loftiest of modern philosophers. It would be legitimate for criticism to take his affirmation and disprove it. It is not legitimate to ignore his point of view and merely affirm the opposite as Arnold, Lowell, and Carlyle did.

It must be remembered that Shelley wrote as an artist, and that he arrives at his visionary heights by the way of the artist and poet. When he gives us a phrase like "the tempestuous loveliness of terror," it must be remembered that he is giving us a picture, an impression, of streaming shadows and flying lights, and that it is through these and their subtle relations that he represents to himself the larger significances of the world and expresses his thought. Many poets, again, have written of the flowers by the grave of Keats. Shelley wrote—touching them with a new significance—of their "light." Just as elsewhere he speaks of "the gleam of the living grass," he shows you the "light" before he tells you the cause of it.

A light of laughing flowers along the grass is spread.

It is his way of merging the many into the one significant glory, and resolving their gentle whispers into

That Light whose smile kindles the Universe.

Newton, with his prism, had added a new wonder to the light of common day. Earlier poets, like Thomson, had dwelt upon these. It was left for Shelley to seize upon the new imagery that Newton had provided, and by its means to give the world a subtler spiritual vision.

> The One remains, the many change and pass;
> Heaven's light for ever shines, Earth's shadows fly.
> Life, like a dome of many-coloured glass,
> Stains the white radiance of Eternity,
> Until Death tramples it to fragments.

It was the task of Shelley to show how that Eternal Light "interpenetrated the granite mass" of things like an ethereal sea; and he used his terrestrial lights and shadows to "represent much in little." His work throughout has the strange beauty, the colour and atmosphere, the dusky lights and lucid shadows of an enchanted kingdom under the sea. But there is nothing vague or lawless in this treatment of the physical world. Indeed, he often writes like a prophet who had foreseen the way in which science herself would one day dissolve the material universe into the stuff of dreams, till its atoms, electrons, centres of force and whirling fairy gulfs of (perhaps we shall discover eventually) intellectual energy outmiracled the miracles.

> Nothing of it that doth fade,
> But doth suffer a sea-change
> Into something rich and strange.

It was in just this flowing aspect of the physical universe, in its changes, harmonious as music, and subtle as the light of thought, that Shelley found his inspiration; and it is partly this fact that has brought upon him the charge of "beating in the void." Few criticisms have been more blind. He delivers us from the lifeless desert of the materialists with their stagnant airs and static hills, and gives us the vital universe, with the movement and the sea-changes, the before and after, that only poetry, of all the arts, can render.

> The fountains mingle with the river,
> And the river with the ocean.

He delights in the beauty of this universal rhythm of ebb and flow, the music of the world. He discovers its analogies with the spiritual realm and with the kingdom of love; and he expresses it, over and over again, through the subtlest natural imagery that he could find, in terms of light and shadow.

In his very simplest mode—in that exquisite poem, *The Cloud*, for instance—he seems to delight in painting the world on its physical side as a pageant of luminous dream-stuff; but the clarity of his vision prevents him from losing himself (as even Prospero perhaps did) in thin air. His vision is the vision of Ariel—"nothing of it that doth fade,"—and the vision of Ariel is the vision of modern science. Shelley is as instinctively true to law in his poem of *The Cloud* as any modern man of science could be in full possession of the doctrine of the conservation of energy.

> I am the daughter of Earth and Water,
> And the nursling of the sky;
> I pass through the pores of the ocean and shores;
> I change, but I cannot die.
> For after the rain, when with never a stain
> The pavilion of heaven is bare,
> And the winds and sunbeams with their convex gleams
> Build up the blue dome of air,
> I silently laugh at my own cenotaph,
> And out of the caverns of rain,
> Like a child from the womb, like a ghost from the tomb,
> I arise and unbuild it again.

One cannot help wondering that this passage did not suggest to Matthew Arnold an angel with more comprehension of the universal processes than was possessed by his flutterer in the void. Shelley loved clouds, not for their vagueness, but because they were luminous parts of the universe. They obeyed all its laws, but they were quicker to respond, to kindle, to dissolve and form again. They were illustrations in little of just that aspect of the world which he burned, like the buried lamp in the lover's island, to make others see.

If his treatment of the garden in *The Sensitive Plant* be compared with Shakespeare's treatment of the bank of wild thyme in *A Midsummer Night's Dream*, it is clear that Shakespeare, like all other poets before Shelley, was interested in the opaque flowers of ordinary vision as living creatures, distinct forms, beautiful details. Shelley had this interest too, but he loved them primarily for the glory that they transfused. They were transparent lamps, burning with an inner flame, little centres at which the Light " whose smile kindles the universe " became visible ; and—as a poet, as an artist—he treated them, unconsciously, with an astonishing modernity, unlike anything else in the preceding poetry of the world. He seemed, instinctively, by sheer force of genius, to have arrived in a flash at the goal towards which our most advanced modern painters are still painfully groping through a maze of inadequate theories. The flowers in that Earthly Paradise did not live or die only to themselves :

> For each one was interpenetrated
> With the light and the odour its neighbour shed. . . .

It is the perfect reconciliation in art of the One and the many, rendered chiefly in terms of light.

The plumed insects swift and free,
Like golden boats on a sunny sea,
Laden with light and odour, which pass
Over the gleam of the living grass;

The unseen clouds of the dew, which lie
Like fire in the flowers till the sun rides high,
Then wander like spirits among the spheres,
Each cloud faint with the fragrance it bears;

The quivering vapours of dim noontide
Which like a sea o'er the warm earth glide,
In which every sound, and odour, and beam
Move as reeds in a single stream;

Each and all like ministering angels were,
For the Sensitive Plant sweet joy to bear,
While the lagging hours of the day went by
Like windless clouds o'er a tender sky.

But there is no confusion in this flood of light. The consummate harmony does not rob the separate notes of their character and individuality. They are perfected in its own perfection, and are made most completely themselves in its own completion.

There was a Power in this sweet place,
An Eve in this Eden; a ruling Grace
Which to the flowers, did they waken or dream,
Was as God is to the starry scheme.

It is the glory of the same absolute light that burns along and between the lines of *Epipsychidion*. If it be taken as a love-poem in the ordinary sense, the luminous wings of the poet may well seem to be beating in the void. But it is not this. Fundamentally, it deals with precisely the same subject-matter as *Adonais*. Indeed, in the later poem Shelley deliberately repeats many of the splendour-winged metaphors of the earlier. *Epipsychidion* is nothing more or less than a pæan to that Light "whose smile kindles the universe." The earthly part of it is but the framework of the lamp through which that Light shines ; and it is not at the celestial flame that the Muse has burnt her wings.

This was the master-light of all his seeing ; and it was this that made all the world glow and burn for him. Criticism of the kind that talked vaguely of his " luminous wings " was itself lost in the " void." It had never read Shelley carefully enough to grasp the extraordinary facts that had suggested those vague phrases to their unconscious authors ; the fact—to begin with—that there is hardly a page in Shelley which does not deal directly with the phenomena of light. There are scores of pages in which almost every line, sometimes almost every phrase, is concerned with effects of light. In the crowning passages, which give a meaning to the whole, these effects are used, sometimes unconsciously, as in a musical improvisation, sometimes with a Platonic clarity of intellectual vision, to shadow forth that Eternal Light,

> That Beauty in which all things work and move.

This quite definite preoccupation with effects of light, a peculiarity of method quite unlike anything else in English poetry, would have been very definitely noted if it had been properly observed. It has not been noted at all. It has merely suggested to hasty and sleepy critics—in a world where there are many other books to be read—a vague general effect of radiance, and a sort of sub-conscious transference of this vague luminosity to their own adjectives. In some respects these critics remind one of the deaf old gentleman in *Punch* who with his back turned to a loudly trumpeting motor-car declares loudly that his hearing has improved, for he can distinctly hear a bumble-bee. Their failure is not without its practical bearing on the textual criticism of Shelley; for I do not think that Palgrave would have suggested the emendation of "sea-girt" for "sun-girt city" in the lines on the Euganean hills if he had realized the kind of effect at which Shelley almost invariably aimed. Incidentally, it may be remarked that Lowell's echo of Arnold's famous sentence is more subtly paralleled by the fact that Arnold's own sentence is an unconscious echo of phrases used by Shelley himself in the preface and the last lines of *Prometheus Unbound*: "If his attempt be *ineffectual* . . . down the 'void' abysm. . . . Love folds his 'wings.' . . ." Mix these extracts from the beginning and end of the uncaught song with a suggestion of luminosity flashed back from the paper knife, and it needs neither a literary detective nor a Freud to reconstruct the one serious critical error of Matthew Arnold.

There is a great deal of inferior work in Shelley, more perhaps than in almost any other poet of his rank. A great deal of *The Revolt of Islam* is bungling, crude verse, devoid of any distinction. It has been lavishly praised, of course. Critics as eminent as Dr. Richard Garnett have affirmed that "the *Faerie Queen* alone of English poems rivals it in the music of its stanza, while Shelley's poem has the advantage in sublimity." The plain fact of the matter is that Shelley at that time could not handle the stanza at all. *The Revolt* cannot be compared for a moment, technically, with the best passages in Byron's *Childe Harold*. The stanzas on the Roman Gladiator alone in the latter poem (for those who will not let themselves be blinded by familiarity) are worth more than all the cloudy fumbling doggerel of the twelve cantos of *The Revolt of Islam*. Only the most conventional depreciator of Byron could seriously, after examination, dispute this. But Shelley was a far greater poet than Byron; and he was greater by virtue of the very qualities upon which Arnold and his echo, and many others, have based their condemnation.

It is not only that they failed to note the peculiar nature of Shelley's preoccupation with effects of light. They have nowhere even commented on the fact that again and again, where other poets would have described, for instance, a stream flowing through caves, Shelley would give you a picture of the same thing stated primarily in terms of light, and would show you "stream-illumined caves," suggesting (though only for a flash) the interpenetration of the granite mass of things by the divine light of Beauty. He sees the rainbow-skirted showers; the dawn reddening the dew of the green fields; and the long blue meteors cleansing the dull night. Where other poets would have described a fruit or named a flower, he sees blooms that "star the winds with points of coloured light" and "bright golden globes of fruit suspended in their own green heaven." He sees Venice, not as other poets have seen her, but with the sun rising behind her "like thought-winged Liberty," and the city transformed before that chasm of light

> As within a furnace bright,
> Column, tower and dome and spire
> Shine like obelisks of fire.

They point from the altar of the dark ocean to the sapphire sky, quivering like sacrificial flames. He shows you a mist like an air-dissolved star; and it is the air-dissolved star, not the mist, that interests him primarily; for all these radiances are hints of a greater radiance—

> Be it love, light, harmony,
> Odour, or the soul of all
> Which from heaven like dew doth fall,
> Or the mind which feeds this verse,
> Peopling the low universe.

Then, at last, he comes upon a windless and crystalline pool, reflecting the image of a temple, a habitation for his divine idea in its completeness. At once his imagination kindles. His lips are touched with fire from an altar beyond our world, and he speaks of

> Praxitelean shapes, whose marble smiles
> Fill the hushed air with everlasting love.

They are smiles of Light, as in *Adonais*. Criticism has missed the continuity of this imagery and of the idea behind it in the work of Shelley. It has overlooked them very largely because our criticism has seldom been an artistic criticism, looking at the work from the side of the poet himself. Shelley is the very type of the poet described in his own poem on the skylark as being "hidden in the light of thought." Criticism has never fully realized that for the poet—as for the painter—there are harmonies of form and colour which, though they are not "thoughts," are yet suffused with the "light of thought." They may tell us no "story," deliver no "message," embody no "moral," and yet be related to, and merge into, the universal harmony. There are many pages in the early work of Shelley where he fails and collapses into something like verbiage. There are many others which have a real value and might be mistaken for verbiage by a reader who is not prepared to enjoy harmonies of colour and light almost entirely for their own sake, or as the artist enjoys purely decorative patterns and rhythms, because he feels that they are related to, and merge into, the larger rhythms of the universe and of art; their lesser harmonies having a subtle analogy with the immortal harmonies of absolute Beauty. For, in his use of light, Shelley often seems to be pre-occupied with its most immediate effects—the reflection of a wet leaf, an inverted pine-tree in a rain-pool, a glow-worm in a dell of dew ; a mist sucked up by the sun ; or a splendid fragment of celestial pageantry like this from *Prometheus Unbound*:

> The point of one white star is quivering still
> Deep in the orange light of widening morn
> Beyond the purple mountains. Through a chasm
> Of wind-divided mist the darker lake
> Reflects it. Now it wanes. It gleams again
> As the waves fade, and as the burning threads
> Of woven cloud unravel in pale air.
> 'Tis lost ! And through yon peaks of cloud-like snow
> The roseate sunlight quivers. Hear I not
> The Æolian music of her sea-green plumes
> Winnowing the crimson dawn ?

But passages of this kind have their place in his poetic scheme ; and when once the reader has accepted the all-pervading thought of that supreme Light " whose smile kindles the universe," these passages become, if not a " criticism of life," at least a beautiful representation in little of that divine process. The Witch of Atlas, that " lovely lady garmented in light," is a sister of the veiled glory of *Epipsychidion*.

If they show the world to be such stuff as dreams are made on, they do it through their truth to natural law, and help the poet in certain august and sacramental moments to withdraw that cloudy veil of dream-stuff and show

> the thought
> Which pierces this dim universe like light.

In *Hellas* Shelley develops the great speech of Prospero to a surer and a nobler conclusion. Shelley, the " ineffectual angel," takes Prospero by the hand, leads him away from the gulfs of " thin air " into which he had well-nigh fallen, and sets his feet upon the rock. " Into thin air," said the elder magician (I will not say Shakespeare, for he contradicts it elsewhere), but Shelley deliberately answers him with a continuation of Shakespeare's own music, repeating some of his very phrases :—

> Talk no more
> Of thee and me, the future and the past ;
> But look on that which cannot change—the One,
> The unborn and the undying. . . .
> Space, and the isles of life or light that gem
> The sapphire floods of interstellar air,
> This firmament pavilioned upon chaos,
> With all its cressets of immortal fire,
> Whose outwall, bastioned impregnably
> Against the escape of boldest thoughts, repels them
> As Calpe the Atlantic clouds—this whole
> Of suns and worlds and men and beasts and flowers . . .
> Is but a vision. All that it inherits
> Are motes of a sick eye, bubbles and dreams.
> Thought is its cradle and its grave ; nor less
> The future and the past are idle shadows
> Of thought's eternal flight. They have no being:
> Nought is but that which feels itself to be.

By the power of that thought, in one short lyric—his *Ode to Heaven*—he was able to present, with absolute truth to law, a lightning vision of the cosmos that for vastness and sublimity of conception has no parallel in philosophy or poetry. It is a poem that for some strange reason, possibly because it was far ahead of its time in its realization of the infinitudes that surround us, has never taken the high place to which it is entitled among the works of Shelley. The abysmal spaces, the centuries of light-years in which modern astronomy has attempted to think, dwindle to nothingness before that triumphant presentation of the whole cosmos in a single image as lucid and perfect as a drop of dew, the smallest orb of light that he could find. Equally triumphant is the suggestion in the same poem of the indescribable and unfathomable mysteries that lie behind and beyond the cosmos. He flashes these upon us by the hint of that unimagined world of leaves of which the flower that holds the tiny gleaming sphere of dew is but an infinitesimal part.

> Palace roof of cloudless nights !
> Paradise of golden lights !
>   Deep, immeasurable, vast,
> Which art now, and which wert then !
>   Of the present and the past,
> Of the eternal where and when,
>   Presence-chamber, temple, home,
>   Ever-canopying dome
>   Of acts and ages yet to come. . . .
>
> Glorious shapes have life in thee,
> Earth and all earth's company ;
>   Living globes which ever throng
> Thy deep chasms and wildernesses ;
>   And green worlds that glide along ;
> And swift stars with flashing tresses ;
>   And icy moons most cold and bright,
>   And mighty suns beyond the night,
>   Atoms of intensest light. . . .
>
> What is heaven ? a globe of dew
> Filling in the morning new
>   Some eyed flower, whose young leaves waken
> On an unimagined world :
>   Constellated suns unshaken,
> Orbits measureless, are furled
>   In that frail and fading sphere,
>   With ten millions gathered there
>   To tremble, gleam, and disappear.

The wings that mounted into that supernal region were not "ineffectual," nor were they beating in the "void." Here, indeed, Shelley was the "Sun-treader" of Browning's youthful worship, and his eyes were fixed upon that Eternal Spirit which sustains and kindles the whole creation. These great moments of his upward flight were his moments not of weakness but of power. It is precisely these moments that give the value to his poetry, and it is nothing less than amazing that criticism, even of the friendliest, should so commonly suggest the opposite, and should deplore the glorious ascent more frequently than it laments the sinking back to earth. In those loftiest moments he comes nearer than any poet but two or three in history to a demonstration of his own divine right to say with his own god of light:

> I am the eye with which the universe
> Beholds itself and knows itself divine.

And this was the poet whom our best criticism believed to be lacking in a sound subject-matter. In the very moments when his ineffectual wings were supposed to be beating vainly in the void, he had drawn nearer than almost any other poet in history to the one enduring Reality, and his lips were touched with prophetic fire.

> The massy earth and sphered skies are riven!
> I am borne darkly, fearfully, afar:
> Whilst burning through the inmost veil of heaven,
> The soul of Adonais, like a star,
> Beacons from the abode where the Eternal are.

In those moments the meaning of his love of light becomes clear; and we know why his poem on the skylark is—more than a third of it—a hymn to light.

> Like a poet hidden
> In the light of thought,
> Singing hymns unbidden
> Till the world is wrought
> To sympathy with hopes and fears it heeded not.

He soars heavenward as the bird soars in its joy, and pours out his hymn to that supreme Light upon which a greater poet even than Shelley turned eyes that could no longer see the lesser lights that rule our night and day. Yet Milton, too, praised these, in his own pure song, as children of the greater Light and sharing its divine glory.

> Hail, holy Light, offspring of heaven first-born,
> Or of the Eternal, co-eternal beam,
> May I express thee unblamed, since God is light,
> And never but in unapproachéd light
> Dwelt from Eternity ; dwelt then in thee.

Never was there a poet for whom more clearly than for Shelley the material universe was the flowing garment of God, illumined by the glory within. There are passages of many pages in *Prometheus Unbound* where almost every phrase is directly or indirectly radiant with that divine thought. The sun is heaven-reflecting. The very bubbles which the enchantment of the sun sucks from the water-flowers of clear lakes make him think of pavilions in which spirits may dwell and float under a green and golden atmosphere, kindled by the celestial noon as it strikes through the woven leaves of the forest of our own mortal life. " How glorious art thou, Earth," cries Asia.

> And if thou be
> The shadow of some spirit lovelier still,
> Though evil stain its work, and it should be
> Like its creation, weak yet beautiful,
> I could fall down and worship that and thee. . . .
> Dim twilight lawns and stream-illumined caves,
> And wind-enchanted shapes of wandering mist ;
> And far on high the keen sky-cleaving mountains
> From icy spires of sun-like radiance fling
> The dawn, as lifted Ocean's dazzling spray
> Spangles the wind with lamp-like water-drops.

The very spray burns with an inner flame. Prometheus in turn addresses Asia herself as the " light of life, shadow of beauty unbeheld"; and to those who would still demand a clearer "goal," a more substantial air for the winnowing of those luminous wings, a more precise meaning in his harmonies of light, one can only echo the words of his own spirits when Ione and Panthea saw their "sustaining wings of skiey grain, orange and azure deepening into gold." Their soft smiles lit the air like a star's fire, and to the questioning of Panthea they replied:

Hast thou beheld the form of Love?

If ever there lived a poet with a real task to accomplish in this world, that poet was Shelley; and his task was rebellion. It had nothing in common with the cheap and easy rebellions of to-day; the pinch-beck rebellions of the sophisticated against the children of light; the cynical rebellions of the world and the flesh and the devil against all the loyalties of the spirit of man and the highest glories of his art and literature. It had nothing in common with that false kind of rebellion which has become "smart" and "fashionable" and is patronized by the reactionary Press, in the sacred name of Liberty, so that the real conflict may be obscured, and the true rebels be choked in the dark. His rebellion was against this very way of the world which in the general shifting of terms has come to be called "rebellion." His rebellion was *against* the fashion, not in favour of it. His task was to interpenetrate the granite mass of things with a spiritual glory, and to reveal that Eternal Beauty which underlies them, shapes them, sustains them, and enkindles them like clouds. He saw this Light behind the dark veil of the world more clearly than even Wordsworth saw it, "a Spirit that impels all thinking things, all objects of all thought."

It is to this Power, this living Godhead, that he cries in the *Ode to the West Wind*. He makes that wild terrestrial breath a symbol of the hidden and infinite spiritual Power that moves through earth and sky and sea and his own soul. The material universe becomes transparent as it moves. The Atlantic's level powers are cloven, and the nations are shaken with premonitions of revolution and re-birth. The Spirit is upon the face of the waters; and, as of old, the creative word is "let there be light."

To be the herald of that Spirit is not to be an "ineffectual" angel, even though the message be too mighty for the bearer. Those poets are fortunate in their generation for whom a darker and less penetrable veil is drawn between their eyes and the Light upon which none can look and live. It was not because his Muse was "moth-like" that she was able to soar above the world. The Light into which those wings mounted was absolute. Shelley failed in his terrestrial life. He was bewildered, confused, self-contradictory in all his terrestrial wanderings, because he was unable to adjust his absolute vision to the world that lay nearest to him. We may thoroughly agree with Matthew Arnold's judgment of the "set" that surrounded Shelley, and with his condemnation of Shelley himself for several foolish actions. But it must be said that some of these actions—the famous letter to Harriet Westbrook, for instance, inviting her to follow himself and Mary Godwin abroad—were so utterly abnormal, so utterly blind and obtuse to every sound instinct of human nature, that, in the case of a man who was certainly abnormally sensitive, they inevitably suggest a failure in adjustment. If his genius had matured, he might have mastered more completely the laws of his own being. It is enough to say here that he died comparatively young, and that when he returned to earth from some of those journeys into the realms of light his eyes were not adjusted to its rough ways and his footing was not sure. But it is the stumbling upon the earth, not the glorious ascent of the wings, that should be described as "ineffectual." In an hour when faith had frozen into creeds he made his choice between the difficult and the easy road, and chose not the broad descent of the destroyer and pessimist, but the arduous ascent into regions from which he caught the first gleams of a diviner day. In the unremitting struggle between the prophets and the priests, Shelley threw in his lot with the prophets. In the unremitting battle between the dreamers who believe that there is nothing behind the universe and the affirmers who believe that there is everything behind the universe, he was with those who affirm. In the conflict between those who believe in the fundamental axiom of both science and religion that the greater cannot proceed from the less and those unknowers who would reduce even the love that they *have* known to dust and ashes, he was with those who believe. In the long warfare between those for whom "chance" was the origin of this ordered and governed universe and those who believe in God, Shelley had the most burning religious faith that had been annunciated by any poet since Milton. In essence it was that of the later Mazzini, and it has been stated in one sentence: "God, in-dwelling, just and good: Duty that prompts to endless effort, rewarded by endless progress, while the soul mounts through ascending existences to an inconceivable oneness with the Divine."

This, I think, is the answer to the doubt expressed in Francis Thompson's essay on Shelley. That beautiful piece of prose, written from the point of view of a great historical religion, throws more light perhaps on its author than upon Shelley. It is not Shelley to whom the universe is a box of toys. It is not Shelley that is "gold-dusty with tumbling amidst the stars." These phrases are especially appropriate to the imagery of Francis Thompson. Shelley, as I said in dealing with his *Cloud*, was singularly alive to the laws and processes of the universe, and he rendered them with the precision of a scientific Ariel. Francis Thompson speaks of " Shelley's inexpressibly sad exposition of Pantheistic immortality " :

> He is a portion of that loveliness
> Which once he made more lovely,

and he adds, " What deepest depth of agony is it that finds consolation in this immortality ; an immortality which thrusts you into death, the maw of Nature, that your dissolved elements may circulate through her veins ? . . . Why, through the thin partition of this consolation Pantheism can hear the groans of its neighbour, Pessimism."

But this, surely, is not only to misunderstand the " pantheism " of Shelley. It is to misunderstand, also, the most exalted philosophy of the writer's own religion ; and the misunderstanding is due to the impossibility of attaining by reason alone to those heights of vision from which the poet—in rare moments—is caught up into the " glory of the sum of things." Francis Thompson missed, in his prose, the likeness between Shelley's glorious vision of

> That Light whose smile kindles the Universe,
> That Beauty in which all things work and move,

and that earlier vision of the God " in whom we live and move and have our being." In that divine philosophy, the peace that passeth all understanding is not a silence or a sleep. It is a perfected harmony, embracing, completing every individual note, and making it more, not less, itself. The sounds and odours and beams in the Garden of the Sensitive Plant were not mingled and confused by their interpenetration. Their essential forms were not blurred. They became sharper and more definite in their communion. They moved "like reeds in a single stream," in the consummate music of the One and the many. It was not a degradation of the individual, but an apotheosis.

Confusions and contradictions in any attempt to formulate this musical philosophy there must be, since for its perfect statement every note in the universal scale must be accounted for. We can touch only scattered points here and there, as Browning touched them in the song of the little silk-weaver—"The lark 's on the wing, the snail 's on the thorn, God 's in His heaven!" The missing clauses in that piece of reasoning—for it is a piece of lightning-logic, overleaping vast gaps—are simply all the other facts in the world. It is only the fire of poetry that can overleap these yawning chasms. But—it arrives, and it can return to verify, by the inner experience of the individual soul.

The faith of the author of *Hellas* was logically elaborated in prose, and confirmed in action by the Saviour of Italy. "We believe that God called us, by creating us; and the call of God can neither be impotent nor false. Grace, as we understand it, is the tendency or faculty given to us all gradually to incarnate the Ideal. It is the law of progress, which is His ineffaceable baptism upon our souls."

It should be axiomatic that all philosophies, as they approximate to truth, must approximate also to one another. But it is amazing that philosophers have not acted upon this axiom. A plain record of their agreements would be more satisfactory to our confused world than all the controversies of those who think, but "make thoughts their aim." If the three sentences quoted above be unravelled and examined in all their implications, it will be found that they depend for their meaning on the implied truth of certain profound ideas originated by the greatest of all historical religions. In the same way Shelley's poetry of light, as I have called it, depends for its ultimate meaning and its ultimate beauty upon the ultimate truth of an idea that was implied in an utterance, more daring on its human side, more simple and exquisite on its divine side, than any that ever came from other lips—" I am the Light of the World."

We have heard much of the " higher criticism." It is time that the still higher criticism of poetry were applied to utterances like these ; for the result of that application is the rolling away of the stone from the tomb of our modern spiritual life and the discovery of the angel. Judged simply by poetic standards, the loftiest utterances of the greatest poets shrivel before the majesty of that utterance as a moth shrivels in the sun. But it is the same absolute Beauty that Shelley reveals in the *Prometheus Unbound* :

Asia. Common as light is love,
And its familiar voice wearies not ever.
Like the wide heaven, the all-embracing air,
It makes the reptile equal to the God . . .

Panthea. List. Spirits speak.

Voice in the air, singing. Child of Light ! Thy limbs are burning
Through the veil which seems to hide them ;
As the radiant lines of morning
Through the clouds ere they divide them.
And this atmosphere divinest
Shrouds thee wheresoe'er thou shinest.

It is the same vision that inspires the music of the last triumphant act of the *Prometheus*—music that seems to catch up the most exquisite melodies of Ariel and the attendant spirit in *Comus* and develop them into a vast cosmic harmony, wherein the soul of man has attained a more complete freedom of the universe than was ever known or imagined before. From end to end it is a poem of light ; and the light means to Shelley what the sea has meant to other poets—a symbol of the Eternal. At times he dwells merely on its immediate beauty, as those other poets would dwell upon the curve and motion of a wave, or the ebbing of a tide. At others he will use it with a kind of figurative art that seems to be at once the origin and the goal of some of the most exquisite conceptions of our later " Pre-Raphaelite " painters. One of the speeches of Panthea in this act of *Prometheus Unbound* is a perfect " storied window, richly dight " for the future cathedral of the universe:

And from the other opening in the wood
Rushes, with loud and whirlwind harmony,
A sphere, which is as many thousand spheres,
Solid as crystal, yet through all its mass
Flow, as through empty space, music and light :
Ten thousand orbs involving and involved,
Purple and azure, white and green and golden,
Sphere within sphere ; and every space between
Peopled with unimaginable shapes. . . .
With mighty whirl the multitudinous orb
Grinds the bright brook into an azure mist
Of elemental subtlety, like light ;
And the wild odour of the forest flowers,
The music of the living grass and air,
The emerald light of leaf-entangled beams
Round its intense yet self-conflicting speed,
Seem kneaded into one aërial mass
Which drowns the sense. Within the orb itself,
Pillowed upon its alabaster arms,
Like to a child o'er-wearied with sweet toil,
On its own folded wings and wavy hair,
The Spirit of the Earth is laid asleep,
And you can see its little lips are moving,
Amid the changing light of their own smiles,
Like one who talks of what he loves in dreams.

It is also a more elaborate embodiment of the same multiplicity in unity which "as reeds that move in a single stream" was suggested in *The Sensitive Plant* and in the *Ode to Heaven.* He uses this imagery of "sphere within sphere" elsewhere to answer beforehand the very argument which Francis Thompson used against the submerging of the individual in his pantheism. But here it is merely an aesthetic embodiment. At his greatest Shelley becomes an instrument of a Power above his own ; and the creative word—*let there be light*—breathed through his lips, transfigures the universe. The light of love interpenetrates the granite mass of the earth and makes of man "one harmonious soul of many a soul."

> All things confess his strength. Through the cold mass
> Of marble and of colour his dreams pass ;
> Bright threads whence mothers weave the robes their children wear.
> Language is a perpetual Orphic song
> Which rules with Daedal harmony a throng
> Of thoughts and forms, which else senseless and shapeless were.
>
> The lightning is his slave ; heaven's utmost deep
> Gives up her stars, and like a flock of sheep
> They pass before his eyes, are numbered, and roll on !
> The tempest is his steed, he strides the air ;
> And the abyss shouts from her depth laid bare,
> Heaven, hast thou secrets ? Man unveils me ; I have none.

All through this, as through the simpler poem of *The Cloud*, there is a constant sense of the orderly processes of the universe, and more than a suggestion of scientific foresight, making its prophetic vision all the more commanding. The wings of this poet are sublimely effectual, and it is time that the earlier judgment be revised. The enchantment of a phrase must not be allowed to confirm it. Poetic power of this immortal kind is of inestimable value to the heart and soul of this generation. Let its luminous wings beat there, and they will not beat in vain. One great stanza, at the end of the *Prometheus*, answers beforehand with curious completeness the sentence of Arnold, and the last five lines of that stanza suggest the significance of the poetry of Shelley to our own day :

> Love, from its awful throne of patient power
> In the wise heart, from the last giddy hour
> Of dread endurance, from the slippery, steep,
> And narrow verge of crag-like agony, springs
> And folds over the world its healing wings.

"Sun-treader, I believe in God, and truth, and love," cried Browning in his earliest poem to the radiant spirit of Shelley. Youthful eyes in this, at least, saw more of the radiance of which he spoke than many older eyes have done. Thompson found the hope of Shelley a "wan-hope," another name for despair. Browning, in this respect, saw more clearly, and expressed the exactly opposite view.

> As one just escaped from death
> Would bind himself in bands of friends to feel
> He lives indeed, so I would lean on thee !
> Thou must be ever with me, most in gloom
> If such must come, but chiefly when I die.

And after all the foul conflicts of our own day, to what purer light of hope can we return than that with which, at the end of *Hellas*, Shelley clothes the vision of the world to be. Though it may be expressed in the terms of a "pagan" and outworn creed, what is this golden calm of absolute beauty after the tempest, this exquisitely depicted light behind the clouds of the world, but a part of the undying vision of the Kingdom of God upon earth ;

and what is its concluding prayer but that of our own generation's deepest need ?

> The world's great age begins anew,
> The golden years return,
> The earth doth like a snake renew
> Her winter weeds outworn :
> Heaven smiles, and faiths and empires gleam
> Like wrecks of a dissolving dream.
>
> A brighter Hellas rears its mountains
> From waves serener far ;
> A new Peneus rolls his fountains
> Against the morning star.
> Where fairer Tempes bloom, there sleep
> Young Cyclads on a sunnier deep. . . .
>
> O, cease ! Must hate and death return ?
> Cease ! Must men kill and die ?
> Cease ! Drain not to its dregs the urn
> Of bitter prophecy !
> The world is weary of the past. . . .

There are few more moving passages in literature than that abrupt change in key from the glorious vision to the passionate grief and longing of the cry, "O, cease !" No words but those of Shelley himself could answer the subtle and beautiful, yet mistaken, sentence in which Matthew Arnold depicted those beating wings. It is not a vain thing to outsoar "the shadow of our night." That great verse is as true of Shelley as it was of Keats. It may be used of Shelley with all the more justice and emphasis because its exquisite tenderness was meant for a younger poet who had been tortured even more keenly by "envy and calumny and hate and pain." In this strange land of ours a very large proportion of the most radiant spirits in the history of our literature have been goaded into something like madness in life, and have been marked out in death as objects of contempt. But against one charge Shelley himself has made himself secure ; and he has done it unconsciously, by his unselfish defence of another poet. The truest and most lucid of English critics, the apostle of sweetness and light, imagined here that he saw luminous wings beating in the void ; and he was answered beforehand, and for all time, in a divine smile of transcendent sweetness and supernal light. For was there ever a void so completely filled with so real a presence as that revealed by Shelley himself in *Adonais* ? And what mightier sustainment could any mortal or immortal wings require than that Power which has now withdrawn his being to its own ; that Power whose "never-wearied love" sustains and wields the world ;

> That Light whose smile kindles the Universe,
> That Beauty in which all things work and move.

POETRY, OLD AND NEW

THE phrase is not of my choosing; and if it implies a breach of continuity it is wrong. There is neither new nor old poetry. There is only poetry. We may compare the poetry of one period with that of another if we choose, but these divisions are arbitrary, for the lines can be drawn anywhere, and it is the peculiar glory of true poetry in all ages that it is perennially vital. This is not a mere figure of speech. It is not merely a sounding phrase to say that poetry lives on while the Cæsars and their dynasties pass into oblivion. It is one of the illuminating facts of history, one of the most radiant illustrations of the power of the human spirit. The song of Homer is alive to-day, while the world in which it was created has vanished. Passages of Vergil still move us, like the cry of a living voice, with their poignant sense of the tears in mortal things, while the Rome of which in his lifetime he was merely a "patriotic poet" has left her most august memory to his keeping. The song of Dante lives in the minds of men to-day—his laurelled head, even, being familiar where the mediæval potentates are forgotten; and from our own Elizabethan age all that is now alive is the supreme voice that said of a king—

After life's fitful fever he sleeps well.

Even in a generation much nearer to our own, how familiar, in comparison with others, are the voices of Wordsworth, Shelley, and Keats; Keats, who went to his death not knowing whether the world had heard him, or would ever hear. I always think that a line in his *Ode to the Nightingale*, telling how he groped through that darkness of a summer's night, spellbound by the song in his own heart, describes with unconscious pathos his own inability to see his approaching fame ; a line full of the hushed wonder of a poet on his way to death and immortality :

> I cannot see what flowers are at my feet.

The whole ode, in fact, might be addressed to the Spirit of Poetry, "Sappho singing in the Nightingale," the same yesterday, to-day, and for ever. From the earliest to the latest, the poets are all members of a single body, the body of European poetry, militant here on earth ; all vitally connected with a great European tradition, as the leaves and branches are connected with the tree that bore them, the living Igdrasil of Song.

The very metre used by Homer had its influence upon a great modern poet like Goethe—I use the word "modern" here, of course, for something larger than what the heathen call the "output" of the last decade. It had also, perhaps, its indirect influence even on a poet like Whitman when—though somewhat barbarously—he echoes its music in such lines, for instance, as

> I open my scuttle at night, and see the far-sprinkled systems.

For three thousand years there has been a vital continuity ; and, moreover, though poetry has never been adequately defined, there has been a continuity of idea in the minds of all nations with regard to the characteristics that differentiate poetry from prose. The essential element, the element that differentiates poetry from prose, has been the musical element, the element of Song. I use the word

"Song" here as it would be understood by the Muse that Homer invoked. Vergil *sings* his great story of Æneas ; and Dante takes Vergil as his guide. Milton, the greatest master of all the harmonies of our tongue, using that glorious measure of English blank verse, was at one with them :

> Of man's first disobedience and the fruit
> Of that forbidden tree, whose mortal taste
> Brought death into the world and all our woe . . .
> *Sing, heavenly Muse.*

The facts are quite clear when one considers what may be called the great works of pure poetry, whether it be lyrical (when the very name implies its music) or epic or dramatic, as in Æschylus and Sophocles. It is a great rhythmical art, and whether its music be that of the lyre, or the measured cadence of a single human voice, or a choric chant, it is always *song*, as its various Muses understood that word. Shakespeare, of course, has complicated the matter a little for the unintelligent, because he used all the resources both of verse and prose in his poetic dramas, and there are also connecting passages of careless recitative in which he was not greatly interested. But, broadly speaking, whenever Shakespeare exercised his full power as a poet, whenever the great moments arrive, they arrive in music, a music that seems to be dictated by the very pulse of life ; a music as precise in its rhythmical law as the movement of the tides and the stars or the beating of the human heart ; so that his words have a universal significance, acquire the majesty of a natural and inevitable process, and it seems as if the Eternal were speaking through his lips :

> To-morrow, and to-morrow, and to-morrow,
> Creeps in this petty pace from day to day
> To the last syllable of recorded time.

How the metrical movement of that last line reinforces the thought, and how absolutely natural is its stress. Its pulse is precise as that of the heart, and as living and responsive to emotion ; yet, if you try to scan it (in the way that some writers of "free verse" seem to think that verse must be scanned), it defies analysis, defies your metronome in the very perfection of its law. It has found, in service to law, its perfect freedom. The thing said could not be said better, could not be said more naturally, could not be said more powerfully. It is like the rhythm of an athlete which enables him to use every ounce of his strength in the most effective way. One has only to compare two runners, two boxers, two crews on the river, or even two dancers, to discover the efficiency of rhythm ; and if you repeat this line to yourself and try to get the utmost value out of its cadence, you will discover that the run of unaccented syllables at the beginning and in the middle, the stresses on the third and fourth syllable, on the long vowel sound in "recorded," and the final word, are a means of extracting infinitely more than the words could be combined to convey in any other form. It is for just this reason that the lines are immortal.

Or if one considers those miraculous lyrics of Shakespeare, one finds him often using the very simplest words, words of every day ; and yet by the pure music of their combination, by those undertones of universal music which deepen them and quicken them when they begin to obey his rhythmical law and find their larger freedom, he fills them with the subtlest ecstasy that was ever breathed through articulate language :

> Nothing of him that doth fade
> But doth suffer a sea-change
> Into something rich and strange.

Even the author of the *Ring and the Book* (perplexed as he was about his own technique), whenever his spirit opened its wings and mounted into the clear air of poetry, expressed himself in pure song. The invocation in the first part of that strange turbid epic of Italy is a perfect example of this, and of his lineal descent:

> O lyric love, half angel and half bird,
> And all a wonder and a wild desire,
> Boldest of hearts that ever braved the sun,
> Took sanctuary within the holier blue,
> And sang a kindred soul out to his face. . . .
> This is the same voice: can thy soul know change?
> Hail, then, and hearken from the realms of help!
> Never may I commence my song, my due
> To God who best taught song by gift of thee,
> Except with bent head and beseeching hand. . . .

And, yet again, the subtlest artist in poetry of the nineteenth century, the Vergil of England, in his great salute across the centuries to the Tennyson of Rome, reaffirms the unity of the whole body of European poetry as a rhythmical art, practised by a great guild of song:

> Roman Vergil, thou that singest
> Ilion's lofty temples robed in fire,
> Ilion falling, Rome arising,
> wars and filial faith and Dido's pyre . . .
>
> I salute thee, Mantovano,
> I that loved thee since my day began,
> Wielder of the stateliest measure
> ever moulded by the lips of man.

Finally, the nearest approach to a definition of poetry on its technical side was made by Edgar Allan Poe, when he said that it was the "rhythmical creation of beauty."

During the last few years, however, there has been a tendency to break down the distinctive meanings of our terms. We have to face the fact that there are very large numbers of readers who have no ear for the music of poetry ; and that they have been endeavouring to persuade themselves and the world that the true poetry is really something quite different. One recent critic has even declared that poetry "must be rid of its music." We have reached the point when, if any writer of realistic descriptions chose to cut his work up into lines of odd or even length and print it so that it looked like what is called "free verse" (I am not for the moment criticizing "free verse"), a large part of the English Press would call it Mr. Jargon's new poem ; and if it dealt with particularly ugly or dirty details, it would be called Mr. Jargon's *great* new poem, and described as a work of poetical genius. Very many more readers than ever before in fact, are now reading badly disguised prose without knowing it, and doing so in the firm belief that now, at last, in one brief decade, the vital continuity of three thousand years has been broken and superseded, and now, at last, they are enjoying the new and the only true poetry. The matter is complicated by the fact that the work *may* be, in some other respects, masterly ; that it may even, in the wider sense, possess something of that poetry which is the substance of all the arts, and is, of course, the substance of some of our greatest prose. But (whether it be a prose masterpiece marred or merely the late Mr. Jack London rehashed in clumsy verse), if it rightly belongs to the prose category, and if, because it is divided into more or less regular lengths of line, or because a number of awkward rhymes are introduced, it is thrust into the category of *Song*, then we are confusing our terms, confusing values in literature, and marring the peculiar beauties both of prose and of poetry.

If the new generation insists on this confusion of terms we must accept it, and find a new name for what has been called poetry for the last three thousand years. Its readers may still be as few as Milton sought, but there will always be room in the many mansions of literature for the poetry that is song, the poetry that has an inner pulse of music, that is born in music, and can never be made by merely taking thought, though it is itself the very music of thought—thought caught up into the universal harmony as a violinist is caught up by the surrounding orchestra and swept into accord with it. That is how a very clear-thinking man of science once described the work of Swinburne; and, although it is by no means always true of Swinburne, it is true often enough to place him among the great singers.

But I cannot see any good ground for invading the realm of one art with work which properly belongs to another. In fact, this breaking down of the categories is part of the same movement which is breaking down the distinctions in words themselves, obliterating their finer shades of meaning, and turning a highly organized and exquisitely developed language into what Herbert Spencer would have called an "incoherent homogeneity," and what, for present purposes, we may ourselves call a "sloppy mess." Only a few weeks ago a book of new poetry was sent to me, the novelty of which was that it had no punctuation. The author explained in a preface, quite seriously, that he regarded punctuation, capital letters, and the division of sentences as a relic of mediæval tyranny. He desired to be free, and his method of achieving freedom was to lock himself up in a mad-house cell and throw the key through the window. All the differentiation of parts, all the organization of language, was destroyed, and while some of the book was unintentionally funny (through the running of one sentence into another and the impossibility of deciding whether one of his characters merely sat down and ate, or whether he sat down and ate a large log of wood), the greater part was quite unintelligible bosh. I wanted to send the author a letter of thanks consisting entirely of punctuation marks without words; but the inspiration came and went and could not be recaptured.

This, of course, is an extreme case; but one may suggest that preoccupation with a desire for novelty defeats its own end. We can draw a distinction between the right way of achieving novelty in poetry and the wrong way. Nobody wants mere repetition of the past, of course. That is elementary; and it need not be discussed here. But it is not a new achievement in flying to cut off our wings; nor is it a new achievement in poetry to break those laws of song which have remained constant from Homer to the present day, and are, in fact, natural laws of harmony, order, and proportion. The true line of progress is development. We are not at the end of metrical invention. We are only at the beginning of it, even in its simplest forms. Newness is not achieved by the very simple method of doing the opposite of what was done by the past. A great deal of the so-called new work to-day simply takes an older method and makes it easier by evading one or two technical difficulties. It will take the metre of Gray's *Elegy*, for instance, and abandon, first of all, that wonderful balance of the cadences that makes it sound like a moving sea. One can imagine very good reasons for this; but I am chiefly impressed by the fact that in most cases it is easier. Then, the new writer will perhaps evade the difficulty of finding a rhyme for the first and third lines. There may be good reasons for this too; but again I am chiefly impressed by the fact that it is easier. Thirdly, the new writer will hunt for startling, sensational, and violent words. He will pour the new wine of

Jack London into clumsily handled old forms of verse. He will sometimes, even when speaking in his own character, adopt the crudities of thought, and even the grammatical crudities, of slack minds ; and one may imagine all kinds of good reasons for this, but again I am chiefly impressed by the fact that it is easier to do this than to write with a sense of all the hidden meanings and finer shades and subtle tones of the incomparable language that was used by Shelley, Keats, Wordsworth, and Tennyson. We do not want it to be coarsened or blunted ; we want it to be touched to new and finer results. We want to develop and amplify it until its range can encompass our growing world and translate it anew into music.

It is sometimes said that we are at the end of metrical invention, and this is made an excuse for indifference to the musical element of poetry. I believe we are only at the beginning of metrical invention, even in its simplest forms, and that no poet has really much excuse for writing to-day unless in everything that he writes he is adding a little to the range of our music. Immediately after the great outburst of new music in Tennyson, Browning, and Swinburne, a poet of quite a different order, Robert Louis Stevenson, who has never been counted among the highly original poets, was able to give us quite original verse-movements like that of his beautiful poem beginning

> In the highlands, in the country places.

His short book of poems is full of these exquisite snatches of song, in forms that have never been used before or since. They have never even been recognized as new by those amazing apostles of novelty who, when they do not abandon all the laws of verse, are usually to be found writing clumsy sonnets, putting crude thought and crude words into the oldest and most conventional patterns of English verse, and claiming that their clumsiness and crudity are evidences of their austere superiority to the flawless music that one finds not only in Tennyson, but in Dante, and in all the true poets from Sappho to Verlaine and from Æschylus to Victor Hugo. The new way, the new glory of song, is opening out on every hand, and they are unaware of it, because they are not listening for music ; they are searching for something else. Very often they seem to be taking the advice of an American critic and trying to popularize Keats by translating him into Billingsgate :

> St. Hagnes Heave, 'ow blistering chill it was.

To be preoccupied with the desire for novelty kills sincerity and silences that spontaneous music which the poets have heard in quiet hours. As Hazlitt pointed out, Milton's view of poetry was expressed in the phrase—"thoughts that *voluntary* move harmonious numbers." To be preoccupied with the desire for mere novelty is not to think, but "to make thoughts one's aim"; it is to see nature not as it really is, but with a distorted eye, wondering to what use of personal interest or ambition or sensation with the crowd it may be twisted again. The simplest note of natural song is worth more than all the self-conscious attempts to be subtle and new by the use of what has been aptly called the "scarlet word." Nothing is so superficial as mere literary sophistication. But that other note, the natural note of song, is, in the last analysis, the most subtle and the most profound, for it is at one with nature herself. Even in its artistry, when it evolves any beautiful form it does so along the lines of natural law as nature unfolds a flower ; and in its most exalted works, though its music may be above the range of ordinary human speech, it is still natural music, the apotheosis of human speech, the thing said as we would like to say it, if only we could.

But it is not by taking thought that a man can write the *Songs of Innocence*, or those greater poems in which the footsteps of love are heard approaching through the night of time, poems in which every line is a little journey to the world's end, and every rhyme a lovers' meeting in the kingdom beyond the world. Song, and song only, holds the secret of these.

> O mistress mine, where are you roaming?
> O, stay and hear, your true love 's coming
>   That can sing both high and low.
> Trip no further, pretty sweeting.
> Journeys end in lovers' meeting,
>   Every wise man's son doth know.

THE POETRY OF EMERSON

TWELVE years ago, during a first visit to America, I was surprised to find that the man whom I had always believed to be the greatest poet of that country, both in the depth of his thought and in the subtlety of his music, was hardly recognized as a poet at all. He was counted among the first of their prose-writers, very much as Matthew Arnold in England was once held to be primarily a critic. But this American poet at that time was hardly ever mentioned among the poets of his country. They spoke of Edgar Allan Poe, Longfellow, Whitman, Lanier, Bryant, Lowell, and Whittier ; but seldom of the man who, as I believed, stood head and shoulders above all these—Emerson. Oliver Wendell Holmes, it is true, with the quick insight of a poet, had long ago said of the *Threnody* that it had "the dignity of *Lycidas* without its refrigerating classicism," and that it had also all the tenderness of Cowper's lines on his mother's picture. But the comparisons that he made were not apt, and the general import of the verdict seemed to have been forgotten. It was the same in England, of course ; but there were additional reasons for it here, both in the far greater disproportion of the circulation of Emerson's essays to the almost negligible circulation of his poems, and also in the tone set for criticism by Matthew Arnold, whose essay on Emerson, in many ways, was as mistaken as that on Shelley. Exquisite poet and far-sighted critic as he was, Matthew Arnold did make two or three serious mistakes—one on French poetry, one on Shelley, and one on Emerson.

In his essay on Emerson he seems suddenly to have forgotten some of his own wisest and deepest sayings on the subject of poetry and its world of ideas, and to be asking for a "concreteness," a faith in the fact, that certainly in one example that he gives—*The Bridge* of Longfellow—has failed us. There is, of course, an undiscovered poet in Longfellow, who wrote infinitely better poems than *The Bridge*, or indeed any of those verses by which he is usually represented in the anthologies for schools. His *Keramos* is as exquisite as it is unknown. His introductory sonnets to Dante are of a very high order; but *The Bridge*, "concrete" as it may be, is neither a good poem nor to be compared for a moment with the best work of Emerson. Moreover, of the right kind of "concreteness" there is more than enough in the poetry of Emerson to refute any suspicion that he too was "an ineffectual angel beating in the void his luminous wings in vain." A poem like *The Humble-Bee* is in itself a full answer to that, and also to the suggestion that he is lacking in warmth and colour.

If it be compared with *L'Allegro*, as its measure suggests, it will be seen to be richer in colour, more sensuous, and even in music to be a worthy rival of its great forerunner. It is a poem in which you can see and touch and smell the summer meadows, and there is a deliciously fantastic moralizing vein in it which should surely be enough to answer Arnold's demand, even in this subject, for "a criticism of life."

> Thou, in sunny solitudes,
> Rover of the underwoods,
> *The green silence dost displace*
> *With thy mellow breezy bass. . . .*

Hot midsummer's petted crone,
Sweet to me thy drowsy tone,
Tells of countless sunny hours,
Long days and solid banks of flowers;
Gulfs of sweetness without bound
In Indian wildernesses found;
Syrian peace, immortal leisure,
Firmest cheer, and bird-like pleasure. . . .

Wiser far than human seer,
Yellow-breeched philosopher. . . .

Some of the phrases in those lines have the real magic. "Crone," in the fifth line quoted, is an extraordinary example of the apt use of a word that at first sight would seem to be quite remote from the subject; an extraordinary example of the secondary meanings and associations that can be awakened in such a word by its use at exactly the right moment. In some mysterious way it suggests, by its likeness to another word, the crooning sound of the bee. It suggests, partly by its own meaning perhaps, and partly by the associations of the two opening consonants, the crooked legs and somewhat decrepit appearance of a tipsy bee blundering into a flower. But nothing is forced upon the reader. It merely suggests vividly, by being the right word in the right context.

Lowell said that Emerson had no "ear," and he tells in his letters that Emerson confessed to him that he did not understand "accent" in verse. There is one line in his *Humble-Bee* where the accent is misplaced, but it was not misplaced through the lack of an ear for the subtler harmonies of verse. It was misplaced because Emerson pronounced it so. His confession to Lowell has its ironical side, for no comparison is possible between the extreme delicacy of the music that appealed to the ear of Emerson and the carefully measured verses that

Lowell wrote. There is a music in the freely moving lines of Emerson's "Give all to Love" for which his own generation was not prepared. In fact, many of his readers missed it altogether, and really imagined—some of them imagine still—that those apparently irregular lines were left in that poem because Emerson could not improve them into the slack and regular stanzas of *The Bridge*. Yet, if ears had been attuned to hear them, what could be more firm, more precise, more finely balanced, in the right way of the Muses than this :

> Though thou loved her as thyself,
> As a self of purer clay,
> Though her parting dims the day,
> Stealing grace from all alive ;
> Heartily know,
> When half-gods go,
> The gods arrive.

We know at once, by the way in which the words, when rightly heard, strike into the mind and endure in the memory, that here the poet is among the immortals and saying immortal things to us. He wanders in the forest or by the sea, painting his own country—the black ducks mounting from the lake, the streams that take their colours from the sky ; and closes his poem with a stanza which is unmistakably of the kind that does not perish :

> Oblivion here thy wisdom is,
> Thy thrift, the sleep of cares ;
> For a proud idleness like this
> Crowns all thy mean affairs.

In *The Fore-Runners* he seems to be on the verge of making a new American mythology of his own. It is one of the poems that most strongly influenced Stevenson, and, in fact, obviously suggested one of his own finest lyrics. But Stevenson's poem goes to a slighter tune :

> Life was over ; life was gay ;
> We have come the primrose way.

Emerson's music speaks to the intellect, and it brings tidings from spiritual realms :

> Long I followed happy guides,
> I could never reach their sides. . . .
> On and away, their hasting feet
> Make the morning proud and sweet ;
> Flowers they strew,—I catch the scent ;
> Or tone of silver instrument
> Leaves in the wind melodious trace ;
> Yet I could never see their face. . . .
> In sleep their jubilant troop is near,—
> I tuneful voices overhear ;
> It may be in wood or waste
> At unawares 'tis come and past.
> Their near camp my spirit knows
> *By signs gracious as rainbows.*
> I, thenceforward, and long after,
> Listen for their harp-like laughter,
> And carry, in my heart, for days
> Peace that hallows rudest ways.

The subtly displaced accent of the line italicized above may be one of the instances that disconcerted Lowell ; but some of the later poets would have recognized in it an anticipation of their own methods. It is a curious irony that these qualities in Emerson, who was a far subtler musician in verse than Poe, were unrecognized in his own day because the time was not ripe for him, and are unrecognized in ours because the readers of to-day take it for granted, without examination, that Emerson was not really a poet. So much for the value of those modern "rebellions" against the verdicts of the past, rebellions which seem to be almost invariably in the wrong direction.

In Emerson's *Bacchus* there is a subtler music yet. It is a marvellous poem, composed surely when the poet had fed on that honey-dew and drunk that milk of Paradise of which Coleridge wrote in *Kubla Khan*. This is not the conventional view ; but, before the conventional unconventionalist dismisses it, he may be asked to read Emerson's *Bacchus* again with care. It is a poem for philosophers ; it is one of the very finest of such poems, brimming over with intellectual ecstasy.

Bring me wine, but wine which never grew
In the belly of the grape,
Or grew on vine whose tap-roots, reaching through
Under the Andes to the Cape,
Suffered no savour of the earth to 'scape.

Let its grapes the morn salute
From a nocturnal root,
Which feels the acrid juice
Of Styx and Erebus,
And turns the woe of Night,
By its own craft, to a more rich delight.

We buy ashes for bread ;
We buy diluted wine ;
Give me of the true,—
Whose ample leaves and tendrils curled
Among the silver hills of heaven
Draw everlasting dew ;
Wine of wine,
Blood of the world. . . .

Wine which Music is—
Music and wine are one,—
That I, drinking this,
Shall hear far Chaos talk with me ;
Kings unborn shall walk with me ;

And the poor grass will plot and plan
What it will do when it is man.
Quickened so, will I unlock
Every crypt of every rock. . . .

Refresh the faded tints,
Recut the aged prints,
And write my old adventures with the pen
Which on the first day drew
Upon the tablets blue
The dancing Pleiades and eternal men.

There is an intellectual ecstasy in this poem which is hardly to be paralleled elsewhere. The beauty of the best work of Poe is undeniable ; but it is the beauty of a cloud catching from a distance the light of a supernal region in which this less familiar poet seems to be carousing with the gods themselves, on the other side of the processes of nature. It is surely necessary, moreover, that one of the accepted verdicts of the past should be revised with regard to the comparative merits of Emerson and Edgar Allan Poe. Emerson may have "confessed" to Lowell that he had "no ear" ; but he also confessed to the world that he thought Poe a "jingle-man" ; and with the music of his *Bacchus* in our own ears, a new and free and subtle music that could hardly be appreciated rightly in his own generation, his thought seems almost to be justifiable. There are occasions when it is right to be a "jingle-man." It was right in *The Bells*. Poe had his own great merits ; but it is only a very insensitive ear that could think the ethereal cadences of Emerson's *Bacchus* inferior to the tawdry rhyming and meretricious mysticism of *Ulalume*.

Ulalume, accepted by poets in France as a great poem—and possibly, like some of the work of Byron, freed from some of its faults in translation—has undoubtedly a spell to cast, but it is not of the subtlest or the most potent kind; and the music of this higher kind, like some of the music of Shelley, it is quite impossible to convey in another tongue.

Ulalume, judged by the highest standards, and compared with Emerson's *Bacchus*, is a greatly overrated poem. It has become customary to take it for granted as one of the unquestionable achievements of American literature. The rebellions against the work of the past are concentrated upon the bigger men, whose work will bear examination. *Ulalume* has just enough verbal magic to give it a permanent place in literature; and it has not been properly examined by criticism for the somewhat absurd reason that it is too obscure. The lucid poets, at their subtlest, challenge thought, and pass beyond thought into spiritual realms, but they are still lucid and intelligible to the spirit of man, if not to his plodding reason. But *Ulalume* is densely obscure from every point of view, obscure to the mind and obscure to that spirit which, in the highest poetry, soars beyond the mind. Both its mysticism and its music are second-rate, when it is compared with work of the quality of Emerson's *Bacchus*. Even within its own limits *Ulalume* is confused—not by the mystery of its theme, but by the demonstrable faults of the poet.

I remember asking an eminent admirer of the poem what meaning he attached to the "Psyche" who accompanied the melancholy dreamer through its mazes. "Psyche," he replied, "was his own soul, of course. He says so himself:

> 'Here, once, through an alley titanic,
> I wandered with Psyche, my soul.'"

He then read the rest of the poem; and when he had "passed to the end of the vista," and "pacified

Psyche and kissed her," I was satisfied by the troubled expression of his countenance that he was wondering whether it could possibly be right for a man to kiss his own soul.

There is a very great deal more than this, of course, to be said about Edgar Allan Poe. In his best work, like *Annabel Lee*, or the curiously beautiful poem of cloud-stuff that he called *Fairy-land* (though this is seldom singled out for praise), he obtained results which have a permanent value for literature. But when he sets a stuffed raven over his door, provides it with a mechanical croak, and sets it off to the tune of "Lady Geraldine's Courtship"; or when he sings of the unhappy maiden who was borne across the billow to wed with age and "titled crime" and share an "unholy pillow," he is meretricious and absurdly overrated. He is on a definitely lower level than that of Emerson, who saw in his native mountain, Monadnoc,

> The haughty pile erect
> Of the old building intellect.

He is not so great a poet as Emerson, because it is he and not Emerson who moves among "the fringes of things." Emerson is at the heart of the universe, listening to its sun-creating pulsations, while Poe is clutching at a sheeted ghost, or shuddering at a phosphorescent bone, or chasing a will-o'-the-wisp across a marsh.

Emerson was the first writer in American literature to begin that great work of the future—the finding and maintaining of that central position which has been temporarily lost in an age of specialists, that central position from which we shall again see "all things in one," as Thomas à Kempis could see them.

In his essay on *The Poet* he gives one of the most beautiful and profound expositions of the art of poetry that have ever been written. In the fragments of verse that preface it he opens two windows in his central turret, from one of which he sees the rhythmic aspect of the universe, and its relation to the poet's craft, while from the other he surveys once more those divine ideas which are the substance of all poetry.

> Overleapt the horizon's edge,
> Searched with Apollo's privilege;
> Through man and woman and sea and star,
> Saw the dance of nature forward far;
> Through worlds and races and terms and times,
> Saw musical order and pairing rhymes.

He shows, too, how the most "concrete" forms of modern life and activity may find their way into art. He was among the first to suggest the method, the only true method, by which the steamship and the railroad may be touched with the light of poetry. He shows how they can be related to central and permanent ideas; revealing, for instance, the poetry of the great Atlantic liner arriving at her destination with the "punctuality of a planet." With that last phrase alone he founded something like a school —and its influence is to be traced in the work of Stevenson, and even in the *Rhythm of Life* of Alice Meynell.

In fact, the influence of Emerson upon some of the most distinctively modern writers of our day is as remarkable as it is unrecognized. He has undoubtedly, for instance, influenced Kipling—not only in such obvious instances as the poem on the American Spirit (which is of course based on Emerson's *Brahma*), but also in what may be called the jungle-poetry. If the four following lines are quoted to the average reader of both authors, he would be uncertain for a moment which of the two had written them:

Cast the bantling on the rocks,
  Suckle him with the she-wolf's teat.
Wintered with the hawk and fox,
  Power and speed be hands and feet.

It is pure Mowgli ; but the lines were written by Emerson. Another interesting trace of Emerson's influence on the same writer may be observed by any one who compares the opening lines of *The World-Soul* with the later *Native-born.*

But Emerson's great value to our own day and to the future is that from his central position he maintained that hope which—oddly enough—even the most negative of his critics, Matthew Arnold, declared to be essential to the greatest art. Arnold declared that Emerson was not among the great writers ; yet he quoted as an example of his deepest insight these words : " We judge of a man's wisdom by his hope, knowing that the perception of the inexhaustibleness of Nature is an immortal youth."

Such hope as this has nothing in common with the easy optimism that averts its face from reality. It is at the opposite pole from that superficial kind, though the superficial pessimist will always confuse them. It means simply that neither life nor death may be permitted to utter the last word of denial in this infinite universe. Matthew Arnold contradicted himself curiously on this matter, for he does at last say of Emerson, " Never had man such a sense of the inexhaustibleness of Nature and such hope." If this be true, and if we judge of a man's wisdom by his hope (as Arnold agreed), it is difficult to see how he could avoid the logical conclusion that Emerson must at least have been among the wisest of men.

His abiding word for us, the word by which he still speaks to us, a word that seems to be the inspiration, both in style and thought, of all that was best in the prose of Stevenson, and of at least one of the finest poems of Browning, is this :

" That which befits us, embosomed in beauty and wonder as we are, is cheerfulness and courage, and the endeavour to realize our aspirations. *Shall not the heart, which has received so much, trust the Power by which it lives ?* "

Matthew Arnold's personal withdrawal from this unconquerable hope, in his essay on Emerson, seems to be a contradiction of what he says elsewhere, and of what he expresses (though faintly) in the finest of his own poems :

> Whence was it ? For it was not mine !

He withdrew from it, hesitatingly, in those moments when he was waiting for the spark from heaven ; but when the spark had fallen and kindled the spirit within him his vision was at one with that of Emerson :

> So near is grandeur to our dust,
> So nigh is God to man.

The hope of Emerson was founded on the only element of which, in the last analysis, we know anything at all, that personality, that soul (it matters very little what we call it), that individuality through which alone we can approach the universal soul : for it is not true to say that we, who are part of reality, can only know fleeting appearances of the world. We have our own private wicket-gate in ourselves, through which we can pass at will into the eternal world.

We cannot transcend our limited spheres of action in the flesh. We are like travellers on a ship who have freedom to walk east, west, north, or south on its deck, while the ship pursues her own course, bearing us to an end of which we know nothing, except that the ship is being steered by great laws. Occasionally we overhear the orders that are being made around us, even if we do not understand them. We hear commands given in the night. And this we do know—that if the meaning goes out of everything, if the good, the true, the beautiful become a mockery by our abandonment of our belief in their eternal significance, or by the assumption that the voyage has no aim and the ship no steersman, then it is the duty of our own souls, and the part of our human reason, to make the opposite assumption (act of faith though it may be) and to say to our fellow-travellers: Hope. For a meaning is the one thing needful, the one thing that even our limited reason cannot forgo. We cannot accept—the reason revolts from accepting—the suggestion that the universe is a gigantic game of bubbles blown by an imbecile and unweeting Power. It is the failure of our own vision of the universe that makes such a suggestion possible—though again and again in modern literature, a literature moving along narrow lines of specialized thought, this suggestion is logically implied. Even in the depths of our agnosticism, and God knows they are deep enough, there are certain things that we ourselves do know. We know a little of human love. We know that it is a better thing than the dust, and that, by every law of thought, the greater can never be originated from the less or subjected to it.

The value of Emerson to the present day is that he was able to keep open the gates of that knowledge within the soul. In the *Threnody*, perhaps the most beautiful and profound poem in American literature, a poem whose music is wrought to the heights of prophetic inspiration, he utters his own hope over the grave of his own child. It is a poem that lends the wings of a Shelley to the weight and thought of a Browning; and if he had written nothing else, it would eventually confirm his right to a place among the master-singers. It is cosmic in its range, and it contains all philosophies. It is human in its grief, and divine in its hope.

What is excellent
As God lives, is permanent ;
Hearts are dust, hearts' loves remain ;
Heart's love will meet thee again . . .
Not of adamant and gold
Built He heaven stark and cold ;
No, but a nest of bending reeds,
Flowering grass, and scented weeds ;
Or like a traveller's fleeing tent
Or bow above the tempest bent ;
Built of tears and sacred flames,
And virtue reaching to its aims ;
Built of furtherance and pursuing,
Not of spent deeds, but of doing.
Silent rushes the swift Lord
Through ruined systems still restored. . . .

THE POETRY OF W. E. HENLEY

HENLEY, the crippled buccaneer, is a vivid figure for many who have never read his works. He was projected into the far future, cutlass at belt and blood-spotted handkerchief about his brow, when Stevenson announced that from the maimed strength of his friend he had drawn the character of John Silver in *Treasure Island.*

Henley himself has given us the plain realistic facts—the colours which Stevenson mixed upon his palette for the purpose of his own art. The bandages, "brilliantly hideous with red," described by Henley, were far remote from *Treasure Island.* Only ships at English wharves could bring to Henley the magical scents of the Ends of the World, the frontiers where he thought the real romance might yet be found. Yet Stevenson's picture serves at least as a kind of symbolical background for the poet. The spirit that was not imprisoned by hospital wards—those "cellars on promotion," as he calls them—did indeed find ships to grapple and cities to sack in the drab world around him. Even in the surgeon's knife there was a glitter of romance for him, as of a gallant enemy's blade.

A friend of both Stevenson and Henley once reinforced the suggestion of Henley's likeness to John Silver by a story which I believe has hitherto not been published. It was an incident that should make a symbolical background for Henley the critic. It was little more than the story of a gesture ; but it was one of the most striking gestures in a certain violent drama (which we call the history of English literature) since the curtain fell on Kit Marlowe in the days of the Mermaid Tavern.

The scene was late at night, outside a famous London theatre. You must picture the audience, cloaked and furred, streaming out into the gas-lit fog. Whistles were blowing for cabs, and newspaper boys yelled hoarsely. The lighted entrance of the theatre made a kind of second stage, where a few groups lingered or dispersed from time to time as the hansoms drove up. On one side of this stage was a large yellow and black poster, advertising the play. Against this luridly appropriate background stood the heavy figure of the dramatist himself, then at the height of his success. He was waging some kind of wordy warfare with another man, a man on a crutch, a certain struggling journalist named Henley. But the successful dramatist was talking in a manner which that particular kind of struggling journalist, by the look of his eyes, would not be likely to endure for long. And to clinch the whole matter of their argument, as the dramatist let the last word slip and moved to the street, Henley—lifting his head like a wounded lion—swung up his crutch and hurled it, with all the power of John Silver behind it, straight at the head of the world's temporary favourite, Oscar Wilde. That is surely a symbolical picture of Henley the critic—a fearless old buccaneer, hurling his crutch, regardless of the world's favour. Indeed, he made up his mind, very early in his life, about the value of such light favour or disfavour as is too commonly bestowed by the followers of an art or a science on the work of their contemporaries. Very clearly and very early he saw for himself—his own strength being disabled "by limping sway"—a world of "folly doctor-like, controlling skill," and his biographer has supplied, by another incident in Henley's life, a striking and pathetic illustration to the lines of Shakespeare which describe that world. It was in his early boyhood that the tuberculous disease broke out which crippled him. There were times when the flesh of his hands would "open like the pages of a book," as one of his friends described it. In his early youth it was found necessary to amputate one foot, and a little later the doctors told him his choice was between death and losing the other. The young man had heard of a certain Professor Lister, not yet recognized by the world, who was experimenting at Edinburgh. Henley consulted his doctors about this man. They dismissed his name with a peculiar contempt which Henley, the critic, swiftly recognized as the symptom of something unusual. Immediately, almost penniless, Henley made his way north to the city where the best of his yet unknown friends, Robert Louis Stevenson, was beginning to see the colour of life. There Henley deposited himself, a strange, silent cripple, with burning eyes and a heart loaded to bursting, in the hands of Lister. "Why did you come to me?" said Lister. "Because I am told by the rest of your profession," said Henley, "that you are utterly incompetent." His biographer tells us that Lister made no reply to this; but he saved the foot.

This incident, coupled with the little drama of the crutch, gives one more than a glimpse of that unquenchable fire within Henley against which all shams, in life and literature, shrivelled up like scribbled forms writ on a parchment.

He passed nearly two years in that hospital, testing all his thoughts at that inner fire. All the nonsense, everything but the truth, was burnt out of the verses that he wrote there. Their peculiar merit is not in their realism, for it is easy enough to exploit suffering. Nor is it in their metrical freedom. They might appeal to some of our moderns on those grounds alone, the grounds on which they were rejected by every editor in London at that time. But they have a unique importance in our literature on other grounds, a value not discovered in Henley's own day, nor even faintly recognized in ours.

The publication of the new edition of Henley has been welcomed in some cases with the usual "not bad for the little man of the day before yesterday" which we have come to expect from the little men of to-day, and in the present chaos of literary criticism in England it may be well that some attempt should be made to elucidate his distinct and peculiar value. Even those who have praised him have done so without perception, and in phrases that might apply with equal fitness to W. E. Henley, to the weather, or to roast beef and plum pudding. He has been praised for a sonnet on Stevenson, for instance, just as he has been praised for his *Song of the Sword* and his *Nightingale*, with all the stock conventional phrases, "virile," "red-blooded," and the rest. But there is an essential difference between the first of these and the others. A hundred other poems of battle or the Spring may be ranked above the last two. But the peculiar gift of Henley, the gift that singles him out as a great writer, a major poet, not only from his contemporaries, but also from all his peers in the past, is his gift of portraiture. He is the Raeburn of English literature—our first, our only, and unapproachable portrait-painter in English verse. Others have excelled in other kinds; but this belongs to him alone. Not in the great masterpieces of our sonnet-literature, not in Rossetti, not in Wordsworth, not in Milton, not in Shakespeare even, shall we find that peculiar gift which is displayed over and over again in the work of Henley. Greater gifts we shall undoubtedly find; but not this particular gift. And he learned to use it in the long days when he was prisoned in that cold, clean hospital ward, half workhouse, half gaol. There was nothing for him to feast his eyes upon in that square squat room except "plasters astray in unnatural-looking tinware, scissors and lint and apothecaries' jars," nothing but the human countenance under every kind of stress—pain, suspense, compassion, and grief. There he found the right world for the exercise of his highest powers. Perhaps only a man who had himself looked up into the steady eyes of the surgeon could have given us that portrait of the Chief—Lister—the large placid brow, the soft lines of tranquil thought, the benign face, proud and shy, his faultless patience and unyielding will, against that tender background of innumerable gratitudes. Only a man who had seen and known the beauty and strength of it five minutes before the knife could have given us that finest touch of all :

> His wise, rare smile is sweet with certainties.

He hangs the naked corridors of the hospital with masterpieces of portraiture : the Scrubber of the Ward ; the Sailor, who, leaning on elbow, tells of the drums he heard on the wharf at Charleston, and gives to those cabined shipmates of the ward once more the colours of the world, the romance of its distances, to drink like wine ; the Visitor, whose little face is like a walnut shell with its wrinkles, and has "quaint straight curls, like horns," of soft white hair adorning either brow ; the Lady Probationer, who has a history ; the Staff Nurses, old style and new ; the Rescued Suicide, with his "unrazored features" ghastly brown against his pillow, and "throat so strangely bandaged."

Henley knew them all, talked with them all ; and, like the great masters of his art on canvas, he painted their souls as well as their faces. He was quite conscious, too, of his aims in the matter, and not a little ambitious, as one may gather from the opening of *The Staff Nurse; Old Style*:

> The greater masters of the commonplace,
> Rembrandt and good Sir Walter—only these
> Could paint her all to you: experienced ease
> And antique liveliness and ponderous grace;
> The sweet old roses of her sunken face;
> The depth and malice of her sly, grey eyes;
> The broad Scots tongue that flatters, scolds, defies;
> The thick Scots wit that fells you like a mace.
> These thirty years has she been nursing here,
> Some of them under SYME, her hero still.
> Much is she worth, and even more is made of her.
> Patients and students hold her very dear.
> The doctors love her, tease her, use her skill.
> They say, "The Chief" himself is half-afraid of her.

It is neither Rembrandt nor Velasquez, but it is a genuine Henley, of the very first rank as a portrait in English verse.

With this deliberate and unique aim in view, it is worth while requoting and re-examining the finest portrait of all, perhaps the finest portrait ever painted in English poetry. Indeed, outside the works of Henley, very few exist to be compared with it. I mean, of course, *The Apparition*, exquisitely apt title for that picture of Stevenson, the amazing visitor who entered like the very Spirit of Romance, prophesying freedom, and loaded the invalid's bed with "big yellow books quite impudently French."

> Thin-legged, thin-chested, slight unspeakably,
> Neat-footed and weak-fingered; in his face—
> Lean, large-boned, curved of beak, and touched with race,
> Bold-lipped, rich-tinted, mutable as the sea,
> The brown eyes radiant with vivacity—
> There shines a brilliant and romantic grace,
> A spirit intense and rare, with trace on trace
> Of passion and impudence and energy;

Valiant in velvet, light in ragged luck,
Most vain, most generous, sternly critical,
Buffoon and poet, lover and sensualist :
A deal of Ariel, just a streak of Puck,
Much Antony, of Hamlet most of all,
And something of the Shorter-Catechist.

Every line, every phrase of every line, is masterly and alive with significance. There is not one botched stroke from the first syllable to the last. But it might as well have been exhibited to dead men as to most of the critics of his own time, one of whom —Leslie Stephen—spoke of Henley's early verses generally as being of "the Swinburnian kind"! Nor has the matter been readjusted, for many of those who acclaim Henley to-day are almost equally wrong in the grounds of their praise, while those who depreciate him as the "little man of the day before yesterday" are usually of a size that Henley, the old tiger of criticism, could have swallowed by the hundred at one fiery yawn of his capacious mouth. It is true that many of his lyrics are commonplace "echoes" (as he himself calls some of them), ballads and roundels that have been done far better by a hundred hands. There are, too, irregular odes, anthems, and voluntaries that contain much of the pomp and circumstance of words, but very little of the inner light that transfigures the similar work of Francis Thompson. His work in all these kinds has been praised and blamed indiscriminately ; and this is a real injustice, for in his true gift he stood alone. A worse injustice has been done to him by those of his friends who realize the inadequacy of much that has been praised by the undiscriminating and would declare, like the *Dictionary of National Biography*, that "his verse was the occasional recreation of a life mainly occupied with editing and the criticism of literature and art," or that his value to posterity lies in the fact that he endured suffering with courage. Some years ago an editor invited me to write an article about the Henley who "suffered like a Red Indian at the stake, but not very much, please, about his poetry." This point of view would indeed be unjust to Henley (and would also lead to an appalling confusion of values in literature), since it not only obscures the best he had to give us, but it would give him a higher rank than Shakespeare himself, or the bountifully happy Dickens and Browning, who were comparatively at ease in Zion. Moreover, there was another man, named Wilkins, who suffered more than Henley ever imagined, and the editor aforesaid had no desire whatever for an article on the sufferings of Wilkins. Possibly this was because the editor conducted a literary journal.

The values of literature are not to be determined by impossible estimates of the comparative suffering in life of those who produced it. Neither shall a man be accounted a great pianist because he has suffered from sciatica. You may point out that a man has been an engine-driver, or a policeman, or a blacksmith, or a sailor, or a balloonist, but none of these things will convince a sane critic that the individual in question can either play the organ or write a poem. All we are concerned with in art and literature is this one question, *Is the work good or bad?* If it be bad, then no desire or regret will make it valuable to the world. Nor shall it rank with the works of Rabelais or Mark Twain, Horace or Chaucer—eupeptic craftsmen all—though the writer of it suffer the tortures of the damned. These values must not be confused by the general after-war carelessness. Literature enshrines the best of our civilization. It is the surest and strongest bridge between the past and the future. If we blow it up, we lose not only the artistic side of the past but the human tradition also.

Henley was a great artist. That is why the

attention of the critic can safely be concentrated upon his work; for it is through his work that the great-hearted man still speaks to us. And, indeed, if there were one thing he tried to convey to us more than another, it was the everlasting joy that he found in life. Even in that bleak hospital he speaks of the fun and frolic scattered through a penny-whistle, tickled by artistic fingers, to the tune of "The Wind that Shakes the Barley." It is all portrait-painting, too:

> Kate the scrubber (forty summers,
> Stout but sportive) treads a measure,
> Grinning, in herself a ballet,
> Fixed as fate upon her audience.
>
> Stumps are shaking, crutch-supported;
> Splinted fingers tap the rhythm;
> And a head all helmed with plasters
> Wags a measured approbation.

This is a grim picture, but he did not mean us to lift our hands in horror. The keynote of it all is joy, grim joy in life, down "to the last edge of the corner-stone, death." It is not the wail of the sufferer. It is the triumphant cry, *non dolet.*

Moreover, it is not in the words and phrases where he flings his crutch that he displays his greatest strength. The kind of violence which he occasionally shows in his verse is more symptomatic of his physical affliction than of his mental power. Strength in art and literature is nearly always accompanied by the rarest delicacy of workmanship. It is the trip-hammer that can crack a nut without breaking the kernel, with a force and a precision unknown to slighter engines. This, as Henley himself knew, was the secret of Tennyson's delicate artistry and his power to put into a few lucid lines of *In Memoriam* the whole vast story of geology. Henley's own greatest work, his portraiture, is entirely free from the weakness of violence, for it was the outcome of his passion for life with all its humours. He continued this portrait painting in his sonnet on T. E. Brown, and in his *London Types,* his studies of the bus-driver, the hawker, the coster, and the Cockney girl, whose hats

> knock you speechless like a load of bricks.

It is really the basis of all his best prose-writing too. His essay on Burns, on Byron, his sketch of Disraeli, and a dozen others are all contributions to his unique portrait gallery. Incidentally, it may be pointed out with advantage at the present time that our old tiger of criticism had something to say about the great artist, whom it is the fashion to despise among the coteries (or was, yesterday, for another reaction is beginning). Of Tennyson's *Vastness* he said that no poem was so filled with " the fury of the seer "—the very quality which latter-day ignorance would rule out of Tennyson's work altogether. He compared the mellowing quality of other later work of Tennyson with that of " the later Rembrandt " ; and he explained, very carefully, for the benefit of this generation, the many snares that lay therein for the future feet of the young ass. Into all of these snares the young ass of our day has stumbled head-foremost, jubilantly hee-hawing : " Down with the early Victorians ! " Blessed, blessed phrase, surpassing even " Mesopotamia " as a substitute for thought among the self-styled " intellectuals ! "

Plain-spoken as Henley always was, he knew not only his own aims but his own limitations. " I have no invention," he said, and he would probably have failed in his plays hopelessly without the collaboration of Stevenson. From first to last his real gift was that of portraiture, where invention was less necessary than insight into the hearts, minds, and souls of his sitters. There is neither violence nor invention in his picture of the fish-wife, but there is the quiet strength of a giant :

> A hard north-easter fifty winters long
> Has bronzed and shrivelled sere her face and neck ;
> Her locks are wild and grey, her teeth a wreck ;
> Her foot is vast, her bowed leg spare and strong.

So she comes down, in her wide blue cloak, her great creel slung on her forehead, her gnarled brown fingers easing the heavy strap. The more the picture is studied, the greater it appears. Many of the words suggest secondary meanings, in the subtlest way. There is the wildness and greyness of the sea in the flowing of her locks, and this blending of the portrait into the background is continued in other phrases to the end of the sonnet.

Much of his patriotic verse was mere Prussianism. It is significant that even in his patriotic poetry Henley was at his best when he first personified England and then drew her portrait. It was in lines like these—staled as they may be by quotation —that he touched his greatest :

> They call you proud and hard,
> England, my England :
> You with worlds to watch and ward,
> England, my own !
> You whose mailed hands keep the keys
> Of such teeming destinies,
> You could know nor dread nor ease
> Were the Song on your bugles blown,
> England—
> Round the Pit on your bugles blown.

And after all, the distinguishing feature of his most famous poem, *Invictus*, is the fact that it is a portrait of the artist, painted by himself. No one who reads it aright will need to be assured that the greatness of this man is to be found in his poetical work, the best that he had to give us :

> Out of the night that covers me,
> Black as the Pit from pole to pole,
> I thank whatever gods may be
> For my unconquerable soul.
>
> . . . . .
>
> Beyond this place of wrath and tears
> Looms but the Horror of the shade ;
> And yet the menace of the years
> Finds, and shall find me, unafraid.
>
> It matters not how strait the gate,
> How charged with punishments the scroll,
> I am the master of my fate :
> I am the captain of my soul.

THE POEMS OF AUSTIN DOBSON

It was customary, at one time, to speak of the poems of Austin Dobson as if, within a strictly limited range, they were chiefly notable for their technical perfection. They were sometimes thought to be a little "precious,' or even exotic—dainties for the literary epicure, exquisitely painted butterflies, emerging from cocoons of golden silk spun by Théodore de Banville, rather than creatures of a warm and breathing humanity. It was one of those generalizations which, because they are in superficial accord with certain obvious facts, obscure many of the more important characteristics of the work. Like so many of the easy judgments of the present day, it became a kind of label for use on all occasions, and it prevented any real analysis of the successive volumes as they appeared.

The danger of attaching labels prematurely is clear enough when one finds, in some of the older books on Victorian literature, that the phrase "Neo-Pre-Raphaelitism" was supposed to be a fairly comprehensive summary of the work of Austin Dobson. There is certainly much that needs revision in the labels that are still attached to him. The quality of his technique has been over-estimated; but, on the other hand, he is greatly under-estimated as a poet of the affections, of simple pleasures and kindly human emotions. Among the English poets he will occupy a permanent place, not unlike that of Charles Lamb among our writers of prose. But he will survive, like many other poets, because of his rare felicities, not because of the general excellence of his craftsmanship in verse. In many ways, of course, his style is faultless. He possesses nearly all those negative virtues which greater poets have often lacked. His sense of the right use of words, their associations and inner meanings, is unerring, but something more than this is required to make the words flow and sing with that "inevitability," as of a natural law, which marks the imperishable things. It was one of the greatest of lyrical poets who said that "there must be something in the mere progress and resonance of the words, some secret in the very motion and cadence of the lines, perceptible but indefinable," before we can say that the form is wedded to the spirit of poetry. Some of the greatest lyrical poets have achieved this end only half a dozen times in their lives, and stupidity has always pointed to their worst work as proof that the end was never attained at all. When it is attained there is no sign of effort, and yet not the slightest concession to the difficulties of the medium. The rebellious words are conquered and move into their places without any sign of shuffling or adjustment; and the poem unfolds as naturally as a flower, whether it be an elaborate orchid or a simple briar-rose. The result is often confused by the unintelligent with the product of a shallow "facility." They have nothing in common; for the harmony of the first is organic, and the pains and "dear delays" and difficulties of its creation are hidden only because they belonged to its maker and not to itself, and because they were conquered, not merely evaded. The irony is that when there is no attempt to conquer them—when there is only a rough approximation to the thing aimed at—it is commonly supposed that the evidences of the artist's slackness are proof of greater power. They may show, of course, that he is not of the merely thoughtless order; but they also show that he is not of those who wrestle with the resisting mass, and conquer it, so that the flawless beauty emerges; whether it be on the great scale with Æschylus among the mountain peaks, or with the light-footed grace of Théodore de Banville, among his fairy-like rose-gardens and irised fountains :

> Comme une floraison par le printemps hâtée,
> Par l'effort de mon bras
> Tu sortiras du bloc, O jeune Galatée !
> Et tu me souriras !

The rhythmical law is one and the same through all the kinds of true poetry, as it is one and the same throughout nature ; and in service to it the poet finds his freedom of the universe ; so that even the most joyous and light-hearted of French poets could cry :

> J'irai jusques au ciel, dans ses voûtes profondes,
> Lui voler pour mes vers
> Le rhythme qu'en dansant chantent en chœur les mondes,
> Qui forment l'univers.

Whenever the lightest verse fulfils the musical law of its being and attains perfection of form, it enters into this universal "dance." Our English Parnassians thus achieved, more often than is recognized, a poetry that has a permanent value. This is true of Austin Dobson ; but certain reservations must be made with regard to the nature both of his technique and of its content. Much, even of his best work, has been placed by criticism in the wrong category. The elimination of *juvenilia*, and the careful exercise of the negative virtues of his art, have created the impression that he was much more of the *Parnassien* in verse than he actually was. There is an occasional stiffness, a slightly forced adjustment of the words to meet the exigencies of metre, which is never apparent in Théodore de Banville ;

and, in short, Austin Dobson is much more closely akin to the simpler poets whose songs "gushed out from the heart" than to the delicate artists with whom his critics have usually ranged him.

We may consider, for instance, one of his best poems—*A Revolutionary Relic* :

> 'Tis the tale of grief and gladness
> Told by sad St. Pierre of yore,
> That in front of France's madness
> Hangs a strange seductive sadness
> Grown pathetic evermore.

The form is derivative, of course, as that of all poems must be to a certain extent ; but the point is that it is derived in its method of attack, in every cadence of its stanza, and in its very atmosphere, from nothing more exotic than what may be called the foreign ballads of Longfellow, in such verse as this from *Birds of Passage* :

> Like a print in books of fables
> Or a model made for show,
> With its pointed roofs and gables,
> Dormer windows, scrolls and labels,
> Lay the city far below.

There is nothing derogatory in this. Nor would Austin Dobson himself have thought so. His own beautiful tributes to the absurdly depreciated poetry of Longfellow (tributes that are conveniently ignored by the literary snobbery of the hour, as are the similar tributes of Henley and Andrew Lang to the best work of the same poet of simple human affections) prove this abundantly. It is merely a question of establishing a fact.

> As I read I marvel whether
> In some pleasant old château
> Once they read this book together,
> In the scented summer weather,
> With the shining Loire below.

Would any reader be quite certain, apart from the clue of the French words in this stanza, which of the two poets had written it ? It happens, of course, to be Dobson. But even then :

> Far above it, on the steep,
> Ruined stands the old château ;
> Nothing but the donjon-keep
> Left for shelter and for show ;

and we are back again with Longfellow and Oliver Basselin. There are many other passages that could be quoted, scores of them, to establish not only a superficial similarity in the handling of words and metres, but also a similarity of sentiment, even when the poem wears the fancy dress of the eighteenth century. Dobson explains the fancy dress clearly enough in the *Epilogue to Eighteenth Century Vignettes.* It is as clear in *The Child Musician* as it is in *The Mosque of the Caliph* or *The Old Sedan Chair* with its echoes of Thackeray :

> It was cushioned with silk, it was wadded with hair,
> As the birds have discovered—that old Sedan chair.

And whether he turns to France or the Orient, the explanation of the underlying similarity may be given in his own words :

> We lay our story in the East.
> Because 'tis Eastern ? Not the least.
> We place it there because we fear
> To bring its parable too near.

And perhaps, occasionally, to avoid a too obvious wearing of the very human heart upon the sleeve. And Longfellow sometimes did precisely the same thing :

> Haroun Alraschid, in the days
> He went about his vagrant ways
> And prowled at eve for good or bad
> In lanes and alleys of Bagdad,
> Once found, at edge of the bazaar,
> E'en where the poorest workers are. . . .

But I have inverted the order. The poem should surely run thus :

One day, Haroun Al Raschid read
A book wherein the poet said,
Where are the kings and where the rest
Of those who once the world possessed ?
They 're gone with all their pomp and show,
They 're gone the way that thou shalt go . . .

O thou who choosest for thy share
The world, and what the world calls fair,
Take all that it can give or lend,
But know that death is at the end.

Haroun Al Raschid bowed his head ;
Tears fell upon the page he read.

One of these passages is from Dobson ; the other is from Longfellow. The reader may decide for himself.

Moreover,—

On the eighteenth of April, in Seventy-five ;
Hardly a man is now alive
Who remembers. . . .'

But again I fear I have inverted the order ; for surely it was :

Seventeen hundred and thirty-nine,
That was the date of this tale of mine ;

For one on the ride of Revere was made ;
But this is the Ballad of Beau Brocade.

Leaving those who like riddles to disentangle the various authors involved (with the assurance that several of these lines are by Longfellow and several by Austin Dobson), let us return, for a moment, to consider the technique of the *Revolutionary Relic.* In the stanza which I quoted above, the line

That in front of France's madness

is typical of one of Dobson's faults. His use of the word " France's," a form that is not used in good prose because it is ugly (the armies of France, the history of France, being preferable to France's armies, or France's history)—is a concession exacted from him in verse by the difficulty of his medium. It is only a slight concession ; but it is in these very slight matters that the little more and the little less make a world of difference in the technique of verse. Even if it were not ugly, it would be wrong, not because it is an unusual form, but because the metre compelled it, and though a thousand arguments can be adduced in its favour, the finer sense of the ear, and what is more important, the artistic conscience, knows that it was forced and it gives the line a stiffness, an awkwardness, a feeling that the poet is not in complete mastery of his instrument. It is all very well to talk of "facility" in verse ; but the "facility" that shows no sign of effort is only achieved in one way, by the conquest of just these little difficulties ; and the poets who write with the flowing freedom of

> I know a bank where the wild thyme blows,

or with the more deliberate art of *The Eagle* :

> The wrinkled sea beneath him crawls.
> He watches from his mountain walls
> And, like a thunder-bolt, he falls,

show no signs of labour, either because they have conquered these difficulties, or because their mastery over their instrument is so complete that it has become a perfectly natural means of expression to them and they can forget all about it.

In the same *Revolutionary Relic* there are other minor faults. A "sadness grown pathetic" is very much the same thing as a "pathos grown sad." There is not enough differentiation of ideas to deserve the verb or the sentence. In short, it is padding to fill out the line. There is also in the fourteenth stanza the use of the older form "waileth" and "wheeleth," where it is useful to the metre, and again the modern form "halts" and "seems" in other stanzas, where it is more convenient. Precedents can be alleged, but it is a fault as it is done here. Even in the *Essays in Old French Forms* there are similar faults. There is too much reliance on that easier method of finding a feminine rhyme in present participles; and even then, if the seamews are *crying* in one line you may find that the waves are forced to be *plying* the reef in another. In the almost perfect "Love comes back to his vacant dwelling" there is just that awkwardness in the arrangement of the words of a subsequent line—"He makes as though in our arms repelling"—that robs it of its final supremacy. On the other hand, there is the quite flawless:

> Chicken-skin, delicate, white,
> Painted by Carlo Vanloo,
> Loves in a riot of light,
> Roses and vaporous blue;
> Hark to the dainty *frou-frou*!
> Picture above, if you can,
> Eyes that could melt as the dew,—
> This was the Pompadour's fan!

Precise in every beat, absolutely natural in the order of the words, exquisitely true and unforced in its rhymes, and coming down on the first syllable of each line with the unerring pulse of the dancer's feet in a minuet, the poem—for it is a poem, not merely *vers de société*—mounts with an airy and half-smiling grace to a burden that suggests a gay and brightly coloured world, vanishing at a waft of its painted daintiness:

> Where is the Pompadour, too?
> This was the Pompadour's fan.

It joins the universal dance of Théodore de Banville's famous ballads, and is therefore poetry.

But it is not in these experiments that Austin Dobson achieves his greatest successes.

"*Yes ; when the ways oppose,*" he begins his *Ars Victrix*, in imitation of Gautier ; and never did an opening line sound more like a translation by a somewhat stiff hand. Then, suddenly, a page is turned and we get the flowing melody of :

> The ladies of St. James's !
> They are so fine and fair,
> You 'd think a box of essences
> Was broken in the air :
> But Phyllida, my Phyllida !
> The breath of heath and furze
> When breezes blow at morning
> Is not so fresh as hers.
>
> The ladies of St. James's !
> They 're painted to the eyes.
> Their white it stays for ever,
> Their red it never dies :
> But Phyllida, my Phyllida,
> Her colour comes and goes.
> It trembles to a lily—
> It wavers to a rose.
>
> The ladies of St. James's !
> You scarce can understand
> The half of all their speeches,
> Their phrases are so grand :
> But Phyllida, my Phyllida !
> Her shy and simple words
> Are clear as after rain-drops
> The music of the birds.

The lines are familiar enough as a piece of eighteenth-century fancy dress ; but it is not the fancy dress that gives them their warmth and life. There is a human heart beating beneath it in wistfulness and longing ; and the quiet poignancy of the desire that all poets know for the true and simple things. The poem may be regarded quite justly as an invocation addressed to the poet's own Muse. If there be any masquerading in it, it is merely the old device of hiding something that is deeply felt with a smile ; and if the reader cares to meet the poet half-way, he will find that these stanzas—quietly repeated—have the true ecstasy pulsing in them.

In fact, whenever Austin Dobson relies on his craftsmanship and his eighteenth-century furniture, or his merely decorative effects, as in *The Masque of the Months*, his work is comparatively a failure ; and whenever he deals with kindly and simple human beings, his work kindles with affection and he sometimes achieves a little masterpiece. There is nothing very much better of its kind in the language than *The Curé's Progress* :

> There 's a little dispute with a merchant of fruit
> Who is said to be heterodox,
> That will ended be with a "Ma foi, oui !"
> And a pinch from the Curé's box.
>
> There is also a word that no one heard
> To the furrier's daughter Lou ;
> And a pale cheek fed with a flickering red
> And a "*Bon Dieu garde M'sieu !*"
>
> But a grander way for the *Sous Préfet*
> And a bow for Ma'am'selle Anne ;
> And a mock "off-hat" to the Notary's cat,
> And a nod to the Sacristan :—
>
> For ever through life the Curé goes
> With a smile on his kind old face—
> With his coat worn bare, and his straggling hair
> And his green umbrella case.

Technically, it is not perfect ; the inversion of "That will ended be" for the sake of the internal rhyme is a concession to a difficulty, not a conquest of it. But it is a marvellous little picture of a living human being; and the "mock off-hat" is as vividly and lightly touched in as anything of the kind in English poetry. It is poetry because almost every pulse of its metre is creative, and helps to reveal an unforgettable character on his own kindly pilgrimage through time. *The Child Musician* and *A Gentleman of the Old School* are two other examples of the same mastery; and in the latter of these there is once again that note of longing for a simplicity lost by the modern world:

We read—alas, how much we read!
The jumbled strifes of creed and creed
With endless controversies feed
  Our groaning tables;
His books—and they sufficed him—were
Cotton's *Montaigne, The Grave* of Blair,
A *Walton*—much the worse for wear—
  And *Æsop's Fables*.

One more—The Bible. Not that he
Had searched its page as deep as we;
No sophistries could make him see
  Its slender credit;
It may be that he could not count
The sires and sons to Jesse's fount—
He liked "The Sermon on the Mount"—
  And more, he read it.

. . . . . .

Lie softly, Leisure! Doubtless you
With too serene a conscience drew
Your easy breath, and slumbered through
  The gravest issue;
But we, to whom our age allows
Scarce space to wipe our weary brows,
Look down upon your narrow house,
  Old friend, and miss you.

Of the poems written in the manner of Gay, it is enough to say here that they are faultless of their kind, and better than the original models. Taken all together, with what may be called the critical poems—including *The Fables, The Prologues and Epilogues, The Varia*, the memorial verses, the beautiful tribute to Tennyson and the delightful little epistles to Mr. Edmund Gosse and others—they constitute perhaps the best *Ars Poetica* in English verse. They have an insight into the essentials of good writing and a mellow wisdom that might be of incalculable value to the present chaotic generation.

We are constantly being told by writers whose ignorance of their subject is only equalled by their conceit, that the young poets of to-day are "sick to death" of the set mechanical forms of the great Victorian poets. If the Victorian poets wrote in set mechanical forms then they were not "great." But the plain truth of the matter is that the forms of English poetry were expanded and extended in a thousand new directions during the Victorian period. More new metrical forms were invented by Browning and Swinburne alone than are to be counted in the whole range of preceding English poetry; and almost every lyric that Tennyson wrote, from his earliest *juvenilia* to *Crossing the Bar*, had something in its cadence or movement that was not to be found in English poetry before him. This is also true of Christina Rossetti and a dozen other poets. The forms of verse were not nearly so "set" as they were when Greece and Rome expressed themselves in their hexameters and pentameters. No Victorian of importance was as limited in his metrical range as some of the most important poets of the Elizabethan, or indeed of any other period. It could almost be demonstrated that taken all together the Victorians invented and used more new rhythmical movements that all the poets of all former periods combined. Tennyson's *Maud* alone has a range of metrical invention and metrical freedom wider than that of all the poets combined in many preceding centuries. The reader who doubts it has only to open the volume and note the forms which are not to be found in earlier poets. Even in the academic Matthew Arnold there are many quite new rhythmical movements, exquisitely free in their musical law, like the *Songs of Callicles*, or *Dover Beach*, or *In Utrumque Paratus*. The plain fact is that the modern "revolt" is not against "set forms," but against form itself—a very different matter—and all too often it obviously proceeds from the consciousness that the "rebel" cannot hope to compete with his predecessors unless the standards are lowered. It is a tendency that is manifest not only in literature, but in all the arts and throughout the whole of our civilization, and it is time that it was met and answered. Curiously enough, one of the most obvious facts about the outstanding work of the "revolting" groups (there are others, of course) is that, with one or two exceptions, it has been in forms that may justly be called "set"—the sonnet, the stanzas used by Chaucer and William Morris, and sometimes quatrains that have been made a little easier to handle by the simple process of rhyming only the second and fourth lines, or by accepting various rough approximations to the end in view. The rest of the "revolt" is mere chaos. The revolt against form, in fact, forbids results in art. It is not a revolt against Victorianism, but a revolt against order and proportion and the laws of good writing in all ages. Worst of all, it is a revolt against the only principle that can lead to the really valuable new results—the principle of *development*, the natural evolution of a great tradition. The present generation is being confused by its present pastors—some of them merely ignorant guides who are striving to turn literature into a kind of walking race, in which the first duty is to be "abreast" of an age that has almost ceased to believe in anything but the material rewards for work badly done. The gospel naturally appeals to many of the young who desire a quick and easy road to such rewards; but those who utter the warning must not be regarded as the enemies of the young or apostles of reaction; and there could be hardly any friend more useful, more likely to help the young to a real appreciation and knowledge of literature, than one who should say, "Give a certain portion of your days and nights to the study of the *Ars Poetica* in these poems of Austin Dobson. Do this one thing thoroughly, and with only a little readiness to learn, and you will then be at least better qualified to express your own opinions."

But this part of the work is primarily critical; and the essential poetry of Austin Dobson is usually to be found in the kind which I have indicated earlier.

On more than one occasion, however, the kinds were united, as when he filled an old French form with his own human pity and made one of his most perfect poems, a lyric touched with the light and consecration to which he laid no claim. It is time that criticism should claim it for him in such work as this:

> In Angel-court the sunless air
> Grows faint and sick; to left and right
> The cowering houses shrink from sight
> Huddled and hopeless, eyeless, bare.
> Misnamed, you say? For surely rare
> Must be the angel-shapes that light
> In Angel-court.
>
> Nay! the Eternities are there.
> Death at the doorway stands to smite;
> Life in its garrets leaps to flight;
> And Love has climbed the crumbling stair
> In Angel-court.

In the last five lines there are beauty, power of imagination, and high poetry; and in themselves they would justify an affirmative answer to the question in the poem that ends his works—*In After Days.*

This last poem has the diamond-like form that makes for permanence. It is rounded and delicate and whole as a single drop of dew that can yet reflect the depth and glory of the sky in its own small lucid mirror. No competent reader can help feeling the poignancy of its regret for something that our literature is in danger of losing. There were realms of literature once, and there are still (though they are surrounded by a thousand enemies) in which it would seem small praise to say of a man that he kept his pen from defilement. But I cannot help remembering the question asked by a critic in a leading journal with regard to the dullest, dirtiest, and worst-written book that was ever printed and suppressed—" *If this is not high art, what is ?* "

What is ? It would be easy to give a more imposing answer ; but it would be quite enough to point to the brief leave-taking of Austin Dobson and say, to begin with, and for the reasons I have given above, *this* :

In after days, when grasses high
O'ertop the stone where I shall lie,
  Though ill or well the world adjust
  My slender claim to honoured dust,
I shall not question or reply.

I shall not see the morning sky ;
I shall not hear the night-wind sigh ;
I shall be mute, as all men must
  In after days.

But yet, now living, fain would I
That some one then should testify,
  Saying, " He held his pen in trust
  To Art, not serving shame or lust."
Will none ? Then let my memory die
  In after days !

STEVENSON

STEVENSON is in some ways the most intimately known personality in our literature. Many others —though not so many as a section of recent criticism would have us believe—have left greater masterpieces to the world; few have left so vivid and affectionate a memory. Many years ago Sir James Barrie wrote a poem on Stevenson, in which he made Scotland herself say :

> I 've ha'en o' brawer sons a flow.
> My Walter more renown could win ;
> And he that followed at the plough,
> But Louis was my Benjamin.

It throws a strange light on the human spirit, and its independence of space and time, to reflect that this intimacy, which enables his readers to follow the very tones of his voice, to see the sparkling of the brown eyes, to hear his whimsical laughter, was deepened and quickened by his isolation in a remote world. The vanished Tusitala—as he signed himself in that moving and prophetic last letter to Mr. Edmund Gosse—is here, living and breathing ; flashing that brilliant smile upon us, eager as ever to press forward on the great adventure of art and life. But it was there, among his island palm-trees, with the sound of the Pacific around him, that he discovered his own country, and that his country learned to know him. There is a more potent annihilator of space and time than wireless telegraphy, and we did not need his own epitaph to tell us that he had found it. All Scotland is in that other letter from the South Seas to his old Scots nurse :

MY DEAREST CUMMY,—This goes to you with a Merry Christmas and a Happy New Year. The Happy New Year anyway, for I think it should reach you about *Noor's Day.* I dare say it may be cold and frosty. Do you remember when you used to take me out of bed in the early morning, carry me to the back windows, show me the hills of Fife, and quote to me :

"A' the hills are covered wi' snaw,
An' winter 's noo come fairly."

It is indeed an abiding memory now.

Blows the wind to-day, and the sun and the rain are flying,
Blows the wind on the moors to-day and now,
Where about the graves of the martyrs the whaups are crying,
My heart remembers how !

Grey recumbent tombs of the dead in desert places,
Standing-stones on the vacant wine-red moor,
Hills of sheep, and the homes of the silent vanished races,
And winds, austere and pure !

Be it granted me to behold you again in dying,
Hills of home ! . . .

It was granted, and more than granted ; for if ever a man saw those hills, it was the author of those lines while he was writing them.

The poetry of Stevenson has never received its full due ; for in this country all diversity of genius is regarded with suspicion. Slight as is the volume of his verse, it is all on the level of the permanent things ; and, at its best, his lyrical note is enchanting as that of Herrick. Indeed, in *Our Lady of the Snows*, in *Youth and Love*, and in his *Requiem* he strikes a more poignant note than Herrick ever struck. I have dwelt elsewhere in this volume on the originality of some of his verse-movements. The lines to his wife:

> Trusty, dusky, vivid, true,

the poem to an air of Diabelli, the exquisite *Let Beauty Awake*, are entirely his own in movement; and the fact that there is nothing startling about the novelty is merely another proof that we are still only at the beginning of metrical invention in quite simple forms. He was one of the first to use the two pairs of long stresses in antithesis—

> Green days in forests and blue days at sea,

which so many later writers have employed; and there are many other technical devices which he either invents or uses more felicitously than almost any other poet. One of these is the concealed internal rhyme:

> Yet shall your ragged moor receive
> The in*comp*arable *pomp* of eve. . . .

He uses this in a way that gives an extraordinary compactness to his line. In his blank verse, too, he has naturalized the classical manner in our modern tongue more happily than any other writer of the nineteenth century, with the exceptions of Tennyson and Landor. The concealed rhymes, the variation of the position of the pauses, the structure of the verse paragraph—all are masterly:

> I heard the pulse of the besieging sea
> Throb far away all night. I heard the wind
> Fly crying and convulse tumultuous palms.

His quiet influence on later poetry, too, has been overlooked. It is not necessary to go to the Greek Anthology to discover where the Shropshire lad learned to flute a country tune so haunting:

> It is the season now to go
> About the country high and low . . .

The brooding boy, the sighing maid,
Wholly fain and half afraid,
Now meet along the hazel'd brook
To pass and linger, pause and look.

The very manner, the very cadence, the very note—all are there in Stevenson ; and it was from Stevenson, too, that the splendid phrases on the hour "when heaven was falling," and the shoulders that "held the sky suspended," were quarried :

For those he loves that under-prop
With daily virtues Heaven's top,
And bear the falling sky with ease. . . .

There is more life in the moods of the earlier poet, and a sounder, because a more comprehensive, philosophy ; but there is no doubt whatever that Stevenson was the fountain-head of the later lyrics. The variety of the verse in Stevenson, and the more difficult measures that he often invents and uses so effectively, have a more durable charm than that of the more monotonous metres of the later poet. But Stevenson's poems have had a wider influence than this. Ballads like *Ticonderoga* have had a numerous offspring in later years. The use of the definite article in the following lines has been familiarized to us by Mr. Kipling, and it points to Stevenson even more than to the old ballads as one of the influences upon some of the later poet's powerful work :

When I was at home in my father's house
  In the land of the naked knee,
Between the eagles that fly in the lift
  And the herrings that swim in the sea . . .

There fell a war in a woody place
  Lay far across the sea,
A war of the march in the mirk midnight
  And the shot from behind the tree,
The shaven head and the painted face,
  The silent foot in the wood. . . .

In the first of these cases, Stevenson is far the more comprehensive poet; in the second, of course, Mr. Kipling has the wider range. But there is a perfection of form in all Stevenson's work that gives it a permanent place among the best of its kind.

One may add here that this applies only to the work that he himself chose to publish. A very strong protest ought to be made against the carelessness which has allowed some of his rough drafts to be published in a recent edition as "New Poems." Every one knows the beautifully finished little lyric which opens *Treasure Island*:

> If sailor tales to sailor tunes,
>   Storm and adventure, heat and cold,
> If schooners, islands, and maroons,
>   And Buccaneers and buried Gold,
> And all the old romance retold
>   Exactly in the ancient way,
> Can please, as me they pleased of old,
>   The wiser youngsters of to-day;
>
> So be it and fall on . . .

Among the "New Poems" there is a rough draft, or rather a series of jottings and emendations and repetitions, which is printed thus:

> Of Schooners, Islands and Maroons,
>   And Buccaneers and Buried Gold,
> And Torches red and rising moons,
>   If all the old romance re-told
> Exactly in the ancient way,
>   Can please, as me they pleased of old,
> The wiser youngsters of to-day,
> So be it, and fall on! If not—
>   If all the boys on better things
> Have set their spirits and forgot—
>   So be it and fall on! If not—
> If all the boys on solid food
>   Have set their fancies . . .

And so on, with other repetitions and other emendations, to the end. This is by no means the only example. A dreadful hash is made of the beautiful poem to an air of Diabelli. In one case, a muddle is made of emendations and corrections in two poems, and the result is served up as a single "new poem." That this kind of thing can be done with the work of so exquisitely conscientious an artist as Stevenson is scandalous in itself, and no condemnation can be too severe for it. But that it should be allowed to pass without condemnation is also indicative of the chaotic state of a great part of modern criticism.

There is, of course, to-day a "reaction" against Stevenson; but it is time that criticism should recognize the reactions of fashion when it sees them, and refuse to be swayed by them. They occur, quite mechanically in many cases, through all our literary history, and they indicate only the mental instability of those who are blindly swayed by them, for they have no relation whatsoever to real values. It is entirely right that there should be new developments in literature; but it is entirely wrong that these new developments should blind us to the excellence achieved by the past. It seems impossible at the present day to get criticism to recognize those two complementary halves of the truth simultaneously. Your modern critic will have it that you must be a supporter of one half of the truth or of the other, either a reactionary or a progressive. It was not a reactionary, but the apostle of European freedom, Mazzini, who once said that he felt it his duty to protest earnestly against these blind reactions in literature, these cavillings at the achievements of past generations. He saw that these "reactions" were too often a mere cloak for mediocrity, which always hates the man who is a master of his craft, the man who has had the temerity to labour so arduously and finish so thoroughly that his work acquires the time-defying quality of the diamond, and challenges posterity with a lucid perfection which it may well despair of rivalling.

Stevenson wrote with that sensitiveness to the inner meanings of words which is essential to their right use. He would never have written, as Mr. Bennett wrote in one of his most admired passages, of "a banner waved by an expiring arm." The meaning of the verb expire, to emit the breath, is not prehistoric; and in all good writing that meaning is retained even when it is used figuratively. Time may expire; but in literature neither an arm nor a leg should be allowed to do so. These members of the body are the very last portions of the material universe to which a word describing a function of the lungs and the mouth should be applied. A boot might as well be called a respirator; and the misuse of the word is of exactly the same kind as the misuse of "transpire" for "happen" at which Mr. Kipling (a master, always, of the right use of words) has so happily smiled in one of his poems. These are not trivial or academic details. They affect the whole texture of the work; and only the man who has the instinct for those inner meanings can evoke from words all the magic and power and beauty that lie hidden in them. There is no other way by which he can fully express himself in literature. To say one thing when you really mean another is not enough; nor are rough approximations enough. Failure here connotes many other defects. The slap-dash criticism of the hour may be too hurried to note them; but they make all the difference between the enduring and the ephemeral. Excellence in these things is not common. It is extremely rare. This is one aspect of what Stevenson meant by "style" when, out of his passionate devotion to literature and its traditions, he struck that note of fear for its future: "The little artificial popularity of style in England tends to die out. The British pig returns to his true love, the love of the styleless, of the shapeless, of the slap-dash and the disorderly. There is trouble coming, I think ; and you may have to hold the fort for us in evil days."

This prophecy, nearly half a century old now, has been justified by events, and more than justified ; for it is clear enough to-day that the tendency of which he spoke was part of a larger movement of the whole body of civilization towards something like a new barbarism, a barbarism that is all the more dangerous because its lowering of the standards is often superficially amusing. It appeals to everything that is lazy in us, everything that is tired of restriction, and of the more difficult way. So-called practical men often seem to think that literature is a sort of polite amusement, without any bearing on the larger affairs of their own world. The Englishman looks at the books in his own house, and is blind to the millions of their kind that circulate like beneficent or hurtful bacilli through the body politic, not only of this country, but also of that great country across the Atlantic where more than a hundred million souls now read our tongue. To walk through a public library in California, and note the scores of books by British writers on those distant shelves, is to realize that the men of letters of to-day have something in trust ; and that if they are false to their trust, or are careless about it, they are undermining a great tradition, and perhaps even hurting their own country. To catch a glimpse of the beautiful little Stevenson monument in San Francisco (far more beautiful than any monument that his own country has yet erected to him, and, indeed, one of the most spontaneous tokens of international affection in the world to-day) is to realize that Stevenson in his devotion to literature was perhaps even truer to his trust than he knew ; and it was his own exquisite sensitiveness to that trust that made him hear the first distant footsteps of the barbarous enemy. He anticipated the peril of civilization through his devotion to literature; for it is in the art and letters of a nation that you may discover the first symptoms of anything really profoundly wrong. It is through art and letters—the expression of a people's inner life—that the moving finger writes the *Mene, Mene*, on the walls of nations. The doom was clearly written there before Rome fell. It was clearly written there before the French Revolution; and it was clearly written there before the downfall of Russia. It is not clearly written in the literature of England; for there are many conflicting tendencies. But there are many of the outward signs of intellectual chaos, the loss of any really fundamental conviction, and the degradation of the standards in art and life. Recently, coming out of a theatre, I heard two of the audience discussing a new play. "Very interesting," said one of them, "but the morality was at least ten years old." It would be interesting to know what Stevenson in his capacity of the "shorter-catechist" would have had to say about this. I imagine that it might have led to a brief "counter-blast ironical" which would have cleared the air immediately.

The one great natural fact that needs to be impressed upon the world to-day is the fact that without law there is no freedom. There is no freedom even for the traffic in a city without law; and when you come to the consideration of the freedom of the spirit in the infinitely more complicated and exquisite traffics and discoveries of art, its dependence upon law is even more certain. There is an absurd idea to-day that genius is opposed to law. It is always opposed to arbitrary pedantries; but on law, in the larger and nobler sense, its very life depends. "The spirit of the artist," as even the opium-eating genius who wrote *Kubla Khan* said, "must of necessity circumscribe itself with rules. It must embody itself in order to reveal itself; but a living body is of necessity an organized body, and what is organization but the connection of parts in and for a whole? This is a necessity of the human mind, and all nations have felt and obeyed it in the invention of metre and measured sounds as the vehicle of poetry; and in the laws of order, harmony, and proportion that govern the cadences of prose." It is quite obvious that all this has a bearing on the wider modern tendencies of which I have spoken.

The two literary artists of the nineteenth century who most clearly understood all that is implied by this, and exemplified it in their own technique, and might therefore have the most salutary influence at the present moment, were, in poetry, Tennyson (against whom the heathen were raging with complete lack of understanding until quite recently) and, in prose, Robert Louis Stevenson, against whom they are just beginning to turn their weapons.

Stevenson was not only the first artist in prose of the latter part of the nineteenth century. A great painter once said of him that he was the first living artist in any form. "I don't mean writers merely, but painters, and all of us. Nobody living can see with such an eye as that fellow, and nobody is such a master of his tools." There was at least one respect in which he was a greater artist than Sir Walter Scott, and that was his unerring instinct for selection of the significant detail. Art can almost be defined, on one side, as selection. "Give me a blue pencil," he once said, "and I will make an epic out of a daily newspaper."

It seems to be commonly supposed to-day that style in literature means a preoccupation with unessential forms and a consequent lack of everything that would really interest the reader. It means, of course, exactly the opposite. It means, first of all, the expression of a vital personality; and, on the technical side, it means the selection by that personality of the significant detail, the significant word, the significant cadence, that suggest far more than themselves, and so enable the writer to economize the reader's attention. It was one of the greatest intellects in English literature who said that the problem of poetry, at its highest, was that of putting the infinite into the finite. It is, in fact, the problem of all art at its greatest—to touch the temporal with the light of the eternal, to use the seen as a means of shadowing forth the unseen; by a process where much is represented in little.

Stevenson's view of the function of art at its highest was just this. He expressed it in that little prose-poem which is to be found in one of his letters to W. E. Henley:

> Sursum corda!
> Heave ahead;
> Here 's luck!
> Art and blue heaven,
> April and God's larks,
> Green reeds and the sky-scattering river,
> A stately music,
> Enter God!

"Ah, but you know," he continued, "until a man can write that 'Enter God' he has achieved no art, none! Come, let us take counsel together and make some."

All creative art, in other words, is symbolical; the burden that would otherwise be too heavy to support rests upon words and symbols, where much is represented in little. But did the light-hearted Stevenson, that son of joy, really carry his own theory into practice? Let us take him, for instance, at his airiest, in that delightful little volume which he once thought of calling "Penny-Whistles." In the *Child's Garden of Verses* we have a perfect example (itself in little) of how the poet can use small things to symbolize and shadow forth greater things. We find him there selecting the very simplest and clearest and best words; toiling, like his own monkish scribe, to give his thought just that lucidity which at last reflects, like a mountain-pool, a corner of blue heaven. But because there is no sign of effort, it is supposed by the unintelligent to be achieved without pains, and because it is so crystal-clear that it takes the infinite to its heart, it is supposed by turbid and shallow minds to be without any depth at all.

It may at first appear that the little poem with which he opens the *Child's Garden* is but a very small pail of clear water:

> I have to go to bed and see
> The birds still hopping on the tree,
> Or hear the grown-up people's feet
> Still going past me in the street.

I do not want to touch it with any more significance than it will bear; but does not a star begin to be reflected, faintly and tremulously, in that small pail of clear water when it is recalled that Tusitala himself was destined to leave, a little early, the life and the art that he loved so well.

> And does it not seem hard to you,
> When all the sky is clear and blue,
> And I should like so much to play,
> To have to go to bed by day?

It is clear enough that much is represented in little by the shadow-march of the North-West Passage. It is familiar enough as a child's poem. Consider it, for a moment, from our own point of view, here in a little lighted room, on a little planet, flying through the immensities of the universe :

All round the house is the jet-black night,
  It stares through the window-pane ;
It crawls in the corners, hiding from the light,
  And it moves with the moving flame.

Now my little heart goes a-beating like a drum
  With the breath of the Bogie in my hair ;
And all round the candle the crookéd shadows come
  And go marching along up the stair.

The shadow of the balusters, the shadow of the lamp,
  The shadow of the child that goes to bed—
All the wicked shadows coming, tramp—tramp—tramp,
  With the black night overhead.

The book is full of good-nights and good-byes. The Unseen Playmate is in it ; and there is even—so great is the magic of its art—a reduction to its very simplest terms of the greatest of all political problems. Half the wars of the world would have been avoided if, in our individual lives and in our national lives, we all fully understood the exquisite elfin satire of one poem in the *Child's Garden of Verses*—the poem on foreign children :

Little Indian, Sioux or Crow,
Little frosty Eskimo,
Little Turk or Japanee,
Oh ! don't you wish that you were me. . . .

Such a life is very fine ;
But it 's not so nice as mine,
You must often, as you trod,
Have wearied, *not* to be abroad.

You have curious things to eat,
I am fed on proper meat ;
You must dwell beyond the foam,
But I am safe and live at home.

There is all the pathos of human aspiration, I had almost said the pathos of human religion, in the last stanza of *The Lamplighter*, which deliberately in its first line adopts the fallacy which Voltaire satirized in *Candide*, and deliberately uses in its last line a cadence that, delicately as it is touched in, has unmistakable undertones :

> For we are very lucky, with a lamp before the door,
> And Leerie stops to light it as he lights so many more ;
> And oh ! before you hurry by with ladder and with light,
> O Leerie, see a little child and nod to him to-night.

These child-poems, in fact, illustrate Stevenson's peculiar gift of self-limitation. He writes always like a man who is telling tales to children. Sometimes it is a kind of self-parody, masking behind a half-smile the more serious thoughts that he would hesitate to wear upon his sleeve. He seizes, for instance, a very simple image, the image of the candle surrounded by shadows—and it was an image that Shakespeare used before him—to represent much in little.

The lines to Minnie, in the *Child's Garden of Verses*, contain a perfect example of Stevenson's use of this imagery, and of what may be called the poetry of candle-light at its simplest, though even the child might suspect that there was something deeper here than the echo of a nursery rhyme :

> The river, on from mill to mill,
> Flows past our childhood's garden still,
> But ah, we children never more
> Shall watch it from the water-door
> Below the yew—it still is there—
> Our phantom voices haunt the air
> As we were still at play,
> And I can hear them call and say,
> " *How far is it to Babylon ?* "

Ah, far enough, my dear,
Far, far enough from here—
Yet you have farther gone!
Can I get there by candle-light?
So goes the old refrain.
I do not know—perchance you might—
But only, children, learn it right,
Ah, never to return again!

The eternal dawn beyond a doubt
Shall break on hill and plain,
And put all stars and candles out
Ere we be young again.

Another wonderful use of candle-light is in *The Master of Ballantrae*, where the duel is fought between the two brothers, among the frosted trees, by the steady light of two candles in the windless night. One remembers what use he makes of those two points of light to enhance the deadly stillness of that scene: how the body of the Master was left lying in their light under the trees; and how, later on, Mr. Mackellar creeps back, guided by their distant brightness, to find one of the candle-sticks overthrown, and that taper quenched; the other burning steadily by itself, making all within its circle of light, by force of contrast with the surrounding blackness, brighter than day; showing the blood-stain in the midst, and the silver pommel of a sword; but of the body not a trace.

Then, too, there is that other haunting scene in *Treasure Island* which, though it wears the outward form of a boy's adventure-story, is from beginning to end suffused with poetry, by the sheer magic of an art that rejoiced in its narrow room and its self-imposed limitations as another might rejoice in the set form of a sonnet.

Consider, for instance, that candle-lit scene where Jim Hawkins and his mother open the dead buccaneer's sea-chest ; how significant is each carefully selected detail in the catalogue of what they discover there ; and representative of how much in little ; until it seems that in a few sentences the whole life and character of the old buccaneer are passed before you. They find " an old boat-cloak whitened with sea-salt on many a harbour-bar, a piece of bar silver, an old Spanish watch, and five or six curious West Indian shells. It has often set me thinking since that he should have carried about these shells with him in his wandering, guilty, and hunted life." All through the scene you are conscious that, beyond the little ring of candle-light, beyond the boy's adventure-story, there is that deeper night and that deeper thought. He uses the candle-light, as he used the ticking of the clock, to fulfil the task of the artist, and to set the temporal in relation to the eternal. This is what distinguishes *Treasure Island* from almost all other boys' books, and makes it an artistic masterpiece, an enduring contribution to English literature. Those superior critics of to-day who are beginning to talk of it as an example of the false picturesque can have neither eyes nor ears for his real achievement, which was that of an exquisitely subtle artist in something like a new form of poetry. Just as in the *New Arabian Nights* he subtly parodies the Oriental tales, so in *Treasure Island* he subtly parodies his own boyhood's delight in pirates, does it so delicately, with so delicious a whimsicality, so tenderly even, that its effect is infinitely heightened, as when a man is able to smile at his own enthusiasm and hold something in reserve. There are many respects in which certain scenes among Stevenson's pirates are quite legitimately comparable with the grave-digger's scene in *Hamlet* : Dick with his Bible ; Silver persuading his comrades that the voice that they had heard in the woods could not have been that of a spirit :

"Sperrit? Well, maybe," he said. "But there's one thing not clear to me. There was an echo. Now, no man ever seen a sperrit with a shadow; well, then, what's he doing with an echo to him, I should like to know? That ain't in natur', surely."

All these things, with Israel Hands' conclusion that if the spirit lives on, the killing of men is waste of time, belong to the kingdom of the mind; and, for all the simplicity of their terms, they are of the essential stuff of poetry.

The most consummate masterpiece of poetry in any language is probably that in which Shakespeare drew the symbolical figure of Hamlet against the dark background of Eternity. In a lighter mode, but with art hardly less consummate within its own deliberate self-limitation, Stevenson essayed a similar task. This is nowhere more apparent than in certain chapters of the *Ebb-tide*, a book whose greatness has never been fully appreciated. Recall, for instance, the scene in which the three would-be murderers, Hay, the broken-down university man; Davis, the American sea-captain; and Huish, the Cockney clerk, are seated at dinner with their intended victim, Attwater, on the lamp-lit verandah of his island-bungalow, a little lighted stage, surrounded by the immensities of the ocean-night; and how Attwater, that strange sardonic figure, under the mask of a sneering man of the world, concealed a religious passion so intense that his apparently chance-dropt words shook and pierced through the conscience of Hay, as the words of Hamlet overwhelmed that other murderer. Consider this scrap of their conversation, where the would-be murderers are trying to discover whether Attwater is really alone on his island:

"I must say this sherry is a really prime article," said Huish. "'Ow much does it stand you in, if it's a fair question?"

"A hundred and twelve shillings in London," said Attwater. "It strikes one as really not a bad fluid. So glad you like it. I was about to say that I have still eight dozen," he added, fixing the captain with his eye. "It seems almost worth it in itself—to a man fond of wine."

Huish and the captain sat up and regarded him with a scare.

"Worth what?" said Davis. "A hundred and twelve shillings," replied Attwater. With a great effort the captain changed the subject.

"I allow we are about the first white men upon this island, sir," said he.

"Too retired by 'alf," said Huish, "give me the sound of Bow Bells."

"This was once a busy shore," said Attwater, "although now, hark, you can hear the solitude. I find it stimulating. And talking of the sound of bells, kindly follow a little experiment of mine in silence."

There was a silver bell at his right hand. He struck it with force and leaned eagerly forward. The note rose clear and strong; it rang out clear and far into the night, and over the deserted island; it died into the distance until there only lingered in the porches of the ear a vibration that was sound no longer. "Empty houses, empty sea, solitary beaches," said Attwater, "and yet God hears the bell! And yet we sit in this verandah on a lighted stage with all heaven for spectators, and you call that solitude."

"That is a queer idea of yours," said the captain at last. "So you mean to tell me now that you sit here evenings and ring up, well, ring on the angels by yourself. . . ."

"As a matter of historic fact," said Attwater, "one does not. Why ring a bell, when there flows out from oneself and everything about one a far more momentous silence? The least beat of my heart and the least thought in my mind echoing into eternity for ever and for ever and for ever."

"O, look 'ere," said Huish, "turn down the lights at once and the Band of 'Ope will oblige. This ain't a spiritual seance."

"No folk-lore about Mr. Huish," said Attwater.

It is this sense of the eternities in his work that differentiates *Dr. Jekyll and Mr. Hyde*, with its wild closing gleam of candle-light, from almost all novels of what is called "sensation." This is the secret of those wonderful fables—or parables, for all his work has something of that quality in it—*Markheim* and *Will of the Mill*. They grip the reader and hold him instantly, with the sense that our mortality is here in the presence of immortal powers. *Will of the Mill*, too, holds the clue to all his *Songs of Travel*, and tells us whither even the armies that the child saw in the glowing fire are marching. The clue is in that extraordinarily beautiful passage about the troop of wandering men who once encountered a very old man shod with iron. The old man asked them whither they were going, and they answered with one voice, "to the Eternal City." He looked upon them gravely. "I have sought it," he said, "over the most part of the world. Three such pairs as I now carry on my feet have I worn upon this pilgrimage, and now the fourth is growing slender underneath my steps ; and all this while I have not found the City."

"All this while I have not found it!" If this were the final note of his work it would be in a sense a denial of the profound truth which he expressed in the little prose-poem on art which I quoted earlier. It is not possible for the mere intellect of man to find that infinitely distant and inscrutable City ; but the creative spirit, like the spirit of love, has reasons of which, as Pascal said, the mere reason knows nothing. The poet, the creative artist, in certain great gleaming moments, flashes to certainties, and does catch sight, though only through mists, of the hidden walls of that City. But when Stevenson wrote merely as a thinker, he lost sight of his own goal. In one of his most moving letters he wrote a passage which has a great significance for the present day, and strikes the keynote of much of our modern scepticism, of the nobler sort :

Yes; if I could believe in this immortality business, the world would indeed be too good to be true; but we were put here to do what service we can, for honour and not for hire. The sods cover us; and the worm that never dies, the conscience, sleeps well at last. These are the wages, besides what we receive so lavishly day by day; and they are enough for a man who knows his own frailty. Nor is happiness, eternal or temporal, the reward that mankind seeks. Happinesses are but his wayside campaigns. His soul is in the journey and in the struggle. How, then, is such a creature, so fiery, so pugnacious, so made up of discontent and aspiration, how can he be rewarded but by rest?

There is a Roman pride in the passage; but I believe that he was here, for once, utterly wrong. The true answer to his question is that so fiery a spirit as he describes can neither proceed from the dust nor be finally subjected to the dust that is so much less than itself. Science and religion are at least at one on this fundamental principle, that the greater cannot be derived from, or ended in, the less; and, moreover, in that passage Stevenson was writing not as Attwater, but as one of the other characters in the *Ebb-Tide*. I wish I could find words to express my conviction that it is just here that a great part of the modern intellectual world is making its most tragically retrograde step. The great men of former generations climbed with difficulty to a certain height of spiritual vision, from which they saw the eternal significance of human life. If once the human race becomes convinced that there is no real ultimate significance, no final aim to be achieved by all its passionate strivings, then indeed our civilization cannot long be held together. It is not a matter that the individual can airily throw aside as if only he were concerned. We have no right, even out of a sense of our personal unworthiness, to deny that great hope of all human affection, that at the very heart and centre of things there is an eternal justice, infinitely greater, not less than our own. We know that the day will come when not only ourselves but the whole human race will have vanished from this planet. But this knowledge does not close or fathom the infinite mystery even of our own existence ; nor could those great poets of the nineteenth century, whom Stevenson acknowledged to be greater than himself, believe that the soul of man, and that great pathetic onsweep of humanity through all the ages, were to end finally in the dust. The answer of Browning was far more profoundly true ; not because it was a happier vision, but because he saw more completely all the stern facts that were involved. Because those facts made a demand upon his own conscience, he felt that they made an eternal demand also. He did not shrink from reality. He faced the facts and saw that if they had no final solution the whole of our life became a diabolical and damnable farce. He spoke as

> One who never turned his back but marched breast forward,
> Never doubted clouds would break,
> Never dreamed, though right were worsted, wrong would triumph,
> Held we fall to rise, are baffled to fight better,
> Sleep to wake.

And when Stevenson's work arose, as it often did, from the deep inner well-springs of poetry, he believed this too ; nay, more, he assumed it ; for, though he stated it less explicitly, and it seemed to give him little more than " half of a broken hope for a pillow at night that somehow the right is the right," what are all these veins of glory and fire that he said he was able to see in the very mire of life ? And what is that thing not seen with the eyes for which he was ready to contend, and fail, and be mauled to the earth, and arise and struggle on for ever ? The significance of poetry runs deeper than the mere surface-meaning of the words. The music of that word " home " in his own epitaph :

> Home is the sailor, home from sea,
> And the hunter home from the hill,

means more than a mouthful of dust. It is the music of the Absolute Reality ; and that is not a silence, not a void, but a consummation.

SOME ASPECTS OF MODERN POETRY

If one were asked to state the fundamental cause of all the discords of the modern world, the chaos of thought in politics and religion, the confusion of standards in ethics, and the bewilderment of critical judgment in art and letters (where it is possible for diametrically opposite opinions to be held about almost any work produced in the last century), the cause could probably be given in two sentences. Our world is now so highly specialized that it grows more and more difficult for us to relate our particular fragments of the truth to the whole. On every side there is a war in progress—not so much between falsehood and falsehood as between innumerable fragments of the truth ; but when undue stress is laid upon a fragment of the truth, whether it be in the theories of psycho-analysis, of post-impressionism, of cubism, of conservatism, of communism, of the value of novelty, of the value of institutions, then men plunge headlong into error and sometimes into disaster ; or, if it be a very small fragment of the truth, they may be whirled into the idiotic folly of certain eccentric movements in art and letters.

This intellectual trouble may be the fissiparous beginning of the end of modern civilization ; or it may be a necessary stage in that transition from the homogeneous to a heterogeneous but co-ordinated and more highly developed world, in which the eye and the hand, the brain and the body of the state will work in harmony. But at present the undeveloped eye has glimpses of one set of facts which the undeveloped brain (or, as it is called by its owners, "the first-class brain") puts aside for another set.

There is an obvious danger that our civilization may not succeed in co-ordinating its warring impulses; for this co-ordination can only be achieved by an intellectual effort, and by the intellectual advance of a much greater number of its members than appear to be ready to make the effort to-day. The tendency is rather in the easy direction. It is just here that art and letters have their great function to perform, if only they can be saved from the cynic and the trifler who believe that they are decorative amusements for the idle, or that they are useful as quick roads to a reputation for a coterie. It is just here that the prophecy which Matthew Arnold made in 1880 may be fulfilled. "In poetry, where it is worthy of its high destinies, our race, as time goes on, may come to find a surer and surer stay." For great art, great literature, great poetry enable us, once more, to see all things in one. The function of the great poet is—as Dante said of himself—to be the scribe of the Eternal Love; and, in those gleaming moments when he sees the signs of the working of Love in the world around him, to record it for his fellow-men, phrase by phrase, line by line, till he has recaptured the universal harmony, the full vision of that Love which moves the sun and all the stars.

But literature—and especially criticism—has shown of late an increasing tendency to lose its hold on the central and unifying principles through which alone the arts can be worthy of their high destiny. It has tended, more and more, to deal with fragments of the truth; to treat all kinds of complex matters as if only one or two factors were involved. So far from escaping from the conventions of the past by the natural road that is always open, the road of development, it has unconsciously enslaved itself to the past by merely changing the names of its conventions. The fiery rebellions of great lonely figures in the past have been observed by later criticism to be great and splendid, with the result that "rebellion" is now the convention of the multitude, the delight of the curate and the academician, and the first lesson of the schools. But in this matter nothing has really changed except the names. The multitude, in its "rebellion," has only the old antagonists. They are as lonely as ever, though they are now called merely "out-of-fashion."

It is a strange spectacle this, in modern art and literature: a hundred thousand rebels, each chained to the same comfortable peak, and all chanting in perfect unison exactly the same thing, a perennial song of hate against the things that are more excellent; criticism practically unanimous in applauding them; and each individual of the vast multitude believing himself to be entirely original, thinking for himself, and utterly alone; though their sublime defiance of what they call the "Victorian period"—the phrase is almost their only intellectual weapon—has long been the established convention of every popular magazine and every secondary school throughout the English-speaking world.

The real rebel is not to be found in those serried ranks. He is to be found still searching for the merely unpopular truth; which, of course, is no longer generally called "truth," for that name, too, has become fashionable. The real rebel, the follower of the real truth, will be found endeavouring to discover and maintain those laws of life, thought, art, in which there is no more "novelty" (in the fashionable sense) than in the laws that govern the courses of the sun. And it must be remembered that it is only because the old sun still rises in its old appointed way that the new morning comes to us, and the real newness in art that we all desire, the newness that is a true development.

At a time when ignorance is being tempted by cynicism to believe that all new fashions in poetry must necessarily prevail, whether they be good or bad, sane or insane, it is interesting to observe that the late Professor of Poetry at Oxford builds his own theory of the art on certain time-conquering sentences of Drummond of Hawthornden against a "new fashion in poetry" of his own day. To rare and difficult newness of right development he was not opposed, of course. All true poets, all reasonable thinkers, eagerly desire that, passionately desire that; but he was against the false and destructive ideas that are so easily born in shallow minds, ideas that merely subvert fundamental principles. For Drummond's poetry was "the height of eloquence; the quintessence of knowledge; the loud trumpet of fame; the language of the gods. There is not anything endureth longer. She subsisteth by herself, and after one demeanour and continuance her beauty appeareth to all ages. In vain have some men of late (transformers of everything) consulted upon her reformation, denuding her of her habits and those ornaments with which she hath amused the world some thousand years. Poesie is not a thing that is in the finding and search, being already condescended upon by all nations and established *jure gentium* amongst Greeks, Romans, Italians, French, Spaniards."

Drummond of Hawthornden was no mere praiser of the past. He valued it because it was the only foundation of the present and the future. The greatest failure of most contemporary criticism has been in its inability to make the elementary distinction between three very different points of view—that of the mere reactionary; that of the progressive who believes in the development of our heritage to new beauty and power; and that of the merely ignorant and perverse destroyer. Criticism too often insists that there can be only the first and last of these; and that the last of these is really the progressive.

Yet, by every analogy in the affairs of the State and in every department of human life, there must seem to be no other progress than that which is based upon the achievements of the past. But so much of our journalistic literary criticism has necessarily been left to the tyro and amateur (the beginner who would "like to do a little reviewing") that the springs of Helicon itself are being muddied. No man, for instance, can be trusted to appreciate, critically, the blank verse of Tennyson unless, at the very least, he is familiar with the development of that great measure in Milton, Keats, Shelley, and Wordsworth, and its elucidation in earlier criticism. But there is often no historical sense, no background, no standard, nothing but a secret conviction that self-conceit and self-assertion, in a world of arbitrary opinions, will make a quick road to a reputation over the ruins of the past. But even this fantastic hope is vain; for if all standards could be laid low, no bubble would be briefer than a reputation without roots, floating in the empty air, at the mercy of every puff of opinion. The laws of Nature are on the side of the truth against every kind of sham. The false theory has no roots. It may deceive for a little while; but it cannot live; and the loneliest idealist may be consoled by the great saying of Coventry Patmore:

> When all its work is done, the lie shall rot;
> The truth is great, and shall prevail
> When none cares whether it prevail or not.

The true poetry of to-day has roots, and its roots are in the past. English poetry, moreover, is rooted in European poetry. It is a striking illustration of the general critical chaos, that while the poets who have really evolved new forms embodying new ideas are often depreciated as "derivative," some of those who are acclaimed as "non-derivative" actually use nothing but the Elizabethan sonnet form, or the oldest established stanza forms in the language, and often carefully reproduce the ancient cadences and ideas. It is quite possible for very fine work to be done in the old forms; but it is absurd to pretend for arbitrary reasons that the way is a new one; or that the real developments of other poets are the old; or that even these latter, even in their most original varieties of new leaf and flower, are really rooted anywhere but in the past if they are alive at all. Drummond of Hawthornden drew his life, as Spenser and Milton drew theirs, from the great tradition of the Renaissance, which was itself nothing but the revival in Europe of an earlier tradition, the putting forth of new leaves on an ancient stem.

"The poets," says Professor Ker, "are justified to themselves in arguing that poetry has not to be invented anew and is not to be trifled with. Drummond in his respect for authority is quite different from the mere critics who preach up the Ancients. Any one can do that. But the poet who belongs to a great tradition of art, transcending local barriers of language, is in a different case altogether. His poetic life is larger than himself, and it is real life."

Nothing could be better said. Nothing could be more salutary at the present moment, if it could be hoped that anything so abstract as a principle, or anything so delicate as the simplest of distinctions between cognate ideas, could be apprehended by the majority of those to whose barbaric axes and hammers the greatest literary tradition in history has been delivered for reduction to chaos. Professor Ker, for instance, shows that the poets, bound together in a common European life, as the branches of a tree are bound together in the trunk, draw the same patterns, follow the same rules of thought and melody through all ages ; and that, so far from this being a slavery to convention, it was in their joyous acceptance of the arduous law of their art that they found their freedom. He shows the use that Drummond made of the tune of Petrarch. He quotes Dante on a certain metrical formula :

> The most noble verse, which is the hendecasyllable, if it be accompanied with the verse of seven, yet so as still to keep the pre-eminence, will be found exulting higher still in light and glory.

How different is the tone of this from the tone of those who would have poetry turn her back on the past and begin anew with a new language. The form praised by Dante has been used by generation after generation of poets in England, who have produced their own music from it. One of the two crowning examples of its use in English is the magnificent *Song of Italy*, by Swinburne :

> Halls that saw Dante speaking, chapels fair
> As the outer hills and air,
> Praise him who feeds the fire that Dante fed,
> Our highest heroic head . . .
> Praise him, O Siena, and thou her deep green Spring,
> O Fonte Branda, sing ;
> But more than all these praise him and give thanks,
> Thou, from thy Tiber's banks,
> Strong with old strength of great things fallen and fled,
> Diviner for her dead ;
> Chaste of all stains and perfect from all scars,
> Above all storms and stars,
> All winds that blow through time, all waves that foam,
> Our Capitolian Rome.

The other is Alice Meynell's quieter, more subtle and more exquisite poem, *In Early Spring* :

O Spring, I know thee! Seek for sweet surprise
In the young children's eyes.
But I have learnt the years, and know the yet
Leaf-folded violet.
Mine ear, awake to silence, can foretell
The cuckoo's fitful bell.
I wander in a grey time that encloses
June and the wild hedge-roses.
A year's procession of the flowers doth pass
My feet along the grass,
But not a flower or song I ponder is
My own, but memory's.
I shall be silent in those days desired
Before a world inspired.
O dear brown birds, compose your old song-phrases,
Earth, thy familiar daisies.

She makes the comparison between this known process of the Spring and the unpredictable inspiration of the poet; but she uses the measure that Dante praised to convey her own unpredictable music; and it was in her own joyous acceptance of the laws of her art that every one of her poems proved itself to be "not a feather, but a bird," wild and uncaged and uncageable, yet with two equal wings that beat in measure.

No work can achieve "originality" by cutting itself "free" from its roots; for that is only a method of suicide. There is a theory among some recent writers that the poet must always be hunting for new words, new phrases, new measures, quite unrelated to the old. But real newness never comes by hunting. It comes from within; and, for its expression, depends on the right use of a language that is already in existence. This language cannot be developed by any generation very far beyond its former limits; but the poet with a right sense of the inner meanings of words can so combine them that they become wells of inexhaustible beauty and significance.

The greatest poets, in fact, often express themselves in the simplest and most familiar words: through the old shades of meaning, the hidden memories, the faded and half-forgotten colours that can be evoked from these words when they are used with the right feeling for their history. It is in their recombination to the new inner purpose that new poetry is achieved. The new magic is often born in the old measures that can be suffused with life (as an old flute takes the breath of a new player) or in the measures that can be developed into some new effect, as the quatrain was developed into the Spenserian stanza. It has been so, in the slow evolution of European literature, for thousands of years without a break, except where a nation fell. Goethe, the mightiest poet of European thought, at the beginning of the nineteenth century adapts the Greek hexameter to his own purposes. The perpetual preoccupation of some of our moderns with the fear of using a word or a measure that has been used before is not a sign of originality, but a symptom of weakness. A man who is urgently impelled to say something does not fret and fuss over the question whether the word "life" or "death" has been used before. If he trusts his own impulse and it is a true one, his utterance will shape itself aright in ways that every artist knows, but this preoccupation will weaken his impulse, and is, in fact, evidence of its original weakness. All the great original writers have used the familiar word when it was the most natural and perfect expression of what they wanted to say. They were not continually trying to avoid what some of our moderns erroneously call the *cliché*. To-day the very word *cliché* has become a *cliché* for use on all occasions; and many writers are attempting to achieve "novelty" in the wrong way. I have even seen a long list of the flowers which it is no longer permissible to mention in English poetry because they have all been mentioned before. The only flower allowed by that list, so far as I could discover, was Old Man's Beard, and as I have myself used it since, it is by this reasoning no longer permissible to mention any English flower at all. But the real newness comes from within. We are not called upon to change the year's procession of flowers, or invent a new language, any more than to invent a new keyboard in order that a musician may give us a new song. The possible combinations of the keyboard are inexhaustible during our existence on this planet ; and poetry has less need even than music to be perturbed about the limitations of its instrument. The whole matter resolves itself into the question of how rightly the notes and the words are used to express the new idea. The word, yes, even the *cliché*, that is lifeless in its wrong or slack use will always glow with life in its right use when the mind and spirit of a man are burning through it.

> Bright is the ring of words
>   When the right man rings them.

" Bright "—how commonplace ! " The *ring* of words " —what an echo ! " The right man "—how reminiscent of " the right man in the right place," and what a *cliché*. Yet the poem is an immortal little lyric. It was written by a master of style ; and it expresses the whole philosophy of the matter :

> Bright is the ring of words
>   When the right man rings them :
> Fair the fall of songs
>   When the singer sings them :
> Still they are carried and said,
>   On wings they are carried,
> After the singer is dead
>   And the maker buried.

There is not even an unusual word from beginning

to end. The whole value of language resides in the fact that it is a traditional growth, and that its words are agreed upon as current coin. This last phrase would be a *cliché*, according to some of our moderns. I might have avoided it easily enough by a more recondite phrase; but, in that context, it was right to use it because it exactly fitted what, at that moment, it seemed desirable to convey to the reader. There are other occasions when it would be rightly condemned as a banality; if, for instance, I were now to say that the poem I quoted above was "current coin," on the ground of its familiarity to a host of readers. In all such cases the known word, the familiar phrase, are to be condemned, not because they are known or familiar (for if this were so not a single sentence in any classic could escape condemnation), but because they are used as loose makeshifts, and do not exactly fit the thought. It is the phrases that are not common property that one has more often no right to use: phrases that are the private property of their maker, in whose own work they were possibly quite unusual; and even these may sometimes be used when they have been brought by age into that great treasure-house of memory upon which Milton used to draw. But it is time that the truth were told about the use of the parrot-cry *cliché* for the depreciation of true and spontaneous poetry and the sustainment of that which has no inner life and is merely hunting after a false novelty or what has been aptly called the "scarlet word." There is, of course, a small soul of good in it, useful to the schoolboy in the elementary stages of learning how to write a letter home. But to pretend that this elementary legislation can have any place in the serious criticism of English literature is absurd. It is easy enough, for instance, to apply it to the great writers of the Victorian period; and to mislead a public which takes most of its opinions at second or third hand into thinking that Tennyson might here or there be condemned by nursery rules. The close of *Enoch Arden*,

> And when he died, the little port
> Had seldom seen a costlier funeral,

is frequently quoted as utterly ridiculous, from something like this point of view. *Enoch Arden* is not one of his greatest poems, though Matthew Arnold thought it a masterpiece. But those who know anything of the way in which a little fishing-village regards a funeral will know that Tennyson was expressing here, with a Chaucerian directness, something which was as true as death and judgment to that village life. I do not say that it might not have been better done, though it has at least the merits of terseness; but I do say that it is ridiculous to praise writers of to-day for doing this same kind of thing considerably worse, and to ridicule Tennyson for doing it better, on the assumption that one of the most delicate artists in the literature of the world, at the very climax of an important poem, had suddenly collapsed below the level of a schoolboy. It is true that Tennyson is not hunting here for a "poetical" close. It would, in this case, be as false as it could be to speak of "burying him darkly at dead of night"; and it is odd that at a time when the direct truth is so frequently invoked by modern versifiers, a glimpse of the truth behind that "funeral" has not reached them. But the position is this. Young gentlemen who have just mastered the five-finger exercises are expressing contemptuous opinions of Chopin and Beethoven. Young ladies sit upon the keyboard and express the emphatic conviction that the resultant sound places them among the greatest composers of all time, and the Press, the great, kindly, cynical, contemptuous Press, encourages them for the sake of copy, knowing that they will swiftly be superseded by another generation that cannot be worse and may be better.

But, in the meantime, the words of wise old Drummond are in danger of being forgotten: "Poesie is not a thing that is in the finding and search." Spontaneous poetry does not have to hunt for the "scarlet word." When men are deeply moved from within they never do this. No hunter of the "scarlet word" could ever have heard the songs of Ariel. The master of language is he who can forget his instrument while he is expressing his thought in music; and this mastery can only be obtained by accepting the language of the past and developing it with devotion and reverence.

Even in the technique of rhythm and metre it is the very greatest mistake to think that "newness" is achieved by the very easy method of undoing what has been achieved by the past. Sweep away as many arbitrary and meaningless rules as you please; but be sure, first, that they are meaningless. There are certain laws in the technique of English verse that have been evolved out of its own nature; laws that, demonstrably, cannot be ignored without a loss of power. They can be waived occasionally for a particular purpose; but the writer who is ignorant or careless of them is definitely more limited in what he can do with words than the writer who avails himself of them.

At the present moment many of those who read literature in a perfectly sound new generation are in a state of hopelessly bewildered confusion about literary and artistic values. They are being told that they are in revolt against some of the masterpieces of former generations with which they are not even acquainted. They are being bewildered from above by a cynical criticism that has lost faith in its own standards; and a race is arising that, without knowing why, has been taught to despise just that part of our literary heritage from which it might have drawn strength and hope to go on with its own new discoveries and developments.

What are the causes of this intellectual obscurantism? The reason that is often given is a very different thing from the real cause; and, in itself, it is sound. We do not want a mere repetition of the past, or imitations of the past. We want something new. So far as it goes, that is true, and it must surely be recognized as elementary.

But a new thing of real value is always a growth. No man ever built a new city by throwing stones through old cathedral windows. Nature herself must be our guide to the new beauty that we desire, and Nature does not achieve newness by startling us with a revision of all her laws. She does not even change her year's procession of flowers. But the dew is on them, and the little white flower with the gold heart that Chaucer loved is welcomed by Wordsworth and Alice Meynell as if they were seeing it for the first time. There is a difference, not in the outer but in the inner values, that does, in fact, make each new individual see it for the first time:

> The clouds that gather round the setting sun
> Do take a sober colouring from an eye
> That hath kept watch o'er man's mortality.

It is only the dullard who cannot see the new world that wakes around him every morning, or who desires to make it newer by painting grass blue or faces green. We are surrounded by a horizon of ever-deepening mystery. The little circle of our knowledge grows from year to year; but its very growth widens the horizon of the mystery beyond. The familiar sights and sounds of our fields, in the deepening light of this mystery, are eternally new for every man that sees them. New analogies are discovered, new harmonies awake under that aspect. The changes are quiet and subtle as the changes of the evening light. They do not call for any immediate sensation, and they cannot be rendered by the violence which is sometimes mistaken for new vigour in modern verse. They cannot be conveyed by decorating the cadences of Wordsworth with crudities borrowed from the gutter, even though those crudities startle the professors out of their sleep, or strike a certain type of modern woman as "amusing," or even make schoolboys snigger with the same delight as they might find in the same kind of thing chalked upon a wall. The shock-tactics are growing a little stale. Mr. Barry Pain once pointed out that nothing is easier than to rouse a sensation of disgust. An untrained dog can do that in any civilized house; and when "new" writers adopt these methods, the remedy is not a pat on the head. The true distinction is not a matter of "gestures" and affectations. The depths are to be found only in quite unaffected simplicity and sincerity. There is, of course, a mannered simplicity. It dwells on the surface of things, and when it desires the depths, turns to moonshine or crystal-gazing rather than to truth. It has the novelty of a fashion, never the newness of the morning. Its quirks and turns are admired by the elementary æsthete. But the real newness is subtle and spiritual. It requires all the finest shades and tones that have been developed in language throughout the ages to express it; and its art is concealed only because it is as open and deep as the sky.

TENNYSON AND SOME RECENT CRITICS

THE "reaction" against Tennyson has been an accepted fact in what may be called the literary politics of the last twenty years. But those who have been in the opposition during that time are already cheered by signs of a change upon the horizon.

It is sometimes assumed, especially by the elderly, that those who set their faces with any constancy against these blind "reactions" are excessively conservative, and opposed both to "progress" and to all that is new. This is the exact opposite of the truth; for it is only those who can develop their heritage from the past that can achieve anything of value for the present or for the future. It was the old conservative journals that were mainly responsible for the "reaction" against Tennyson; and it was Mazzini, the prophet of European freedom, who made the strongest protest that has ever been made against these blind tides of opinion in literature. He spoke of his own predecessors, Goethe and Byron, as "incomplete beings"; but he went on to say this:

> Because we now stand on the threshold of a new epoch, which, but for them, we should not have reached, shall we now decry those who were unable to do more for us than to cast their giant forms into the gulf that held us all doubting? I feel the necessity of protesting earnestly against the reaction set on foot by certain thinkers against the mighty-souled, which serves as a cloak for the cavilling spirit of mediocrity. There is something hard, repulsive, and ungrateful in the destructive instinct which so often

forgets what *has* been done by the great men who preceded us, to demand of them merely an account of what might have been done. . . . Those only should dare to utter the sacred name of Progress whose souls possess intelligence enough to comprehend the past and whose hearts possess sufficient poetic religion to reverence its greatness. The temple of the true believer is not the chapel of a sect; it is a vast Pantheon.

The reaction against Tennyson and the great Victorians has its counterpart in almost every generation. There are a few writers to-day who, endeavouring to see both the past and the present in a historical perspective, believe that disproportionate value has been given to the work of some of the idols of the present hour. But, at the moment, our concern is with those who, out of all proportion, are being decried; and it is surely time that some effort be made to raise criticism above the influence of caprice and fashion, so that—for once—a generation may see even its own predecessors in the right historical perspective.

The chief indictment that has been brought against Tennyson will, in fact, be the chief ground upon which he will be praised by posterity—the fact that he did so completely sum up and express the great Victorian era in which he lived. The "Victorian style," as I have seen it described by various modern critics, is of course a myth. Just as some writers will set up a man of straw for the sheer pleasure of knocking him down, so various modern critics refer to that myth, as if the great men of that extraordinarily various period—Carlyle, Tennyson, Dickens, Thackeray, Darwin, Newman, Browning, Swinburne, Matthew Arnold—all wrote exactly alike and from the same point of view. To call the roll of the whole Victorian era is to summon up an army of august shades that have no rivals in the variety of their greatness in any other reign in English history.

There was never a more ridiculous spectacle than that of a generation which, with much exaggerated promise, an unparalleled amount of bluff, and little performance, has taken upon itself to condemn the greatest of the Victorian literature as utterly unprofitable.

There are certain phases of the Victorian period which, we may be heartily glad to know, have vanished never to return. But the recent critics of Tennyson have completely overlooked the fact that Tennyson himself is by far the most savage satirist of what was false in his own age ; and that no recent writer has ever approached the fierceness of his indictment :

Gash thyself, priest, and honour thy brute Baal,
And to thy worst self sacrifice thyself,
For with thy worst self hast thou clothed thy God.
Crown thyself, worm, and worship thine own lusts !—
No coarse and blockish God of acreage
Stands at thy gate for thee to grovel to—
Thy God is far diffused in noble groves
And princely halls, and farms, and flowing lawns,
And heaps of living gold that daily grow,
And title-scrolls and gorgeous heraldries,
In such a shape dost thou behold thy God.
Thou wilt not gash thy flesh for *him* ; for thine
Fares richly, in fine linen, not a hair
Ruffled upon the scarfskin, even while
The deathless ruler of thy dying house
Is wounded to the death that cannot die ;
And tho' thou numberest with the followers
Of One who cried, " Leave all and follow Me."
Thee therefore with His light about thy feet,
Thee with His message ringing in thine ears,
Thee shall thy brother man, the Lord from Heaven,
Born of a village girl, carpenter's son,
Wonderful, Prince of Peace, the Mighty God
Count the more base idolater of the two ;
Crueller ; as not passing through the fire
Bodies, but souls—thy children's . . .

The work of Tennyson abounds in passages of that kind. It was Tennyson who drew, with Chaucerian humour, the "fat-faced curate, Edward Bull." It was Tennyson who with one phrase disconcerted even "the stony British stare" of his period. It was Tennyson who riddled with the buck-shot of his wit the "padded man who wore the stays."

> What profits it to understand
> The merits of a spotless shirt,
> A dapper boot, a little hand,
> If half the little soul is dirt.

It was Tennyson who painted that extraordinarily vivid picture in a dozen lines of the worst type of Victorian family confronted by a young love-affair :

> While we stood like fools
> Embracing, all at once a score of pugs
> And poodles yell'd within, and out they came
> Trustees and Aunts and Uncles. "What, with him!
> Go" (shrill'd the cotton-spinning chorus) ; "him!"
> I choked. Again they shrieked the burthen—"Him!"
> Again with hands of wild rejection, "Go!—
> Girl, get you in!" She went—and in one month
> *They wedded her to sixty thousand pounds*
> *And slight Sir Robert with the watery smile*
> *And educated whisker.*

An emphasis must be placed on the "And" in the last line but one, or the full flavour of that perfect little passage is not obtained. It was Tennyson who saw the rich humour of a certain Victorian attitude to women, and satirized it in *The Northern Farmer*, again with a Chaucerian directness :

> Bessie Marris's barne! Tha knaws she laäid it to meä.
> Mowt a beän, mayhap, for she wur a bad un, sheä.

It was Tennyson who, in *The Princess*, introduced one of the most important movements of the present generation to English literature ; and, although his treatment of it would not, on the sociological side, satisfy its living exponents, it was nevertheless, in any just historical view, a work of extraordinary insight into the main problem ; and it abounds in wise and subtle criticism of those who would evade the problem in his own day. On the artistic side, of course, it is an exquisite piece of work, and the critic who dismisses it on the ground that it is not something else (a " great bleak " Æschylean drama, or a study of slum-life) is merely a fool. It is time that we had some plain speaking about these arbitrary dismissals of masterpieces. That it is a living artistic influence—not, of course, upon the little sects of London, but upon the literature of the world—is obvious enough to any one who remembers even one instance—the extraordinary musical effects with which a writer so different from Tennyson as d'Annunzio uses certain passages of it as a recurring *motif* in his finest novel. But, for the moment, I am chiefly concerned with the fact that the book was a real criticism of Victorian life.

A thousand passages could be quoted to show that, on the whole, Tennyson was, in fact, by far the clearest-sighted critic of the characteristics of his own age. He did not use our own phrases about it ; and his language occasionally, among those who have no historical sense and cannot read any literature but that of the hour, has the unreal effect of an old Victorian drawing on the mind of a child who has not yet realized the mutability of the fashions. For those who have realized it, and know that men and women did dress like that, talk like that, and think like that, there is a pleasure even in the broidery-frame and the half-cut novel on the " rosewood shelf." These things will all be part of the value of the work to posterity, for they are a representation of a world as it really was. And he saw it, and painted it from every side. He saw the children of the city, soaking and blackening soul and sense in city slime :

> There the Master scrimps his haggard sempstress of her daily bread.
> There a single sordid attic holds the living and the dead.

Again and again he attacked with what Henley called the " fury of the seer " these evils of his age and ours. It is absurd to condemn him because he accomplished no more than the twentieth century has accomplished. He was first and foremost a poet ; and by his effort to point towards a better world he had at least earned the right to say to his critics, as he did, " I have not made the world " as it is. It was Tennyson, again, who endeavoured to see steadily the whole appalling problem of peace and war. The fact that the phrases which he used about it have become a part of the language, and are so vital that they strike root in the mind of generation after generation, and develop there the idea of a hope for the world, is in itself an illustration of the great saying that the poets are the unacknowledged legislators of mankind. Those phrases have been staled by quotation, but they have sunk into the minds of millions, like the parallel phrases in which Darwin embodied his own great scientific generalization. Individuals may be unconscious of the quiet power of those great simple ideas in which worlds of struggling thought are suddenly summed up and delivered through a single lucid sentence. But it is impossible to set bounds to the power of those ideas ; and it is quite certain that Darwin, through science, and Tennyson, through literature, are still among the great forces that are determining the course of human events.

Finally, it was Tennyson who, when all the religious creeds were crumbling under the assaults of a not unjustly incensed science, stood like a rock for certain great fundamental faiths ; and—what is more important—he compelled the respect, even of that incensed science, for his restatement of those beliefs. For men like Tyndall, quoting him in their own scientific works, affirmed that Tennyson understood the drift of modern science better than any poet since Lucretius. Science, ever groping towards some one great simple generalization which will cover the whole process of the universe, may yet discover that she has been anticipated by poetry. In a generation she may be expressing everything in terms of motion ; but it will be Tennyson that put the generalization into its most perfect form, and enabled us to see in it

> That God which ever lives and loves,
> One God, one Law, one Element,
> And one far-off divine event
> To which the whole creation moves.

It must have been disturbing to the complacency of some of our moderns to find a living critic of so wide a range as Mr. Saintsbury placing Tennyson, with Vergil, among the twelve greatest writers of the world, in any age, and in any tongue. But the plain truth is that a very large part of the recent depreciation of Tennyson comes from those who are quite unaware of the regions of thought in which he moved.

On the technical side of his art, also, there are subtleties which cannot possibly be appreciated by critics who, demonstrably, do not know of their existence. A long and devoted novitiate is required before any man can appreciate the finer points of craftsmanship in any art ; and to look for criticism of any real value upon the art of Tennyson from some of the coteries of to-day would be like asking a puppy to direct the hand of a great surgeon during a delicate operation. There is a real problem to be solved here, for criticism ; and I confess that I do not know the solution. We cannot place any artist above criticism ; but the modern world must realize the plain fact that the masters of any art are often utterly beyond the range of those who depreciate them at the present day. I can only suggest that the substitution of a little humility for the prevalent conceit, the substitution of a little readiness to learn a few elementary technical details for the assumption of universal knowledge, might help us to a more real appreciation of the art of poetry, and might make us hesitate before we indulged in the easy dismissal of the masters.

I cannot hope to elucidate more than a few of these technical points here : indeed I am not sure that they can be made clear unless the poems are read aloud ; but the attempt shall be made.

Tennyson's painting of both land and sea can be compared with that of Turner. Like that of Turner, it was at first supposed to be artificial and untrue, because he had faithfully rendered an aspect of nature that had not hitherto been revealed in art. He was in many ways a more deliberate artist than any of his predecessors ; and his landscapes are often elaborations of the sketches he made, in one or two lines of verse, during his rambles in the country. Nothing quite like them had ever been done before. In their simplest form—for we must begin at the familiar beginning—we get such stanzas as that in *The Palace of Art* which describes

> A full-fed river, winding slow
> By herds upon an endless plain,
> *The ragged rims of thunder brooding low*
> *With shadow-streaks of rain* ;

or that extraordinarily vivid and terse picture of *The Eagle* :

> He clasps the crag with crookéd hands,
> Close to the sun in lonely lands,
> Ringed with the azure world he stands.

> *The wrinkled sea beneath him crawls.*
> He watches from his mountain walls
> And, like a thunderbolt, he falls.

Nobody who has ever stood upon a mountain at any great height, over a lively sea, with a brisk wind blowing, can fail to recognize the vivid truth of that line,

> The wrinkled sea beneath him crawls.

Not only in the simplicity and precision of the phrasing is it masterly ; but its music also is alive. The long vowel-sound of the word upon which the rhyme falls gives the very sound of the brawling waves in the caverns below. The line moves and shines and sounds like the sea ; and yet there is not a trace of effort. It is as lucid and simple as all greatness always is. Not a rhyme is forced. Nothing is affected. Everything is concentrated on expressing as perfectly as possible the picture that the poet had in his mind.

A little more subtle, but not less natural, is the technical device in another early poem. I call it "device," because I am endeavouring for the moment to deal with it on its technical side ; but Tennyson had so complete a mastery over his instrument that he expressed himself quite naturally through it, and there is no more exquisite rendering of Nature's own music in the whole range of lyrical poetry. It will be noticed that in the seventh line of the passage I am about to quote, the line ending with the word "lament," Tennyson deliberately disappoints the ear that would expect there a rhyme for the earlier "gray" ; and he does this in order to give the rhyme and satisfy the ear more fully in the next line ; a line that begins a new sentence, and so helps him to carry on the low eerie music of the wind among the reeds :

The plain was grassy, wild and bare,
Wide, wild, and open to the air,
Which had built up everywhere
  An under-roof of doleful *gray*.
With an inner voice the river ran,
Adown it floated a dying swan,
    And loudly did *lament*.
  It was the middle of the day,
Even the weary wind went on,
    And took the reed-tops as it went.

Those who are puzzled by the declaration of Edgar Allan Poe that Tennyson was in some respects the finest of all poets cannot do better than read that brief passage to themselves, slightly emphasizing the italicized words, pausing a moment on "lament," then catching up the music of the wind again in the next line. There is an "inner voice," not only in that river, but throughout the whole poem. There had been nothing quite like this airy music in poetry before Tennyson. But it must be remembered, as I said above, that I am attempting to elucidate here only one or two of the simplest points of his technique. Tennyson would be among the great poets of the world even if he were to be estimated on his landscape work alone; for, like all great landscape, it has spiritual values.

When he wrote the first version of *Œnone* he had not yet mastered his instrument. There is no better illustration of his growth in mastery and of his development of the technique of blank verse than a comparison of the first version of *Œnone* with that which he published ten years later. The first, beginning:

There is a dale in Ida, beautiful
As any in old Ionia,

is mellifluous, but without any structural firmness. It is somewhat artificial and abounds in double words like "glenriver." The second version is as firm and balanced in structure as a Greek temple. The cadence of the phrase is subordinated to the cadence of the sentence ; the cadence of the sentence to that of the blank verse paragraph. Yet the beauty and harmony of the parts is enhanced, not lessened, in their subordination to the whole. Even the vowel-music, in which Milton is his only rival, is deepened and enriched ; and the labour that he spent upon the poem has resulted, not in making it more artificial, but infinitely more direct and natural. The double words have disappeared ; and it flows, without Miltonic inversions, in the natural order of our speech, but speech made perfect. The landscape, too, which that opening paragraph depicts has assumed an organic beauty. It is unfolded, in its natural order, point by point.

> There lies a vale in Ida, lovelier
> Than all the valleys of Ionian hills.

Compare those opening lines with the original opening quoted above. Even in that short space the development is apparent. Dwell a little, in reading them, on the vowel sound of "all," and the long ō in "Ionian," and note how, by ending the line on the word "hills," he gives it spaciousness and leads you up to a horizon. He proceeds to deepen it, and ends the paragraph on another monosyllable that gives a still greater horizon—and touches the whole with the gleam and mystery of the sea :

> The swimming vapour slopes athwart the glen,
> Puts forth an arm, and creeps from pine to pine,
> And loiters, slowly drawn. On either hand
> The lawns and meadow-ledges midway down
> Hang rich in flowers, and far below them roars
> The long brook falling through the cloven ravine
> In cataract after cataract to the sea.

Tennyson was the first of our poets to obtain this effect of the horizon. Swinburne and many others have used the word "sea" for this purpose, sometimes in every other stanza throughout a very long poem. But in Tennyson, supreme artist as he was, its use was at once more deliberate, more natural, and more full both of meaning and of real mystery. Its source was in the spell that the Lincolnshire coast had cast upon his boyhood, a sense of the infinite, "felt in the blood and felt along the heart."

There are many misapprehensions of the nature of blank verse at the present day, especially among the critics of the prose-drama. Some of them appear to think that, because prose occasionally stumbles into a line that can be scanned, blank verse is an elementary affair, from which our greatest poet, Shakespeare, in his later plays, was vainly endeavouring to free himself, vainly aspiring to the maturity of prose. And here, in a nutshell, one has the clue to much that is wrong with modern criticism of poetry. Writers of prose (which has its own separate aims and glories) are continually endeavouring to lead an entirely different art into their own paths; and readers of prose, when they encounter the poets who have been misled into those paths, exclaim: "Here, at last, is the new and only true poetry. How utterly wrong were Sophocles and Vergil and Milton and Tennyson, to whom poetry—even though they wrote in unrhymed verse—was a music and a song":

> Till one greater man
> Restore us, and regain the blissful seat,
> Sing, heavenly Muse!

The occasional loose versification of Shakespeare in passages which ought to be regarded as in the nature of "recitative" is partly responsible for the misunderstanding of blank verse, which is by far the most difficult and subtle and highly organized instrument of English verse. Landor, the critic who of all Englishmen came nearest to the Greeks, said that even the hexameters of Homer, when compared with the blank verse of Milton, sounded like a tinkling cymbal on the shores of the ocean. And, for all the looser recitative in Shakespeare, which had a special cause in the conditions of the Elizabethan theatre, his blank verse mounts at once into music, and assumes as firm and majestic a structure as that of Milton whenever the height of his argument demands it. Its rhythm, in its greatest moments, seems to be dictated by the very pulse of life itself :

> To-morrow, and to-morrow, and to-morrow,
> Creeps in this petty pace from day to day
> To the last syllable of recorded time.

But these rhythms and this music are not a matter of "scansion." To scan those lines would be to ruin them, just as effectively as the elocutionist ruins them by delivering them as prose. The beauty of the verse depends upon subtle variations from the normal beat of the iambic pentameter. Shakespeare did not write :

> Ĭ knōw | ă bānk | whĕreōn | thĕ wīld | thўme blōws.

That is the attempt of some one to make the line scan. He wrote that exquisitely flexible line of music :

> Ī knŏw ă | bānk whĕre thĕ | wīld | thȳme | blōws.

And this is not an attempt to scan it ; for its appeal is to the ear, not to the fingers ; but the divisions indicate, at least, the syllabic equivalence which keeps it in the scheme of the measure. And this is a point that the seekers for a false freedom have forgotten. It is the fact that there does exist a normal beat that enables the artist to depart from it and return to it, through innumerable subtle variations. Once again, it is the law that secures his freedom. When Tennyson describes the ending of the Lucretian universe, he crams thirteen syllables into the iambic pentameter :

> Ruining along the illimitable inane.

When he wishes to describe the nightmare of a man lost among dark mountains he makes his iambic pentameter suddenly go

> Slipping down horrible precipices.

But he gets his effect only because he is able to make the line break away from a known measure. If all the lines went slipping down precipices he could not have achieved that effect.

It is demonstrable that many modern critics are unaware of these elementary matters in the technique of the art of poetry, as it has been developed through three thousand years of literature. Miss Amy Lowell, for instance, in America, recently complimented a new poet on the fact that his lines bore no relation to any regular measure, and that he had broken away from a tyranny for which she seemed to think Tennyson was chiefly responsible. Immediately afterwards she brought her whole case to the ground by remarking that unfortunately this new poet had not had a very good education, for he mispronounced certain words ; and she proceeded to prove this by scanning his lines with a mechanical "short, long, short, long" of a kind that neither Tennyson nor any other true poet would have regarded as above the level of an infant school. This is not a matter of opinion. It is demonstrable ; and it is typical of much that is being written to-day on the subject of poetry by thoroughly incompetent persons—and, unfortunately, with the approval of some carelessly edited English journals that once maintained a high standard of criticism.

The blank verse of Tennyson is, beyond question, the finest since Milton ; and it has certain subtleties of movement that surpass in delicacy, if not in strength, anything in *Paradise Lost* :

> The lights begin to twinkle from the rocks :
> The long day wanes : the slow moon climbs ; the deep
> Moans round with many voices. Come, my friends,
> 'Tis not too late to seek a newer world.
> Push off, and sitting well in order smite
> The sounding furrows ; for my purpose holds
> To sail beyond the sunset, and the baths
> Of all the western stars, until I die.
> It may be that the gulfs will wash us down ;
> It may be we shall touch the Happy Isles,
> And see the great Achilles whom we knew.

Behind it, and embodied in it, there are always those great spiritual values of which I spoke above. The sea was to Tennyson, as to other great poets, an image of Eternity. It is thus that he uses it in the opening of the *Morte d'Arthur*, that great piece of music which Meredith selected as the very highest example of style in English poetry. Read that passage again, familiar as it may be, and see how in its simplicity and strength and subtle spiritual values and secondary meanings it bears upon the present condition of Europe and the world :

> So all day long the noise of battle rolled
> Among the mountains by the winter sea,
> Until King Arthur's table, man by man,
> Had fallen in Lyonesse about their lord,
> King Arthur ; then, because his wound was deep,
> The bold Sir Bedivere uplifted him
> And bore him to a chapel nigh the field,
> A broken chancel with a broken cross,
> That stood on a dark strait of barren land.
> On one side lay the Ocean, and on one
> Lay a great water, and the moon was full.

Consider, once again, the quiet Homeric strength of that one phrase—" because his wound was deep."

There is no ransacking of the gutter here for the crude language of violence. This is the great style. "A broken chancel with a broken cross"—that is the picture of our own altar.

There is no more profound and complete summing up of the very process of change to which modern critics have affirmed that Tennyson was blind than the first three lines of that passage :

> The old order changeth, yielding place to new,
> And God fulfils Himself in many ways,
> Lest one good custom should corrupt the world.

It contains the philosophy of the whole matter, and its justification ; and it justifies Tennyson also, both as poet and prophet. He may yet be justified in his vision of the return of the King, with sails blowing in from the same great sea, while voices call from the hills—"Come, with all good things, and war shall be no more."

And at the end of the same poem he obtains one of the most magnificent closing effects in all poetry, by his use of sea-distances, and the subtle blending of them in his music with the words of the dying King and the vision of the happy island of Avilion, the land of the hereafter. It is not idle, I think, to take this great poem as most beautifully symbolizing the passing of the old order of the age which Tennyson so completely summed up and represented in his poetry. The last words of the King begin with a solemn change in the music of the blank verse which is not to be paralleled in Milton or any other master of that great instrument :

> The old order changeth, yielding place to new,
> And God fulfils Himself in many ways,
> Lest one good custom should corrupt the world.
> Comfort thyself : what comfort is in me ?
> I have lived my life, and that which I have done

May He within Himself make pure! but thou,
If thou shouldst never see my face again,
Pray for my soul. More things are wrought by prayer
Than this world dreams of. Wherefore let thy voice
Rise like a fountain for me night and day.
For what are men better than sheep or goats
That nourish a blind life within the brain
If, knowing God, they lift not hands of prayer
Both for themselves and those who call them friend?
For so the whole round earth is every way
Bound by gold chains about the feet of God.
But now farewell. I am going a long way
With these thou seest—if indeed I go—
(For all my mind is clouded with a doubt)
To the island valley of Avilion;
Where falls not hail, or rain, or any snow,
Nor ever wind blows loudly; but it lies
Deep-meadowed, happy, fair with orchard lawns
And bowery hollows crowned with summer sea,
Where I will heal me of my grievous wound.

The sound of that great deep was seldom absent from beginning to end of the work of Tennyson. He was the successor of Wordsworth rather than of Keats in what might be called the substance of his art, and he developed the work of Wordsworth in a thousand directions. He is more the artist, less definitely philosophical, less didactic. But "the light that never was on sea or land" is even more subtly transfused through his poetry, kindling it as the sun kindles a cloud. His lightest poems are like brooks, running down with many a "fairy water break" to the eternal sea:

Flow down, cold rivulet to the sea,
Thy tribute wave deliver. . . .

Always there is that extraordinary sense, elusive sometimes as a fragrance, of the presence—I know not what else to call it—of the Eternal. His lightest music is full of shadowy recollections, haunting tones from beyond our world. Sometimes it is the lament of the soul hemmed in by things temporal :

> A still salt pool, locked in by bars of sand,
> Left on the shore that hears all night
> The plunging seas draw backward from the land
> Their moon-led waters white.

More elaborately a similar theme is worked out in *The Lotos-Eaters*. Sometimes it is a simple cry of longing for lost friends in the presence of the ebb and flow which measure with so terrible a precision the passage of our days :

> Break, break, break
> On thy cold grey stones, O sea!
> And I would that my tongue could utter
> The thoughts that arise in me.
>
> O, well for the fisherman's boy
> That he shouts with his sister at play!
> O, well for the sailor lad
> That he sings in his boat on the bay!
>
> And the stately ships go on
> To the haven under the hill,
> But O for the touch of a vanished hand
> And the sound of a voice that is still!

This brief poem is a simple but very perfect example of the way in which rhythm and metre bring the thought of the poet into harmony with the pulsations of the universe ; the swinging tides, the moving ships, and the beating heart of man all seeming to discover their common measure as he translates them into music, and entering thereby into some wider communion with the Eternal. The coming and going of sails across infinite horizons, with all that is implied in that simple symbol, was never more exquisitely rendered than by this great artist :

Fresh as the first beam glittering on the sail
That brings our friends up from the underworld;
Sad as the last which reddens over one
That sinks with all we love below the verge;
So sad, so fresh, the days that are no more.

It would hardly be too much to say that there is not a single page of the final edition of Tennyson's work in one volume which does not establish that relation between the temporal and the eternal which it is the one aim of all great art to establish. He does not need to say "here is God" or "there is God," "here is the eternal" or "there is the eternal." With a later poet he can say "Lo, everywhere." Everywhere he brings us into communion with the eternal harmonies. He can convey the sense of them to us simply by making us hear, lying awake within sound of the sea,

Time flowing, in the middle of the night,

as in those four almost miraculously beautiful stanzas of *In Memoriam* where he seems to say nothing, yet says everything:

When on my bed the moonlight falls,
I know that in thy place of rest,
By that broad water of the west,
There comes a glory on the walls:

Thy marble bright in dark appears,
As slowly steals a silver flame
Along the letters of thy name,
And o'er the number of thy years.

The mystic glory swims away;
From off my bed the moonlight dies;
And closing eaves of wearied eyes
I sleep, till dusk is dipt in gray:

And then I know the mist is drawn
A lucid veil from coast to coast,
And in the dark church, like a ghost,
Thy tablet glimmers to the dawn.

I have tried to show elsewhere in this volume that rhythm and metre, so far from making the poet's expression of his thought unnatural, are his chief means (*when he has mastered his instrument*) of bringing his thought into harmony, consciously or unconsciously, with the rhythms of Nature herself. This is one reason why a thought expressed in verse by a master has often a precision and a universality that make it immortal; and the most minute and elementary points in the technique of its music are not without a bearing on the saying of Aristotle that poetry is the "most philosophic of all writing." I will return, for a moment, to the consideration of one or two of those elementary matters in technique, and try to elucidate their relation to the higher aspects of poetry. In order to do this we must go down to the very roots of articulate speech. I spoke earlier of that vowel-music which seems to some of our moderns a very trivial part of the technique of poetry. It was nevertheless part of the technique of poetry for three thousand years, in Homer, Vergil, Milton, and Tennyson. It might almost be called the basis of their technique; and to sweep it aside without examination is as foolish as it would be to declare that light and shade have no relation to the higher aspects of the art of painting, or that those proportions in music which led Kepler to the discovery of his laws have no philosophic or artistic value. As a living poet has said:

We will not look where the snail and the slug lie
For Psyche's birth, and that is our death.

There is nothing mechanical in that vowel-music

which, at its simplest, may appear to be hardly more than the careful balancing of the long ō, o̅r̅, and o͞o sounds, one against another, as in innumerable lines of Milton :

> *Sonōrous* metal *blōwing* martial sounds ;

or :

> High on a *throne* of royal state that far
> Outshone the wealth of *Ormus* or of Ind,
> Or where the *gorgeous* East with richest hand
> Showers on her kings barbaric pearl and *gold,*
> Satan *exalted* sat ;

or, in Tennyson :

> *Mournful Œnone* wandering *forlorn* ;

or :

> The *moan* of doves in *immemorial* elms.

In itself this may seem a trivial matter ; but it is only one of innumerable and more subtle harmonies of tone that the poet evolves *when he is the master of his instrument*, and evolves quite naturally, because his mastery enables him to forget his instrument, and to express himself through it, just as in the evolution of articulate language itself from sounds that imitated the sounds of Nature an instrument was gradually perfected through which men might express their highest thoughts and deepest emotions. The development of

> Sweet articulate words
> Sweetly divided apart

into an instrument of thought is unconsciously, and again in its simplest form, represented in Tennyson's own song by the Lakes of Killarney. Beginning with the echoes of a bugle among the hills, it gradually rises into a music that has a spiritual significance :

O hark, O hear, how thin and clear,
  And thinner, clearer, farther going,
O, sweet and far, from cliff and scar
  The horns of elf-land, faintly blowing.
Blow, bugle, let us hear the purple glens replying ;
Blow, bugle ; answer, echoes ; dving, dying, dying.

O, Love, they die in yon rich sky ;
  They faint on hill and field and river.
Our echoes roll from soul to soul
  And grow for ever and for ever.
Blow, bugle, blow ; set the wild echoes flying ;
And answer, echoes, answer ; dying, dying, dying.

The connection between the development of thought and the development of language has been emphasized by many of the evolutionary philosophers. It is worth our while to examine here some sentences in which the materialist, Haeckel, unconsciously conceded to the poets a power of thought above his own :

In the wider sense language is common to all the higher gregarious animals. It is effected either by touch or by signs, or by sounds having a definite meaning—the song of the bird, the bark of the dog, the chirp of the cricket, are all specimens of animal speech. Only in man, however, has that articulate speech developed which has enabled his reason to attain such high achievements.

There are certain consequences of that unusually true statement of the eminent materialist ; and they have a very direct bearing upon literary values, and upon such poetry as that of Homer, Vergil, Milton, and Tennyson. The bearing is obvious enough upon such direct pieces of onomatopœia as

Myriads of rivulets hurrying through the lawns,
The moan of doves in immemorial elms,
And murmuring of innumerable bees.

Here is language fulfilling one of its primary functions, but on an instrument exquisitely perfected : the soft quick syllables that are crowded into the first of these lines giving the very sound and movement of the brooks; the deep slow vowel-sounds on ō and ōr in the second line, with the repetition of the alliterative m, giving the calm music of the dove-haunted woodland; and the murmuring vowels of the last line giving, to any reader who wishes to make it so, the exact sound of the thing it depicts. It is language used as Vergil used it:

> Formosam resonare doces Amaryllida sylvas,

but with more subtlety and more variety than the hexameter allowed.

Again, in the great line from *Boädicea*, in that marvellous unrhymed metre of Tennyson's own invention, the onomatopœia is perfect: he describes an army that

> Roared as when the roaring breakers boom and blanch on the precipices.

The reduplication of the roar, the boom of the breaking wave, the sharper sound in the word *blanch* as it whitens after the heavy shock, and the swift hissing retreat in the word "precipices"—it is a perfect imitation in articulate language of the thing it depicts; and, again, it is the method of Vergil:

> Panditur interea domus omnipotentis Olympi,

where the very doors of the gods are heard to open. Or again where, in the *Morte d'Arthur*, Sir Bedivere, in armour, climbs down through the rocks to the lake:

> Dry clashed his harness in the icy caves
> And barren chasms, and all to left and right
> The bare black cliff clanged round him . . .

the whole passage rings like steel on stone.

The points on which I am dwelling here are, of course, elementary in the technique of poetry, though they are not so elementary as those which are so frequently dwelt upon by writers who have only recently discovered that it is possible to break the regular beat of an iambic pentameter, and have therefore come to the erroneous conclusion that firmness of line and precision of handling are evidence of inferior workmanship, or that a merely vague wavering or fluttering of the syllables, inexpressive of anything but the minor poet's vacuity, is evidence of a super-subtle art. It is only the firmness of the normal line, the backbone of the work, that makes the departure from it significant.

But this is only the beginning of the matter. It is quite demonstrable that, above and beyond all this, the possession of a great and subtle instrument of language connotes in certain poets—and Tennyson is among them—a power to deal with certain profound ideas as no man could possibly deal with them without that instrument. Inability to express certain fine shades of thought, inability to reach certain heights of expression, even for the most eminent men of science, remains nothing less than inability. And this is one of the explanations of the perpetual conflict between certain kinds of materialistic science in the nineteenth century and certain kinds of religion. The failure, on both sides, was in their inability to express the fullness of their own thought ; and it was just here that Tennyson, in some degree, through the exquisite perfection of his instrument, came near to reconciling them. When Tennyson speaks of a soul descending

> from the distance of the abyss
> Of tenfold-complicated change,

he is expressing perfectly an idea which, in that form, is full of significance to every man of science ; but has never been expressed in science or philosophy so precisely or completely. This again is demonstrable; and, if any reader doubts it, he has only to produce an equally terse arrangement of words to express the same idea. The possession of this instrument of language connoted in Tennyson the intellectual power that developed it and was in turn developed by it. It became an intellectual and spiritual instrument; and through it he was able to express gradations of thought which, as he developed them, reacted upon his powers of thought; so that, one step leading to another, he was able to attain to heights of vision beyond the range of the philosopher whose exposition of this very development I quoted above. The music which in Tennyson's early poems gave us that marvellous unstopped tone of the fen wind blowing over the reeds, begins with *In Memoriam* to soar into loftier regions.

It is interesting to make a direct comparison of the two methods.

Haeckel, employing his own not very precise instrument, writes as follows:

> Our monistic view, that the great cosmic law applies throughout the whole universe, is of the highest moment. It not only involves, on its positive side, the essential unity of the cosmos, but it marks the highest intellectual progress, in that it definitely rules out the three central dogmas of metaphysics—God, freedom and immortality. We assign mechanical causes to phenomena everywhere. To the solution of the world-riddle the nineteenth century has contributed more than all its predecessors. *In a certain sense, indeed, it has found the solution.*

The last sentence is stupendous in its crudity; and the whole paragraph, under analysis, resolves itself into a pitiable exhibition of human weakness. Compare with this clumsy picture of the "universe" the exquisite precision of Tennyson gazing

> Where all the starry heavens of space
> Are sharpened to a needle's end;

compare with the bland cocksureness of Haeckel the deep inner voice of that passage from *In Memoriam* :

> And what I am beheld again
> What is, and no man understands ;
> And out of darkness came the hands
> That reach through Nature, moulding men.

Or (to put it on its very simplest ground), with the muddled denials of a materialist who, while declaring that we know nothing but the report of our own senses, is yet ready to affirm that these can tell us the whole truth, compare that cry of the great poet to the " living will," and the higher " monism " of the last great lucid stanza of *In Memoriam* :

> One God, one Law, one Element,
> And one far-off divine event
> To which the whole creation moves.

Whatever else may be said about this conception, it was one that, demonstrably, Haeckel was unable to formulate, because he had not the intellectual instrument. The reverence that characterized all the work of Tennyson when he confronted those fundamental problems proceeded from clearness of vision, not from haziness or limitation. He was quite demonstrably able to realize infinitely more of the vastness and mystery of the universe than the materialistic philosopher could realize. He wished to accept all the facts and then find their reconciliation, if possible. In one stanza, for instance, he sets two great arguments one against the other :

> Who trusted God was Love indeed,
> And Love creation's final law,
> Though Nature, red in tooth and claw
> With rapine, shrieked against the creed.

No phrase has been used more often as a text by the modern pessimists than that " red in tooth and claw" of the third line. A whole group of writers has specialized in that particular aspect of things which Tennyson summed up and expressed in one line of a complicated and highly organized poem. Lord Morley, for instance, used it as a criticism of the faith of Wordsworth; forgetting, apparently, the faith of the man who originated the phrase. Tennyson, in giving that clean-cut phrase to the world, demonstrated by its very vigour that he was more alive to that aspect of Nature than those who have been forced to borrow the phrase from him. But he was able to consider a hundred other aspects also:

Earth, these solid stars, this weight of body and limb,
Are they not sign and symbol of thy division from Him?

Speak to Him, thou; for He hears, and spirit with spirit can meet.
Closer is He than breathing, and nearer than hands or feet.

This many-sidedness of Tennyson's work has never been fully recognized. His early Arthurian poems practically founded the Pre-Raphaelite school in England. There was a "Lady of Shalott" school; a Lancelot school; and a school that specialized in a form of beauty that Tennyson drew, in one golden line, revealing the "warm white apple of her throat." But in Tennyson the sacred mount of Camelot rose into heights of symbolism. The mighty hall that Merlin built was built to the golden numbers of modern philosophy; with its four great zones of sculpture:

And in the lowest beasts are slaying men,
And in the second men are slaying beasts,
And in the third are warriors, perfect men,
And in the fourth are men with growing wings.

In *Maud*, again, he was the leader of the "spasmodic school"; but behind the emotional love-story, and the political interpretation that has been thrust upon it, there are depths of thought unsounded yet by modern criticism. In form it was unique in our literature—a long dramatic poem, consisting entirely of lyrics joined together in such a way that each lyric represents a scene in the action. Moreover, the metres of these lyrics were quite new in English poetry. Many of them depend for their effect on a development of the device which was noticed above in *The Dying Swan*, the holding over of the rhyme from the line in which it was expected, for a fuller effect in a subsequent line. But here the method was occasionally elaborated into long swiftly moving stanzas :

> We are puppets, Man in his pride, and Beauty fair in her flower ;
> Do we move ourselves, or are moved by an unseen hand at a game
> That pushes us off from the board, and others ever succeed ?
> Ah, yet we cannot be kind to each other here for an hour ;
> We whisper, and hint, and chuckle, and grin at a brother's shame ;
> However we brave it out, we men are a little breed.

It is a curious fact that many of the modern critics of the " derivative " poetry of Tennyson have never yet discovered that he was among the greatest of metrical inventors, and have never yet realized that the originality of many later poets often consists in reproducing the most conventional measures in a degraded form. It ought to be the aim of the poet, in his technique, to develop the instrument which he has inherited. In his heritage he is derivative, he is bound to be derivative ; but in his use of his heritage he ought to be creative ; and it is only the right kind of derivative poet who can ever be creative or, in the truest sense of the word, original. His thought should naturally lead him into new developments of rhythm and metre and music.

This is the true line of rebellion against the constraints of the past; but it involves patience and labour. In recent years the ground has shifted under our feet, and modern critics are now calling the hunt for the easier way, "rebellion." The rebellion that achieves anything is difficult, and as long as art. It involves solid work, with hand and brain; and neither "genius" nor youth can evade it, if they desire to reach their goal. It is just here that a revival of attention to the work of Tennyson might be salutary to a generation in a hurry.

The opening satire in *Maud* upon his own age, as fierce as anything in Juvenal, is another example of the fact that I tried to emphasize at the beginning of this essay—the plain fact that Tennyson was the exact opposite of the complacent accepter of things as they were in the Victorian period:

Sooner or later I too may passively take the print
Of the golden age—why not? I have neither hope nor trust;
May make my heart as a mill-stone, set my face as a flint,
Cheat and be cheated, and die: who knows? We are ashes and dust.

These quatrains, with their regular, alternate rhymes, establish the normal measure, which he then proceeds to elaborate into some of the most exquisite of his metrical fugues, if that word may be borrowed from music to suggest the effect of the deferred rhyme to which I referred above. There are few passages in Tennyson, or in any other poet, so masterly as those in which he begins to depart from his established measure, defer the rhyme, and surprise the ear, taking wider and wider curves in the stanza before coming to the full close of music and meaning in the final line.

Music and meaning, I say, for they are inseparable here. Whenever he varies the instance of the rhyme he does it for a purpose, to secure a definite effect, as he did in *The Dying Swan* ; but here the purpose is larger and more significant. In the following passage, for instance, which gives the lover's vision in the dark, the first four lines are again a regular quatrain, rhyming alternately ; but, after that, he sweeps off into a magnificent fugue of verse which is fully closed only in the fourteenth line :

Cold and clear-cut face, why come you so cruelly meek,
Breaking a slumber in which all spleenful folly was drowned,
Pale with the golden beam of an eyelash dead on the cheek,
Passionless, pale, cold face, star-sweet on a gloom profound ;
Woman-like, taking revenge too deep for a transient wrong
Done but in thought to your beauty, and ever as pale as before
Growing and fading and growing upon me without a sound,
Luminous, gem-like, ghost-like, death-like, half the night long
Growing and fading and growing, till I could bear it no more ;
But arose, and all by myself in my own dark garden-ground,
Listening now to the tide in its broad-flung ship-wrecking
roar,
Now to the scream of a maddened beach dragged down by the
wave,
Walked in a wintry wind by a ghastly glimmer, and found
The shining daffodil dead, and Orion low in his grave.

If it be read aloud, with a slight dwelling upon the rhyme-sounds, the exquisite structure of the whole becomes apparent even to those who have no inward ear for verse ; but it is almost impossible that work of this kind should be fully appreciated in the English-speaking world to-day. It is only too clear that this poetry requires more of its readers than all but a few can give ; and a very few experiments suffice to show that the readers who can follow this music in their minds, or can even follow it metrically, are far fewer than men of letters suspect. This is an additional reason for withstanding the foolish depreciation of our Vergil, and, I may add, it is one of my motives for endeavouring to make these technical details clearer. A world that is rapidly losing its power to take in anything but picture-writing need have little fear that appreciation of "one good custom" in literature will corrupt it, or cramp its own endeavours.

A little later, in *Maud*, after the lovers' meeting at night, there comes a passage of incomparable beauty where again the rhyme arrangement has what I have called the fugue effect. It is an impression of the summer night, as the lover lingers on in the great dark garden, listening to the sound of the sea and watching the mightier movement of the starry heavens. For precision and power in conveying the thousand and one intangible things that make up such an impression—the silence, the peaceful sounds, and the inner depths of passion—this music is unmatched anywhere. It is the supreme "nocturne" of English poetry. Here, if there be any truth in the theories of impressionism, is an impression in poetry more exquisite than any that was ever painted. We need no further truth than the sheer beauty of that summer's night; but here, for once, dreams are caught in a net of twilight, and made to surrender their secret in flawless music, intricate, wild, and precise as the rhythms of the universe, whose divine wildness is folded in a divine law:

> Is that enchanted moan only the swell
> Of the long waves that roll in yonder bay?
> And hark, the clock within, the silver knell
> Of twelve sweet hours that past in bridal white,
> And died to live, long as my pulses play;
> And now by this my love has closed her sight
> And given false death her hand and stolen away
> To dreamful wastes where footless fancies dwell
> Among the fragments of the golden day.

The last ten words give the most precise and beautiful description of the nature and origin of dreams that is to be found in poetry.

After the tragedy, when the lover, outlawed for ever by his blood-guilt, is wandering alone on the

Breton coast, there is an almost miraculous touch, so slight, so quiet that its tremendous dramatic significance may easily be missed by those who do not realize that they are here in the presence of a master, whose every syllable demands the closest attention. It is one of the passages which justify the declaration of Jowett about this poem : " No poem since Shakespeare seems to show equal power of the same kind, or equal knowledge of human nature " ; and the equally emphatic statement of Ruskin that " no admiration can be too extravagant." In quoting these statements I do not wish to use them as a mere " argument from authority " ; but it is ridiculous that any generation should leap to the opposite opinion without proper consideration and without taking the trouble to read the work in question. In one flagrant instance a well-known writer actually denied in public that one of the greatest lines in this poem was to be found in the works of Tennyson. If this were not arrogance gone mad, I certainly do not know what to call it ; and I know of no better remedy than a little authority.

The passage, which I have selected as an example of Tennyson's Shakespearean power of depicting human nature and the tremendous forces that attack the soul and are dominated by the soul, is that in which he gives the lover's curious brooding over a minute shell at his feet on the seashore. It can be compared only with the musing of Hamlet over apparently trivial matters ; but here there is something added, a suggestion that the besieged mind of the blood-guilty outlawed man is groping, groping for a sign, some little nucleus of evidence that there is a meaning, a guiding hand, a steersman of the universe. It has often been treated as if it were only a pretty interpolation, a lyric, complete in itself ; and, in fact, it seems to stand quite aloof from the great tempestuous movement of the preceding and subsequent scenes of the poem. But, in itself, it contains the explanation of this ; and it is by that very aloofness that, with almost uncanny power, it suggests the beginnings of the outcast's madness and the question whether the delicate cells of the brain will withstand the shock. It was the device of a supreme master, an incomparable master, to suggest this by a sudden contrast of extreme stillness, and by a passage that in itself is so exquisitely logical and sane :

> See what a lovely shell,
> Small and pure as a pearl,
> Lying close to my foot,
> Frail, but a work divine,
> Made so fairily well
> With delicate spire and whorl,
> How exquisitely minute,
> A miracle of design. . . .
>
> Slight, to be crushed with a tap
> Of my finger-nail on the sand,
> Small, but a work divine,
> Frail, but of force to withstand,
> Year upon year, the shock
> Of cataract seas. . . .

And so the music gradually swells up again, through subtle gradations, now of prayer that his lost love may be comforted, now of hope that the slain man may still be living, and now of intense longing :

> O, that 'twere possible
> After long grief and pain
> To find the arms of my true love
> Round me once again !

The frail mind ceases to withstand the terrible forces that are attacking it ; its cosmos breaks up into the chaos of madness ; and he imagines himself to be dead and buried alive, and unable to sleep. The movement of the lines (which is again a " fugue effect ") in those passages of madness, is more fitly to be compared with the first part of Goethe's *Faust* than with *Hamlet* ; but in their exact representation of the movement of the troubled mind they are beyond anything that Goethe ever wrote :

> Dead, long dead,
> Long dead !
> And my heart is a handful of dust,
> And the wheels go over my head,
> And my bones are shaken with pain,
> For into a shallow grave they are thrust,
> Only a yard beneath the street,
> And the hoofs of the horses beat, beat,
> The hoofs of the horses beat,
> Beat into my scalp and my brain,
> With never an end to the stream of passing feet,
> Driving, hurrying, marrying, burying,
> Clamour and rumble, and ringing and clatter,
> And here beneath it is all as bad,
> For I thought the dead had peace, but it is not so ;
> To have no peace in the grave, is that not sad ?
> But up and down and to and fro
> Ever about me the dead men go ;
> And then to hear a dead man chatter
> Is enough to drive one mad.

Then, in the final scenes, depicting the gradual return to sanity, the music once again broadens and deepens into a vaster movement, in which the individual finds himself at one with the universal. It is possible, for any one who wishes to do so, to narrow the significance of that last section of a great poem and turn it into a merely local militaristic manifesto. But those who wish it must have forgotten their Shakespeare ; and they must be entirely ignorant of the mind of Tennyson as expressed not only here, but in scores of passages throughout his work, on one of the great hopes of the world. That hope will not be furthered by foolish assaults upon those who have seriously endeavoured to grapple with one of the greatest problems in the evolution of the race, and envisaged it clearly, from a hundred points of view, as in itself it really is.

This breadth of vision is, in fact, the glory of Tennyson. It is as absurd to seize one detail in his presentation of the universe, and attempt to limit him to that, as it would be to describe him as the pessimistic exponent of a Nature " red in tooth and claw." It is equally foolish to concentrate attention on his weaker poems. These things exist in every poet; and, on the whole, in proportion to the magnificent body of his work, they are rarer in Tennyson than in any other English poet. His technical skill; his landscape work; his development from the mere artist into one of those great sage poets, looking out over the whole field of human affairs from a central position; his power of keeping always " an equal mind "; and, in the life of his own heart and intellect, as in all that concerned the State of Man and the City of God, his faith in law as the only guide through what is merely a chaos in many lesser poets;—all these things place him with the greatest on the roll of the world's literature. In the reign of law he found his chart and his compass, and in his answer to those who would " rebel " against it (and are, generally speaking, unaware of its existence, even as a scientific or philosophic idea), he delivered the answer of all the ages: If you take advantage of this chart of law you are free of all the seas; and you may be able to sail to your desired haven. If you throw it overboard, believing yourself to be a very glorious " rebel " against mere conventions, you are no longer free, but at the mercy of wind and wave. The very opposite of what you expect will happen; and you will not have the remotest chance of reaching even that end which you yourself proposed as your goal, unless that goal be your own destruction.

There never was a poet who comprehended so perfectly the necessary changes of growth without losing his sense of the fundamental and essential things which must abide through all change. The chariot of his soul is drawn by steeds not less fiery than those of any rebel, but he has the reins in his hands and he can guide. This indeed is only another illustration of his power to accept all the facts simultaneously and find their reconciliation. The specialist in " rebellion " thinks that unreined steeds are more magnificent than those which are tamely controlled. This is obviously true ; but it is not the whole truth. The broken-down cab-horse of Martin Tupper is obviously an inferior creature to the splendid unbridled steeds of many a Phaethon. But it is possible to go a step further and say that there is something even worthier in the possession of a spirit great enough to master and control even the horses of the sun, and drive them to his abiding goal.

Some of the depreciation of Tennyson is based upon a complete misunderstanding of his method in one or two poems. His moral critics are doubtless very noble sinners, but that is no reason why, in their inverted Pharisaism, they should lift ridiculously self-conscious hands in a horror of personal modesty over the lines in *Galahad* :

> My strength is as the strength of ten
> Because my heart is pure.

The lines are not about themselves—strange to say ; nor are they about Tennyson ; nor are they a boast of Galahad. The methods of poetry are not those of prose conversation. (I have dealt with this very common mistake of current criticism elsewhere in this volume.) The method in *Galahad* is that of objective lyrical poetry, in which a voice may be given not only to virtues and powers, but also to inanimate objects. To regard it from a self-conscious personal point of view is almost as absurd as to deprecate, out of the critic's own sense of personal modesty, those greater statements, "I am the true Vine," or "I am the Light of the World." But, quite apart from this, the method of *Galahad* is that of the objective lyrical poetry which gave a voice to the brook elsewhere in Tennyson, and a voice to the cloud in Shelley. One does not suspect the brook of self-conceit because the poem says :

> Men may come, and men may go,
> But I go on for ever.

One does not accuse the cloud of boasting because Shelley writes :

> I bind the sun's throne with a burning zone,
> And the moon's with a girdle of pearl ;
> The volcanoes are dim, and the stars reel and swim,
> When the whirlwinds my banner unfurl.

Nor does one impute self-righteousness to Shelley because he makes Apollo say :

> The sunbeams are my shafts, with which I kill
> Deceit, that loves the night and fears the day.
> All men who do, or even imagine ill
> Fly me, and from the glory of my ray
> Good minds and open actions take new might
> Until diminished by the reign of night.

These lines, in fact, are very justly comparable with the lines from *Galahad* ; and the method is familiar to all students of lyrical poetry.

I believe it is partly because of the growing inability to distinguish between the methods of prose, or even the methods of prose conversation, and those of poetry that the charge of "priggishness" has been brought against the last passages between King Arthur and Guinevere. There is something that requires explanation in the fact that while these passages could move to tears a critic and man of the world like Macaulay, they have incurred the disapproval of Mrs. Elinor Glyn.

Much of Tennyson's blank verse has what I have called an objective lyrical quality. The Guinevere passages cannot be judged as if they were intended to be a realistic conversation. They embody ideas and emotions that could never be actually spoken by a human being ; and if those ideas and emotions are condemned for their "inhuman moral superiority," it must be remembered that, in Tennyson's poem, King Arthur differed from every other figure in the *Idylls of the King*, and that he was definitely represented as having both a supernatural origin and a supernatural departure. Criticism is bound to consider the poet's intention in judging his results ; and the poet's intention was certainly not to make King Arthur the typical husband of collusive divorce. He was the great figurative head of an allegorical system, and the hope of the world centred in him, as the sustainer of the moral order. His last great battle in the West is the most amazing prophecy in literature ; it foretells in detail, physical and spiritual, the tragedy through which the world has been passing ; and the hope of the end of wars and the victory of the moral law is bound up in the conception of the second coming of that King. To dismiss this great allegorical idea as unworthy of a great poet, on the ground that it is too modern for Malory, was absurd enough ; but it was even more absurd to criticize Tennyson for not making the King a replica of the human Lancelot. In the very nature of things—as Tennyson himself pointed out again and again in the poem—this King could only be represented as a kind of objective Conscience, speaking not his own thoughts, but the highest thoughts of Lancelot and Guinevere themselves. If Tennyson was unable to make him as real an individual as Lancelot, it was for precisely the same reason that Milton was unable to depict the

Leader of the angelic hosts as vividly as he depicted the terrestrial or infernal characters in *Paradise Lost.* It is possible that Tennyson would have been less open to criticism in those farewell passages if he had embodied exactly the same ideas in an impersonal description of the workings of the moral law, rather than in a direct utterance from the head of his allegorical system. Every prose-artist knows how a character may be allowed to think a sentence that he could not speak ; or how, in a descriptive context, a virtue may be attributed to a character that he must not attribute to himself. But, as I tried to show above, the methods of this semi-lyrical narrative poetry are not those of prose fiction. The subject is in its own way as far removed from ordinary life as the desertion of Psyche by her wingéd Lover because she had lighted her lamp against his command. If the critic condemns that desertion, or those farewell passages between the King and Guinevere, on the ground that it would be unchivalrous in himself to behave thus, then it may fairly be replied that the fault is in the self-consciousness of the critic. He might just as well condemn Apollo for his "inhumanly superior remark" in Shelley :

> I am the eye with which the universe
> Beholds itself, and knows itself divine.

The King—that personified Conscience—is the highest in Guinevere talking to herself. It is even the highest in Lancelot talking both to her and to himself. The clue is given in the great chant in *The Coming of Arthur :*

> Blow trumpet ! He will lift us from the dust.
> Blow trumpet ! Live the strength and die the lust !
> Clang battle-axe, and clash brand. Let the King reign !

The mystical side of this poem cannot be ignored by criticism, and the passage I have quoted is also the answer to the charge that Tennyson emasculated the subject. Moreover, it is quite uncritical to fasten upon the passage in *Guinevere* and suggest that Tennyson is there glorifying his own virtue, while the so charitable critic ignores that other cry of the faithless friend and human sinner, Lancelot ; which, after all, proceeded from Tennyson also :

> Then, in my madness I essayed the door ;
> It gave ; and thro' a stormy glare, a heat
> As from a seventimes-heated furnace, I,
> Blasted and burnt and blinded as I was,
> O, yet methought I saw the Holy Grail. . . .

Much of the depreciation of Tennyson, in fact, is based upon sheer incapacity to comprehend his breadth of vision. He drew Lancelot as well as the King ; and those who mistakenly seek for a warm, comfortable, erring human being in the latter are merely looking in the wrong direction. Tennyson himself pointed out the difference between the King and his other characters when he said, in an image that sums up the whole matter—"*the low sun gives the colour*." To refuse to consider and give their proper weight to the poet's own words, except in carefully chosen passages which can be twisted into a suggestion that Tennyson looked upon himself as the blameless King, and that the blameless King was also the Prince Consort, and that all three of them were insufferable prigs, is unworthy of the country that produced Hazlitt, Coleridge, and Matthew Arnold ; a country that possesses in Tennyson a poet who was to his own age what Vergil was to Rome. Yet this has been the method of many writers who specialize in one or two aspects of life, and resent the recognition of any other. Some of these writers fully justified one of the finest intellects of our time—Dean Inge—in his remark that Tennyson was being depreciated because he did not glorify adultery. Shortly before

Dean Inge touched with his keen and scholarly lance the very centre of that barbarous shield, a leading journal had quite definitely, quite openly, quite brutally attacked Tennyson on this very ground—that he did not glorify his women as harlots, or make his men heroic as adulterers. This leading journal, a great conservative periodical (I have pointed out elsewhere the topsy-turvy conditions of modern "rebellion"), gave, quite definitely, as additional grounds for this judgment, the alleged fact that after the Great War adultery was the general rule in this country, and that it was admirable and altogether noble. The statement was, of course, not at all characteristic of that journal's general tone; but it has to be remembered that almost anything can be printed in the guise of literary criticism in our journals to-day, and it is not difficult for such things to escape editorial attention. We hear a great deal about the evils of destructive propaganda; but it may be affirmed that if our civilization does eventually go down in what Tennyson prophetically depicted as "red ruin and the breaking up of laws," it will be due in no small measure to the intellectual conditions of our day, and the constant endeavour, through literature, to make the worse appear the better cause. The effects are unseen, but incalculable. I have personally encountered teachers in schools who are so bewildered by the trend of things that they mistrust their own judgment. They are told, authoritatively, by contemporary criticism that what their own conscience declares to be bad is good. The public charlatan overrides them with those whom they are appointed to teach; and their gratitude for the slightest attempt to restore the balance is often manifest. This country is thoroughly sound, and it will continue to lead the world, provided that it be not corrupted from without and taught to despise its own greatest men. The little coteries of pseudo-intellectuals are quite unrepresentative of the real life of the people. But, through the Press and its machinery, they exercise an influence out of all proportion to their numbers or their character. Editorial supervision of the anonymities who play the part of the rat and the moth is difficult, for their work is minute, and it does not always appear till the tree falls or the cloak is unfolded in tatters. It is even more difficult to correct the tone than to eliminate the falsehood. But some endeavour must be made, all along the line, in the journalistic treatment of English literature, if one of the greatest traditions in the world is to be worthily sustained and developed. Tennyson is one of the greatest figures in that tradition, a superb artist, seeing life steadily and seeing it whole. So far from being a moral prig, he is one of the few writers who have spoken quite simply and sincerely of their own failures. He, too, has fought with beasts, and sunk into "the sloughs of a low desire." The modern coteries, on the other hand, who despise him, are often eaten up with an inverted self-righteousness and are quite convinced that they themselves are perfect beings ; that their conventions are final ; and that they have never made a mistake in act or word. There has been far too much of the desire to assert originality not by thinking, but by "making thoughts one's aim." It is time that we regained our desire simply to discover the truth so far as we are able ; time that we regained, too, a little respect for the depth, the large and true simplicity, of the great masters. Tennyson can at least teach those who have been bewildered by charlatanry one lesson that they will never learn from his depreciators. It is to be found in his readiness to turn round upon himself and ask, "Am I wrong ?" In the second *Locksley Hall* (which, despite the fact that its phraseology is not that of our own day, is a great poem) he asks whether he is mistaking the "growing glimmer" for the "light withdrawn." He asks, also, many other stabbingly direct questions—none of which can be waved aside by any honest reader as lacking in prophetic vision :

Authors—essayist, atheist, novelist, realist, rhymester, play your part,
Paint the mortal shame of nature with the living hues of Art.
Do your best to charm the worst, to lower the rising race of men.
Have we risen from out the beast? then, back into the beast again.
Chaos, cosmos, cosmos, chaos, once again the sickening game,
Freedom free to slay herself, and dying while they shout her name. . . .

He foresaw that the cry of "Art for Art's sake" would lead inevitably to the view that "the filthiest of all pictures painted ill was mightier than the noblest painted well." And in many modern instances this very thing has been authoritatively proclaimed. A French professor, M. Douady, recently announced that Tennyson was a poet for school children. He takes Falconer's ridiculous *Shipwreck* quite seriously, with its

Then might I in unrivalled strains deplore
The impervious horrors of a leeward shore.

But our own second-rate writers have taught him that Tennyson is beneath contempt. It makes neither for the honour of English literature, nor for the wider recognition of the "best that is known and thought in the world," that this kind of criticism should be tolerated any longer.

Criticism should have no wind-vane for the fashions. The eccentric, the precious, the epigrammatic, have too long obscured the central and significant things. The secret of all great art in all periods comes very near to us in such poems as that which ends and crowns the work of Tennyson. Those who approach it simply and sincerely, dropping all their affectations, will find in it something better than an epigram for the mind, something better than dust and ashes for the soul. There is an august beauty in the music of that old age, broadening out like a majestic river, as it flows, magnificent in peace, a moving image of his own work, back to the Power who gave it :

> . . . such a tide as moving seems asleep,
> Too full for sound or foam,
> When that which drew from out the boundless deep
> Turns again home.

THE SPIRIT OF TOUCHSTONE

VOLUMES have been written on the women of Shakespeare. His kings were analysed by the pen of Walter Pater. His birds have been caught and caged in a score of volumes; his flowers have been plucked and pressed in another score. But the Fools of Shakespeare, those most subtle of all his creatures, coloured like flowers, wild as the birds, kings of the cap and bells, whose dogged constancy would even seem to pass the love of Imogen—what of these? The spirit of Touchstone, as revealed not in one play but in many, has escaped us hitherto without even an essay. Others abide our question, only the spirit of Touchstone is free; and through his lips the master-intellect talked to his audience, and played the part of chorus to his own characters, with a freedom which the merely objective dramatist could not have obtained. The spirit of Touchstone, in fact, is the fugitive spirit of the master himself; and it illuminates the greatest of all his works, *Hamlet*, in a way that I think has been missed by the Shakespearean commentators.

The clan of Touchstone is a large one. His kinsfolk established those festivals of folly in old England wherein on May mornings, Whitsun holidays (holy days too, as an old Puritan writer complains), the peasantry would choose to themselves lords or captains of misrule, and break into the churches, though the minister were at prayer or preaching, dancing and waving their garlands and may-boughs about, like devils incarnate. Even to this day there are relics of these customs in a few unchanging nooks of the English countryside. The "fool-plough" is still taken around in certain districts at the right season; and the rich farmer who refuses to subscribe the right amount to the ploughman's ale may watch them ploughing up his garden instead; for "it's a charter of old England," they declare, "and nobody can gainsay it."

The spirit of old England is there, at any rate, for it is a festival of freedom; and, moreover, nobody can gainsay that even an English garden may sometimes be all the better for having a plough run through it.

But the Court Fool was kept as a kind of specialized and personified sense of humour, whereto great kings delegated the function of self-criticism. His wit was a kind of fool-plough breaking up the gardens of ceremony and telling the truth to the lords of the earth.

This mere suggestion of the background of the subject is enough; for there is no end to the ramifications of the family tree of Touchstone. They were innumerable. He had cousins in France; but the home where his freedom flourished was England. You may see him to-day breaking into song or drawing pictures in *Punch*.

But, whatever their ancestry or posterity may be, the Fools of Shakespeare are his own; and the spirit of Touchstone in his plays has the freedom of all the forest of life. It seems incredible to-day that one of the writers on the old English customs could say that Shakespeare marred some of his finest works by the introduction of these motley figures fresh from the Whitsun ales of the peasantry. Even if Shakespeare had not told us, it is obvious that in these elemental creatures, springing from the soil of England like fantastic flowers, half primrose-coloured and half leaf-green, with jingling cap and crimson coxcomb, the very embodiment of her May, he would find a subject made to his hand. And, in fact, Shakespeare *has* told us. In *As You Like It* we get many suggestions of those subtle uses to which the master put the cap and bells. "This natural is a whetstone for the sharpening of other men's wits," declare those everyday human characters who are unable to recognize the fairy blood in the creature of motley; but Shakespeare, in calling him Touchstone, surely indicated something more than this, even as he indicated the necessity for sharpening the wits of those others. Touchstone is a quick, sensitive, impressionable creature, a thing by which gold and its alloys may be brought to the test, a touchstone for truth. And into the mouth of the melancholy Jaques, who is at war with the real follies of the world, Shakespeare puts the whole philosophy of motley, and describes how somewhere, midway upon the journey of his own life, he met a fool in the forest. I should like to lay particular stress on this passage, for it helps to illuminate the kinship of the spirit of Touchstone with the "antic disposition" of Hamlet; and, despite the long dispute between the critics as to whether Hamlet was mad or merely feigning to be mad, it has always seemed to me that Shakespeare, consciously or unconsciously, was simply developing the idea of this passage, and that Hamlet in his black trappings was neither more nor less than the tragic apotheosis of Touchstone. The Duke says of Jaques:

> If he, compact of jars, grow musical,
> We shall have shortly discord in the spheres.

(*Enter* JAQUES.)

The Duke. What, do you look merrily?
Jaques. A fool, a fool, I met a fool in the forest,
A motley fool—a miserable world!
As I do live by food, I met a fool;

Who laid him down and basked him in the sun,
And railed on Lady Fortune in good terms,
In good set terms, and yet a motley fool.
" Good morrow, fool," quoth I. " No, sir," quoth he,
" Call me not fool till Heaven hath sent me fortune."
And then he drew a dial from his coat
And looking on it with lack-lustre eye,
Says very wisely, " It is ten o'clock.
Thus we may see," quoth he, " how the world wags.
'Tis but an hour ago since it was nine,
And after one hour more 'twill be eleven.
And so, from hour to hour, we ripe and ripe,
And then from hour to hour we rot and rot.
And thereby hangs a tale." When I did hear
The motley fool thus moral on the time
My lungs began to crow like Chanticleer,
That fools should be so deep contemplative,
And I did laugh sans intermission
An hour by his dial. O noble fool!
A worthy fool! Motley 's the only wear.

The Duke. What fool is this?

Jaques. O worthy fool! One that hath been a courtier,
And says, if ladies be but young and fair,
They have the gift to know it; and in his brain,
Which is as dry as the remainder biscuit
After a voyage, he hath strange places cramm'd
With observation, the which he vents
In mangled forms. O that I were a fool!
I am ambitious for a motley coat.

The Duke. Thou shalt have one.

Jaques. It is my only suit;
Provided that you weed your better judgments
Of all opinion that grows rank in them
That I am wise. I must have liberty
Withal, as large a charter as the wind,
To blow on whom I please; for so fools have;
And they that are most galled with my folly,
They most must laugh. And why, sir, must they so?
The why is plain as way to parish church:
He that a fool doth very wisely hit
Doth very foolishly, although he smart,

Not to seem senseless of the bob: if not,
The wise man's folly is anatomiz'd
Even by the squandering glances of the fool.
Invest me in my motley; give me leave
To speak my mind, and I will through and through
Cleanse the foul body of the infected world,
If they will patiently receive my medicine.

This, surely, is the very keynote of *Hamlet*; and a few lines further on, when Jaques is defending his proposed adoption of motley (or, if we choose to anticipate a little, an "antic disposition"), he formulates the whole idea of Hamlet's play within the play:

Let me see wherein
My tongue hath wronged him; if it do him right,
How he hath wrong'd himself; if he be free,
Why then my taxing like a wild-goose flies,
Unclaimed of any man.

At the beginning of *As You Like It* we get the first suggestion of that pathetic and beautiful constancy of the Fool which was developed to tragically beautiful endings among the storms that washed out all the colours from the motley coat of the friend of King Lear.

Rosalind. But, cousin, what if we assay to steal
The clownish fool out of your father's court?
Would he not be a comfort to our travel?
Celia. He 'll go along o'er the wide world with me.

All through the play we get suggestions of that half-humorous, half-pathetic self-accusation which may be taken lightly in this comedy, yet has an undertone that merges into the deeper music of *Hamlet*:

Rosalind. Where learned you that oath, fool?
Touchstone. Of a certain knight that swore by his honour they were good pancakes, and swore by his honour the mustard was naught: now I 'll stand to it, the pancakes were naught and the mustard was good, and yet was not the

knight forsworn . . . swearing by his honour, for he never had any; or if he had, he had sworn it away before ever he saw these pancakes or that mustard.

And again and again we get the suggestion that the Fool, after all, does speak in set terms, that he can reword the matter which, as Hamlet said, mere madness would gambol from :

Celia. Prithee, who is 't that thou mean'st ?
Touchstone. One that old Frederick, your father, loves.
Celia. My father's love is enough to honour him. Enough! speak no more of him ; you 'll be whipp'd for taxation one of these days.
Touchstone. The more pity, that fools may not speak wisely what wise men say foolishly.
Celia. By my troth, thou sayest true ; for since the little wit that fools have was silenced, the little foolery that wise men have makes a great show.

At the end of *As You Like It* we get the beginnings of that soul-searching music which was to sweep through the whole universe in *Hamlet*, the first notes of that strange swift irony at the expense of all that is false in himself and the world ; that ecstatic truth-seeking which deals even more sternly with itself than with others, and proceeds from the profoundest depths of our nature :

Touchstone. Salutation and greeting to you all!
Jaques. Good my lord, bid him welcome: this is the motley-minded gentleman that I have so often met in the forest: he hath been a courtier, he swears.
Touchstone. If any man doubt that, let him put me to my purgation. I have trod a measure; I have flatter'd a lady: I have been politic with my friend, smooth with mine enemy; I have undone three tailors; I have had four quarrels, and like to have fought one.
Jaques. Is not this a rare fellow, my lord ? he 's as good at any thing and yet a fool.
Duke S. He uses his folly like a stalking-horse, and under the presentation of that he shoots his wit.

The Fool in *Twelfth Night* is another incarnation of the spirit of Touchstone, and, beyond noting here the part that he plays in stripping Malvolio of his conceit, one only needs to recall the two very exquisite touches which reveal the Fool once more as the fugitive spirit of the master himself. One is in the scene where Toby Belch and Andrew Aguecheek are making the night hideous with their revels and call upon the Fool for a song, to which, with the most exquisitely dramatic use of the lyric in any play, Shakespeare makes his reply with the song :

> O mistress mine, where are you roaming ?

The second is at the close of the whole play, when the Fool is heard singing another song. We are told in some of the older editions that Shakespeare has disfigured his work by the meaningless nonsense of that ending. For Polonius it is nonsense, perhaps, a cheap adaptation of a contemporary ballad. But it is precisely the most miraculously beautiful touch of the master-hand in the whole play. Shakespeare uses it as Beethoven used the tavern song to close his Ninth Symphony when instrumental music could go no further :

> When that I was and a little tiny boy,
> With hey, ho, the wind and the rain,
> A foolish thing was but a toy,
> For the rain it raineth every day.
>
> But when I came to man's estate,
> With hey, ho, the wind and the rain,
> 'Gainst knaves and thieves men shut their gate,
> For the rain it raineth every day.
>
> . . . . .
>
> A great while ago the world begun,
> With hey, ho, the wind and the rain.

We shall hear that song again ; for, though it closes the play, it is not the end of that symphony which was the soul of Shakespeare. The spirit of Touchstone, as I have tried to suggest, is one and the same in all its avatars, and the next time that we hear that song will be from the lips of the Fool in the most tragic moment of King Lear. It is the same faithful motley-minded creature who reappears to set the compassionate lightnings of the genius of Shakespeare playing around the tragic figure of King Lear, as if to defend him from the crueller lightnings of his doom. The wandering white-haired King may be the central figure of the tragedy ; but if you were to take away the Fool you would take away the spirit of Shakespeare, and, in the last act of all, you would deprive even Lear himself of his own soul and discrown him of his final kingship.

In the first act, after Lear has dismissed Cordelia, and abdicated in favour of Goneril and Regan, the master strikes the first note of that wild and exquisite music which is to accompany the outcast King through storm and darkness down to death. There is an undercurrent of deep pathos in that fourth scene of the first act where, in his first uneasiness at what he has done, the King calls alternately for his unfaithful daughter and his faithful Fool, who already knows the truth too well and is pining over the banishment of Cordelia.

The Fool has been using the rapier of his wit to defend his master, using it to such purpose that he has imperilled himself with Goneril. It is in an attack upon the Fool that she begins to unmask herself to the unhappy Lear. The crowning bitterness of the King's outcry against her cruelty is given by the soul of Shakespeare, speaking through the lips of the Fool. The King says, " Doth any here know me ? This is not Lear. Who is it that can tell me who I am ? " And the Fool replies in two words, "Lear's shadow." But when Goneril drives her father out, there is a faithful shadow of that shadow that runs after him, crying, "Uncle Lear, Uncle Lear, tarry and take the fool with you." And so, as they approach the castle of the second daughter, the Fool forewarns him, with a passion and compassion that must needs hide itself in motley, being in the presence of the King, "Shalt see thy other daughter will use thee kindly."

And at the climax of the scene, when the second daughter also drives him out into the bleak night, to whom does the old man turn but to that motley-minded and compassionate friend, with the terrible cry which is the climax of that scene : "O, fool, I shall go mad!" And leaning upon the Fool's shoulder, he goes out into the darkness and storm. And so Kent meets them on the desolate heath.

And as the rage of Lear dies out from sheer exhaustion, he turns again, with one of the most human touches in the play, to his faithful shadow. "My wits begin to turn," he says. "And I 'll to bed at noon," cries the Fool, the last words that we hear from his lips in this play ; though Kent calls him to help his master, crying, "Thou must not stay behind." They go out into the night together, and we see the Fool no more ; but he lives in the heart and soul of Lear, sustaining him up to the moment when he meets Cordelia. This motley figure is needed no more, for Lear has learned all that he could tell him. The spirit of the vanished Fool, the soul of Shakespeare, would now speak through the mouth of King Lear himself. Yet, in the very last moments of the play, Lear turns from his dead daughter, Cordelia, to cry, "And my poor fool is hanged!"

This would end the tale of Touchstone and his tribe, so far as their motley is concerned, but it does not quite end the tale of the spirit of Touchstone. The Fool and the King play "handy dandy" in *King*

Lear, till towards the end you might cry, "Presto, which is the King—which the Fool?"

In one work, his greatest, perhaps the greatest single work ever achieved in any language—the greatest poem, the greatest artistic achievement of the human intellect—*Hamlet*, though it was written before *King Lear*, he seems to me to have developed the idea of Touchstone further. Volumes have been written on the madness of Hamlet, some of them by eminent specialists in lunacy. Polonius also has discussed in hundreds of essays the question whether Hamlet were half mad, or only pretending to be mad. Hamlet's own declaration that he was "only mad nor' nor' west" counts for little with either party. It is a dangerous thing to proffer any new suggestion about that work, but I am emboldened by the amazing blunders of Polonius to proffer a suggestion here which at least has one merit—that it disposes of many volumes of rubbish and simplifies the whole question. It has always illuminated the whole play for me, and I am tempted to hope that it may light a lamp or two for others. The conception of that motley-minded Spirit as the Truth-teller, the Spirit at war with a world of shams, had long been taking shape in the mind of Shakespeare. He was particularly fascinated by that intellectual ecstasy which burned its way through ceremony and insincerity, and proceeded from nothing more and nothing less than a clear vision of the truth and a fierce desire to make the truth prevail.

Moreover, Shakespeare was possessed by that restless discontent with himself which all artists know, the torture of the mind which has expressed itself in a hundred tales of the clown who laughs and dances with his heart bursting; or in songs of a hundred poets who have deliberately adopted the cap and bells, in order to forestall the slings and arrows of outrageous critics, or in order that they may forestall the jest at a heart worn too openly upon the sleeve. Byron did this in *Don Juan*, as a hundred poets have done it; and for the playwright, the man to whom the whole world has indeed become a stage, a kingdom of make-believe, there must often be a more than usually violent reaction against the unreality of that life which is like a walking shadow. Shakespeare expresses this dissatisfaction over and over again, as in the sonnet where he says he has made himself a motley to the view.

Through the mouth of Hamlet himself Shakespeare in more than one passage criticizes the insincerities of the stage and his own craft. Yet, just as Hamlet declared that the play was, after all, the thing wherein to catch the King's conscience, so it is quite clear that Hamlet consciously or unconsciously adopted the means desired by Jaques to purge the world, to catch the consciences of all around him, and wage war upon all their insincerities in a kind of intellectual ecstasy of truth-seeking. He not only gores his own falser thoughts, but bites upon every insincerity as a man bites upon a sore tooth. He becomes the tragic Fool of that court, a Fool in black trappings and inky cloak; and the passage upon which all the discussion is based as to whether he is mad or merely feigning to be mad must be interpreted to mean neither more nor less than what it says. For Shakespeare, when Hamlet swears his friends to silence about the ghost of his father, makes him use the exact word for the spirit of Touchstone, the word that was always applied to the Fool:

> Here, as before, never, so help you mercy!
> How strange or odd soe'er I bear myself,
> *As I, perchance, hereafter shall think meet*
> *To put an antic disposition on.*

To that *antic* disposition, to that spirit of Touchstone within him, he gives a free rein henceforward, striking at all the follies and stupidities around him with an invisible, but far more potent, intellectual bauble. He is Touchstone raised to the *n*th. In his loyalty to his dead father, in his pining away for the disloyalties of others, and in his absolute mastery over all the stops of that wild and exquisite music with which the wandering Fool of Lear consoled and supported his master to the end, Hamlet the Prince of Denmark accomplishes the desire of Jaques, ascends the intellectual throne and reigns. It is the apotheosis of Touchstone :

> Seems, Madam, I know not seems !

The apotheosis of Touchstone, I say, for every syllable that falls from the lips of Hamlet burns with an intellectual ecstasy for the truth that is almost supernatural in its fierce devouring onslaught. It breaks up through the thin crust of customs and ceremonies like a volcanic lava and carries everything before it. The tragedy is that of a man so superior to those around him that they believe him to be mad. It is to this end that Shakespeare developed the crude original. How any critic, even though he had borrowed the plum-tree gum of old Polonius himself, could ever have suggested that Hamlet was mad, or even pretending to be mad, surpasses one's imagination, when Shakespeare himself again and again satirizes Polonius, and makes a sheer butt of him for entertaining that same idea. But everything, of course, is possible in a world that hangs tercentenary almanacs on its walls, with quotations from Polonius printed as moral maxims for our daily guidance ; and there is no Hamlet to enter, reading, as of old, to sweep it all away.

Hamlet is Touchstone, the very test for truth, supernaturally quick to see the truth, responsive as a musical instrument to the lightest touch, and above all things supernaturally sane. He knows, as surely as if a ghost had told him, even so trivial a matter as that Polonius was coming to tell him about the actors, and he sweeps the tedious recital away with a "buzz, buzz" which is not madness, but contempt for the intolerable stupidity of the old statesman. He knows, though he says no word to show it, that there is some one concealed behind the arras when Ophelia approaches; and he knows, too, that she knows it, and that she is deceiving him. It is this knowledge, not his madness, that makes him upbraid her with all the bitterness of those wintry winds that caught up the music of the Fool of Lear.

Quick, too, supernaturally quick and alive he is during the play within the play, where every word that falls from his lips is that of the sublimated jester, Touchstone; from the coarseness that he flings at Ophelia and the snatches of song used by the antics in the morris dances—"With hey and ho, the hobby-horse is forgot"—to the swift subtle phrases that strike home like dagger-blades straight to the heart of the King.

And, as if to drive his point home, Shakespeare himself gives us the key to this antic disposition in perhaps the most wonderful scene of all, the grave-diggers' scene, where the two clowns are tossing about the bones of the dead, and suddenly Hamlet enters, takes up the snatches of their discourse and turns them into a music that sweeps through the whole universe.

There is no more dramatic moment in literature than that in which Hamlet is brought face to face not with a ghost, but with the skull of his own true spiritual father, the skull of Yorick. The lines in which it is told were not purposeless, and they surely suggest an extraordinarily close relationship between the child Hamlet and Yorick.

Alas, poor Yorick! He hath borne me on his back a thousand times. . . . Here hung those lips that I have kissed I know not how oft. . . . Now get you to my lady's chamber, and tell her, let her paint an inch thick, to this favour she must come.

Surely, in the profoundest sense, there is a play within the play here. This glimpse of the childhood of Hamlet, and his injunction to the skull to resume its old function of truth-telling, are an indication of where Hamlet learned his own method of telling the truth to kings. It may be that Shakespeare, deeply interested in the effect that he could obtain with his Fools, merely seized an opportunity of developing that kind of character, and that it grew under his hand almost unconsciously up to a certain point; but I feel certain that when he wrote this passage it had become a conscious development, and that he was here deliberately giving us the explanation of Hamlet's "antic disposition." It is hardly too fanciful to imagine the child Hamlet jogging on the old Fool's shoulder to a tune that we have heard before, and that, when he broke into those wild rhymes about the clay of Cæsar stopping a hole to keep the wind away, he was still haunted by it:

When that I was and a little tiny boy,
With hey, ho, the wind and the rain.

SHAKESPEARE AND THE SEA

> Everything that heard him play,
> Even the billows of the sea,
> Hung their heads and then lay by.

ONE of the secrets of the power of the Elizabethan age in poetry lies in the combination of two facts: the fact that England was a small and solid island, and the fact that the sea surrounding her had suddenly assumed an aspect of almost daily deepening mystery. Never before in the history of the world had there been such a combination.

There had been legends and fairy tales of happy islands where men walked with gods as with their elder brothers; but never before had there been such a revelation of miraculous realities. For here was discovery on discovery of unimagined oceans and continents. Veil after veil was withdrawn, only to make more mysterious the veils beyond. It was as if men were sailing out into the vastness of the Eternal.

Never before had it been possible to sit in a tavern and hear from the lips of those who had sailed beyond the utmost limits of the Old World that the fairy tales were infinitely less marvellous than the truth. It was an age of real presences, and England had become a Prospero's island by virtue of the mighty presence of the sea. Seamen came back like Lazarus from the grave, but their lips were not even sealed, and they held the Bread of Life in their hands. It was as if men had suddenly discovered that their earth was, after all, not a thing of make-believe, a dust-bin of customs and creeds, but a real island floating in the real mystery of an infinite heaven.

It was seriously discussed in the little black taverns, "at the latter end of a sea-coal fire," whether men might not sail straight up to the Gates of Paradise. The Bible and the Map, in Hakluyt's phrase, had opened doors for them. But for the greater intellects of the time it meant an even more vivid realization of the isolation of their little hearth-fires in an unfathomable universe. It meant a spiritual voyage through an immeasurable abyss of darkness in quest of a spiritual Cathay.

That "strangeness" which Bacon, long before Walter Pater, had proclaimed as one of the qualities of beauty, was nothing more or less than the gleam of the treasure that the galleons of these great spiritual adventurers brought back from worlds beyond the world.

The exquisite poem of Drayton, *To the Virginian Voyage*, combines in itself both aspects, the outer and the inner beauty of this fine quest. But if one searches the Elizabethan poets for work dealing directly with the sea as a subject in itself, it is more than a little surprising to find how rarely they approach it in that way. The influence of the sea upon their poetry was as great as its influence upon the City of London. But you do not find either of them very salt.

There is no contemporary work of importance dealing with the Armada. There are few poems directly connected with the seafaring life of the time. There are songs, of course, like the dialogue in Dowland's *Book of Airs*, in which Neptune and the gods of the wind are paraded in what might be called lyrical masques rather than poems. There are innumerable conventional sea-pictures among the sonneteers, many of them imitations of the French and Italian poets rather than original poems of the sea.

But there are very few Elizabethan lyrics that deal directly with the subject, very few even so vital as the verses by Surrey—the "complaint of a woman for her absent lover, being upon the sea."

The sea, in fact, has been used by almost all the English poets incidentally, as an image, a symbol, a means of "representing much in little." The function of poetry, as described by Wordsworth in the great passage from which those four words are quoted, has been carried out chiefly by two means of expression—rhythm, which introduces law into chaos and has its counterpart in all the arts and in all creation; and imagery, a means of representing those things which are beyond the direct reach of our minds, representing occasionally even those things which we call divine. The sea, with its tidal rhythms, its measured waves, its immeasurable horizons, has been one of the chief images used by the English poets in the exercise of this great art.

It is in this more subtle way that the sea has most profoundly influenced our island literature and lent some of its deepest tones to the music of our poetry. For though England herself, in almost all her phases —political, social, religious, and artistic—is a daughter of the sea, "lulled with sea-sounds in a thousand caves, and lit with sea-shine to her island lair," the physical aspect of the matter would have no vital importance for us in literature if it were not for the fact that her poets have caught sight, across her grey horizons, of a vaster and more significant sea; that sea from which, in a deeper sense than they knew in Greece or Rome, beauty herself was born; that sea which Keats, not Cortez, beheld from the mount of vision. "Hence," cried Wordsworth, child as he was of the inland lakes:

> Hence, in a season of calm weather,
> Tho' inland far we be,
> Our souls have sight of that immortal sea

Which brought us hither :
Can in a moment travel thither,
And see the children sporting on the shore
And hear the mighty waters, rolling evermore.

The sound of that sea is heard in all the greatest poetry of England, whether of the lakes, or the mountains, or the coast. It is heard in Matthew Arnold's *Dover Beach*, which begins with a picture of the Channel under the moon, and then develops it into spiritual imagery. The two stages are clearly marked in this poem, and they elucidate the point which I desire to make later in dealing with Shakespeare's treatment of the sea. The sea, in that vast, symbolical sense, rolls an infinite horizon round our English poetry, just as the stars round off the three divisions of the *Divine Comedy*.

The greatest of all poets, Shakespeare, holds that position because he was able to show us more things than any other man in their eternal aspect ; and, by doing this, to double the truth, double the reality, of the human pageant that he passes before us. More than that of any other poet his music has caught the very cadence of that unfathomable sea whose waves are years. Of the sonnets it might almost be said that they are themselves waves in that eternal element. They are so much at one with it that we cannot tell the music of the sea from their own.

Like as the waves make toward the pebbled shore,
So do our minutes hasten to their end :
Each changing place with that which goes before,
In sequent toil all forwards do contend.
Nativity, once in the main of light,
Crawls to maturity, wherewith being crowned,
Crookéd eclipses 'gainst his glory fight,
And Time that gave doth now his gift confound.

"Like as the waves !" The waves themselves

are allowed only a single line ; but what a sea-picture is this, and how the music of the sea informs every syllable, every cadence ; so that the only possible musical accompaniment to the whole would be one played by the ocean. This music is carried on through sonnets in which there is no direct reference to the sea at all, but the cadence is unmistakable.

"When in the chronicle of wasted time," he says, and we see the waves wasting themselves in foam once more. Just as in the end of Arnold's *Dover Beach*, when the poet has left the sea for the loftier theme, we hear the clashing of waves in that darker world, "swept with confused alarms of struggle and fight, where ignorant armies clash by night" ; so Shakespeare uses the music of the sea to represent those processes of change which make of the whole physical universe a flowing tide of coloured shadows. A modern critic has touched this continual vanishing away of ourselves and the universe with something of the morbid beauty of a fever ; but only at the price of that cruelty, that injustice to ourselves and the universe, which may be said to lurk like a disease in the heart of all the æsthetics of pessimism.

Walter Pater approached this aspect of the universe from the critical side. Shakespeare has the wider and deeper creative view. Over and over again, in his sonnets, we feel that in the midst of all these flowing tides he has within himself some abiding certainty, though even for him it may be inexpressible, too great even for such definition as Shelley could give it. *The one remains, the many change and pass.* He doubts and fears ; but these doubts and fears and sorrows are a kingly crown, a divine crown, that he would not resign for all the pleasures that tickle the palate of the modern æsthete. What an ebb and flow, making a sound like thunder, everlastingly, there is in the antiphonal cadences of this :

When I have seen by Time's fell hand defaced
  The rich-proud cost of outworn buried age ;
When sometime lofty towers I see down-razed
  And brass eternal slave to mortal rage ;
When I have seen the hungry ocean gain
  Advantage on the kingdom of the shore,
And the firm soil win of the watery main,
  Increasing store with loss and loss with store :
When I have seen such interchange of state,
  Or state itself confounded to decay,
Ruin hath taught me thus to ruminate
  That time will come and take my love away.
This thought is as a death, which cannot choose
But weep to have that which it fears to lose.

And ever and again in the darkness he kindles some great beacon for storm-tossed mariners like that triumphant hundred and sixteenth sonnet, giving us his answer to their age-long question—*How with this rage shall beauty find a plea, whose action is no stronger than a flower ?* For this mightiest of all poets was the tenderest also ; but he did not halt there. Beyond the music of the sea, beyond the music of our mortality and the eternal note of sadness that Sophocles heard upon the Ægean, he finds his own answer, his own reconciliation, and utters it in the major key :

Love is not love
Which alters when it alteration finds,
  Or bends with the remover to remove.
Oh, no, it is an ever-fixed mark,
  That looks on tempests and is never shaken ;
It is the star to every wandering bark,
  Whose worth 's unknown, although his height be taken.

With such music as this in our ears, and with that great sea-mark towering before us, we understand what Victor Hugo meant by his elaborate comparison of Shakespeare with the sea, and by his conclusion :

to look upon the soul of Shakespeare is to look upon the Ocean.

It is in this attitude towards the universe, then, this constant realization of the fact that poetry is concerned with what ear has not heard and eye has not seen, that the greatness of the art of Shakespeare resides. It is in his use of sea-music, of sea-imagery, to bring his readers into touch with thoughts that would otherwise be beyond the reaches of any soul, that we are to find his greatest sea-poetry. He uses the sea sometimes as an image for the universe itself, for all that is outside the bounds of the individual soul. He does this, for instance, in *Hamlet*, where he debates whether he shall "take arms against a sea of troubles," and in *Pericles*, where he cries :

> Put me to present pain,
> Lest this great sea of joys rushing upon me
> O'erbear the shores of my mortality,
> And drown me with their sweetness.

Throughout the work of Shakespeare, however, we are never very far away from even the material sea ; never, one might say, out of earshot of it. There are, of course, the obvious cases, like the prologue to *Henry V.*, which gives us almost the only contemporary picture of an Elizabethan fleet :

> Suppose that you have seen
> The well-appointed king, at Hampton pier,
> Embark his royalty ; and his brave fleet
> With silken streamers, the young Phœbus fanning.
> Play with your fancies, and in them behold
> Upon the hempen tackle ship-boys climbing,
> Hear the shrill whistle which doth order give
> To sounds confused ; behold the threaden sails
> Borne with the invisible and creeping wind
> Draw the huge bottoms through the furrowed sea
> Breasting the lofty surge : Oh, do but think
> You stand upon the rivage and behold
> A city on the inconstant billows dancing :
> For so appears this fleet majestical.

More vital, and certainly one of the most vivid of sea-farewells, is the picture in *Cymbeline* of the sailing of Imogen's lover—one of the very few instances of the use of "perspective" in English poetry, or, indeed, in any poetry, before the romantic revival. One may hazard a guess that these scenes of waving and farewell from vanishing ships and receding shores—moments that all through the history of England have plucked at the islander's heartstrings—have directly influenced the development both of seascape and landscape in English poetry :

Imogen. I would thou grew'st unto the shores o' the haven,
 And question'dst every sail : if he should write,
 And I not have it, 'twere a paper lost,
 As offer'd mercy is. What was the last
 That he spake to thee ?
Pisanio. It was his queen, his queen !
Imogen. Then waved his handkerchief ?
Pisanio. And kiss'd it, Madam.
Imogen. Senseless linen ! happier therein than I !
 And that was all ?
Pisanio. No, Madam ; for so long
 As he could make me with this eye or ear
 Distinguish him from others, he did keep
 The deck, with glove, or hat, or handkerchief,
 Still waving, as the fits and stirs of 's mind
 Could best express how slow his soul sail'd on,
 How swift his ship.
Imogen. Thou shouldst have made him
 As little as a crow, or less, ere left
 To after-eye him.
Pisanio. Madam, so I did.
Imogen. I would have broke mine eyestrings ; crack'd them, but
 To look upon him, till the diminution
 Of space had pointed him sharp as my needle,
 Nay, follow'd him, till he had melted from
 The smallness of a gnat to air, and then
 Have turn'd mine eye and wept.

Tennyson had undoubtedly very carefully studied this passage from *Cymbeline*. He borrows the very phrasing of one line to describe a very different kind of distance, "where all the starry heavens of space are sharpened to a needle's end." It is recalled by the sea-distance at the close of the *Morte d'Arthur*, too, where the hull becomes "one black dot against the verge of dawn"; and again by the exquisite coming and going of sails in the later song:

> Fresh as the first beam glittering on the sail
> That brings our friends up from the underworld;
> Sad as the last that reddens over one
> That sinks with all we love below the verge. . . .

This is not dramatic. It is not concerned with the "moving accident." It bears the burden of no moral or political revolt or acquiescence. It is "art for art's sake," the very thing that the age pretends to require, and in this case it is simply a quiet and beautifully painted seascape, developed from the earlier seascape of Shakespeare. The passage in *Cymbeline* has a less vivid parallel in the second part of *King Henry VI.*, this time a picture from the deck of a ship:

> As far as I could ken thy chalky cliffs,
> When from thy shore the tempest beat us back,
> I stood upon the hatches in the storm,
> And when the dusky sky began to rob
> My earnest-gaping sight of thy land's view,
> I took a costly jewel from my neck,
> A heart it was, bound in with diamonds,
> And threw it towards thy land: the sea received it,
> And so I wish'd thy body might my heart;
> And even with this I lost fair England's view
> And bid mine eyes be packing with my heart,
> And call'd them blind and dusky spectacles,
> For losing ken of Albion's wished coast.

But the influence of the sea upon Shakespeare

is least shown by the passages in which he deals directly with it. Far more is it shown in the exquisite lines with which Florizel woos Perdita, lines that seem to reveal some subtle correspondence, some law of beauty that is common to this child of the sea and the waves that had refused to harm her, lines that seem in their exquisite movement to share the secret of the waves, the tides, and the pulsing of the human heart ; the innermost secret of rhythm itself :

> What you do
> Still betters what is done. When you speak, sweet,
> I 'd have you do it ever : when you sing,
> I 'd have you buy and sell so, so give alms,
> Pray so ; and, for the ordering your affairs,
> To sing them too : when you do dance, I wish you
> A wave of the sea, that you might ever do
> Nothing but that ; move still, still so,
> And own no other function.

There is the essence of sea-poetry, an essence not to be found in the mere fact that Shakespeare elsewhere used this or that nautical phrase. This is the music which, as I said above, is to be heard through many of the sonnets and plays where no mention of the sea is made at all.

Throughout the work of Shakespeare we are never much further from the sound of that sea-music than is the heart of the little island itself. We may wander through his enchanted woodlands, thinking that all we hear is the sigh of the leaves ; and suddenly through an arch of green boughs and ferns, as through some exquisite magic casement, we catch a glimpse of the moonlit foam. What an exquisite glimpse is that which Oberon and Titania give us, for instance, in the very heart of *A Midsummer Night's Dream* :

> *Oberon.* I do but beg a little changeling boy
> To be my henchman.
> *Titania.* Set your heart at rest :
> The fairy land buys not the child of me.

> His mother was a votaress of my order ;
> And, in the spiced Indian air, by night
> Full often hath she gossip'd by my side
> And sat with me on Neptune's yellow sands,
> Marking the embarked traders on the flood,
> When we have laughed to see the sails conceive
> And grow big bellied with the wanton wind ;
> Which she, with pretty and with swimming gait
> Following,—her womb then rich with my young squire,—
> Would imitate, and sail upon the land,
> To fetch me trifles, and return again,
> As from a voyage, rich with merchandise.

Indeed, the whole magic of the play is drawn from that perilous foam ; and if one required a philosophical justification for such magic, one would only have to point through the vistas of the forest to that infinite mystery of the sea, where Oberon, sitting on a promontory, heard the sea-maid's music.

"Thou rememberest," he says to Puck, once and twice ; and Puck replies, "I remember."

"That very time I saw," says Oberon, "but thou couldst not,

> Flying between the cold moon and the earth,
> Cupid all armed ; a certain aim he took
> At a fair vestal throned by the West,
> And loosed his love-shaft smartly from his bow
> As it should pierce a hundred thousand hearts ;
> But I might see young Cupid's fiery shaft
> Quenched in the chaste beams of the watery moon,
> And the imperial votaress passed on,
> In maiden meditation, fancy-free,
> Yet marked I where the bolt of Cupid fell :
> It fell upon a little western flower,
> Before milk-white, now purple with love's wound,
> And maidens call it love-in-idleness.
> Fetch me that flower : the herb I showed thee once :
> The juice of it on sleeping eyelids laid
> Will make or man or woman madly dote
> Upon the next live creature that it sees.

Fetch me this herb ; and be thou here again
Ere the leviathan can swim a league."

" I 'll put a girdle round about the earth
In forty minutes,"

cried Puck ; and well he might, in the power of that wizardry. For surely, though it has scarce even been noticed by the critics, it is one of the most exquisite touches of the master-poet's art that has girdled his magic flower with this fairy ring of sea-shine. The wand of Merlin himself could hardly have worked so potent a spell, or evoked so marvellous a vision as that ring of white fire, from the mermaid singing on the dolphin's back to the mysterious shadow of leviathan vanishing away into the darkness of the sea.

This magic casement opening through an arch of leaves in the forest gives us one more brief glimpse of the boundless sea-world beyond at the moment when Oberon decides to break the spell that he had cast upon the mortals in the power of that sea-drawn magic :

But we are spirits of another sort :
I with the morning's love have oft made sport,
And, like a forester, the groves may tread,
Even till the eastern gate, all fiery-red,
Opening on Neptune with fair blessed beams,
Turns into yellow gold his salt green streams.

Incidentally one may remark that this is one of the very few instances in Elizabethan poetry of a feeling for the natural beauty of the sea, or of its treatment with so rich a sense of colour. There in that sea is the infinite treasure-house of his power ; and there is the horizon that surrounds the dreams, the fairy tales, of our brief night with mystery and closes them in peace.

It is with something of the same visionary power

that in the fourth scene of *Richard III.* Shakespeare suddenly opens a magic casement in the solid walls of the world and bids us gaze into the mysteries of the sea, as into some wizard's crystal. It is one of the most wonderful sea-pictures in the whole of literature, both in its inner and outer significance, which the doomed Clarence, walled about with stone, in the Tower of London, suddenly reveals to Brackenbury. Half-way through the passage it will be noted once more how Shakespeare leaves the sea behind him, or rather uses it as a means for representing something vaster, the "tempest of a soul," just as, in his own way, Arnold did in *Dover Beach*:

> Methought I saw a thousand fearful wrecks;
> Ten thousand men that fishes gnawed upon;
> Wedges of gold, great anchors, heaps of pearl,
> Inestimable stones, unvalued jewels
> All scattered in the bottom of the sea. . . .
> *O, then began the tempest to my soul,*
> *. . . then came wandering by*
> *A shadow like an angel with bright hair*
> *Dabbled in blood.*

But marvellous as is that glimpse of the deep where false fleeting visions come and go, around a mind "hot for certainties," the master-poet had not yet come to the height of his power, not yet encountered the full tempest of those things that war against the soul, as he did in the four supreme tragedies. In these can we not descry Shakespeare himself, wandering through the darkness of that universal sea in quest of some one steadfast thing, as Dante wandered through Hell and Purgatory and Heaven in quest of Beatrice? This is what distinguishes his work from that of all other Elizabethan dramatists—the burning passion, the devouring passion, that he had in a world of lies and shams for the steadfast and unshaken harmonies of the

Eternal. Is it not this great struggle that raises to the sublimest heights of tragedy the pitiful story of Othello? It is not by a mere accident that Shakespeare, at the moment when Iago's poison runs riot in the veins of the Moor, sets the wild elements of that uncertain sea raging around them and through them, and makes Iago their prophet. At the very moment when Othello, hot for the one wild certainty left to him, utters that awful and almost smothered cry for vengeance :

O blood, blood, blood,

Iago whispers to him, " Patience, I say ; your mind, perhaps, may change." And then the storm rolls in like thunder :

> Never, Iago. Like to the Pontic sea,
> Whose icy current and compulsive course
> Ne'er feels retiring ebb, but keeps due on
> To the Propontic and the Hellespont,
> Even so my bloody thoughts, with violent pace,
> Shall ne'er look back, ne'er ebb to humble love,
> Till that a capable and wide revenge
> Swallow them up. Now by yond marble heaven, (*kneels*)
> In the due reverence of a sacred vow,
> I here engage my words.
>
> *Iago.* Do not rise yet.
> (IAGO *also kneels.*)
> Witness, you ever-burning lights above,
> You elements that clip us round about,—
> Witness that here Iago doth give up
> The execution of his wit, hands, heart,
> To wrong'd Othello's service !

In *Macbeth* Shakespeare ventures to explore those terrible midnight seas even further. The witches that cast their wild shadows over this tremendous tragedy have no kinship with those poor old crones whom Christian people so recently burned at the stake. They have something universal in them.

They are more than evil. They are personifications of those wild tempests which wreck the soul on its eternal quest; those wild storms of change, and ruin, and seemingly purposeless mockery in the world, which baffle the most earnest steersman. Just as in the sonnets, there is a basis of direct reference to the sea, and then imagery and a great undertone of sea-music sweeping through the whole universe.

There are moments in the play when the whole world seems to become a seething witches' cauldron, their bubbling, midnight sea. And had some of our modern dabblers in darkness rightly understood the profound symbolism of this one great tragedy, there would be fewer of those childish attempts to startle the world by paddling on the fringe of its dark waters.

> *1st Witch.* When shall we three meet again
> In thunder, lightning, or in rain?
> *2nd Witch.* When the hurly-burly 's done,
> When the battle 's lost and won.
> *All.* Fair is foul, and foul is fair:
> Hover thro' the fog and filthy air.

Throughout we are given terrible glimpses of the immense tempest, a battle as terrible as that of the archangels, which is being waged in the soul of Shakespeare, behind and through and beyond the action of the play. At the opening we have the wounded soldier bringing his report of the earthly battle of Malcolm:

> Doubtful it stood,
> As two spent swimmers, that do cling together
> And choke their art.

Of the enemy he says that: "The multiplying villainies of nature do swarm upon him"; and of

Macbeth's valiant action he says, with the very sound and motion of the sea in his words :

> As whence the sun 'gins his reflection,
> Shipwrecking storms and direful thunders break,
> So from that spring whence comfort seemed to come
> Discomfort swells.

Then, with supreme power, the master-dramatist carries us to the thunders of the North, brings the great theme to a head, sums it up, and utters it through the mouths of the witches in one of the wildest strains of sea-music that ever fell on mortal ears.

> *1st Witch.* Where hast thou been, sister ?
> *2nd Witch.* Killing swine.
> *3rd Witch.* Sister, where thou ?
> *1st Witch.* A sailor's wife had chestnuts in her lap
> And munch'd and munch'd and munch'd :—
> " Give me," quoth I :
> " Aroint thee, Witch," the rump-fed ronyon cries.
> Her husband 's to Aleppo gone, Master o' the Tiger :
> But in a sieve I 'll thither sail,
> And, like a rat without a tail,
> I 'll do, I 'll do, and I 'll do.
> *2nd Witch.* I 'll give thee a wind.
> *1st Witch.* Thou 'rt kind.
> *3rd Witch.* And I another.
> *1st Witch.* I myself have all the other,
> And the very ports they blow,
> All the quarters that they know
> I' the shipman's card.
> I will drain him dry as hay ;
> Sleep shall neither night or day
> Hang upon his pent-house lid ;
> He shall live a man forbid :
> Weary sev'n nights nine times nine
> Shall he dwindle, peak, and pine.
> Though his bark cannot be lost,
> Yet it shall be tempest-toss'd.
> Look what I have.

2nd Witch. Show me, show me.
1st Witch. Here I have a pilot's thumb,
Wrecked as homeward he did come.
3rd Witch. A drum, a drum!
Macbeth doth come.

Into the hands of these fleeting, inconsistent powers Macbeth delivers himself, and thenceforward he has no pilot, no certainty, no repose. At the very climax of the murder scene, beyond the knocking at the gate, and infinitely more menacing to the soul, we hear as it were the deep baying of the blood-hounds of that sea from which there is no escape:

Whence is that knocking?
What hands are here? Ha! They pluck out mine eyes.
Will all great Neptune's Ocean wash this blood
Clean from my hand? No, this my hand will rather
The multitudinous seas incarnadine,
Making the green one red.

The thumb of the pilot had been cast into the cauldron, and henceforward Macbeth is at the mercy of the elements. No longer can he say with Banquo:

Fears and scruples shake us:
In the great hand of God I stand.

He has abandoned all stability, lost his sheet anchor. "But let the frame of things disjoint," he cries:

Better be with the dead,
Whom we to gain our peace have sent to peace,
Than on the torture of the mind to lie
In restless ecstasy. Duncan is in his grave:
After life's fitful fever he sleeps well.

It is the tempest of the soul that tosses him here; but his prayer for sleep is only a tragic deepening of the same sea-music which we heard from the lips of another king. For in all these great moments of all the sonnets and poems and plays there is really only one soul speaking, the soul of Shakespeare, boundless as the universal sea in compassion :

> Wilt thou upon the high and giddy mast
> Seal up the ship-boy's eyes, and rock his brains
> In cradle of the rude imperious surge,
> And in the visitation of the winds,
> Who take the ruffian billows by the top,
> Curling their monstrous heads, and hanging them
> With deafening clamour in the slippery clouds,
> That, with the hurly, death itself awakes ?
> Canst thou, O partial sleep, give thy repose
> To the wet sea-boy in an hour so rude,
> And in the calmest and most stillest night
> Deny it to a king ?

Through all the sound and fury of those darker storms of tragedy we hear, in every lull between the gusts, that deep-sea music :

> Duncan is in his grave :
> After life's fitful fever he sleeps well.

But Macbeth is called upon to be wise, amazed, temperate and furious, loyal and neutral, all in a moment, and he knows that it is as impossible as to bridle the sea. No sooner is one wave surmounted than another comes on :

> Fleance is 'scap'd.
> Then comes my fit again : I had else been perfect,
> Whole as the marble, founded as the rock.

But there is no rock to which he can cling in this wild tide. He cannot reduce to order this chaos of his own creation. There is no harmonious universe possible for evil, no security, no peace. Banquo is safe, he is told, with twenty trenchéd gashes in his head, the least a death to nature. But for Macbeth the only reply is, " Get thee gone : to-morrow we 'll hear, ourselves, again." And as he turns to the feast he meets the ghostly accuser, and the waves overwhelm him :

Which of you have done this? . . .
Thou canst not say I did it; never shake
Thy gory locks at me. . . .
The times have been
That, when the brains were out, the man would die,
And there an end; but now they rise again,
With twenty mortal murders on their crowns,
And push us from our stools.

All things have lost their certainty for him. It is not only evil and good that shift their forms in that sea; but there is nothing definite left for him under the sun. All is Protean, and it is to Proteus, god of the sea, that he prays:

Approach thou like the rugged Russian Bear,
The arm'd rhinoceros or the Hyrcan tiger,
Take any shape but that.

There is nothing in that Protean nature that he can trust:

It will have blood; they say, blood will have blood.
Stones have been known to move and trees to speak.

But some certainty he must have. He must know the worst. It is impossible to return; he must plunge further into that sea of blood. Once more he cries to those secret black and midnight hags:

I conjure you, by that which you profess,—
Howe'er you come to know it, answer me:
Though you untie the winds and let them fight
Against the churches; though the yeasty waves
Confound and swallow navigation up;
Though bladed corn be lodged, and trees blown down;
Though castles topple on their warders' heads;
Though palaces and pyramids do slope
Their heads to their foundation; though the treasure
Of nature's germins tumble all together,
Even till destruction sicken,—answer me
To what I ask you.

And the very truth that thunders in his ears deceives him. Never shall he be vanquished till the forests of the earth shall come against him; till Birnam Wood shall come to Dunsinane. The forests at least are anchored in their place; and for a while he is able to find some certainty in that. Yet, like as the waves make towards the pebbled shore, so do his minutes hasten to their end. There is nothing serious left in mortality. And with what a solemn music does Shakespeare usher in that last note of the angry sea:

> To-morrow, and to-morrow, and to-morrow,
> Creeps in this petty pace from day to day
> To the last syllable of recorded time.
> And all our yesterdays have lighted fools
> The way to dusty death. Out, out, brief candle!
> Life 's but a walking shadow, a poor player
> That struts and frets his hour upon the stage,
> And then is heard no more. It is a tale
> Told by an idiot, full of sound and fury,
> Signifying nothing.
>
> (*Enter a* MESSENGER.)
>
> Thou comest to use thy tongue; thy story quickly.
>
> *Messenger*. As I did stand my watch upon the hill,
> I looked towards Birnam, and anon, methought,
> The wood began to move.

The power of that tremendous dramatic moment can never be fully realized on the stage. It is fraught with all the wonders and terrors that were implied in the strange old word—*panic*. In its effect upon the mind of Macbeth it bears no relation whatever to its material cause. It is as if, moved by some great hand behind the universe, the mountains themselves were coming like billows to obliterate the wrong that forbade them to rest.

I shall not attempt to pluck the heart out of the mystery of that most enchanting of all sea-tales, *The Tempest*. The first suggestion of it was undoubtedly in one of those fairy tales that the Elizabethan seamen brought home to the Mermaid Tavern—tales about men whose heads stood in their breasts, islands that were full of airy voices and dissolving visions. Shakespeare seized upon the idea of such an island and made it the magic crucible of the universe, the centre of all its chemistry, spiritual and material, and all its changes.

Those who have wronged Prospero are cast upon it by the sea; and Ariel tells them when they draw their swords that

> The elements,
> Of whom your swords are tempered, may as well
> Wound the loud winds, or with bemocked at stabs
> Kill the still closing waters.

They committed Prospero and his child to the sea, for which foul deed

> The powers delaying, not forgetting, have
> Incensed the seas and shores, yea, all the creatures
> Against their peace.

They are confronted, indeed, with the same problem as Macbeth when the forests came against him. For all these creatures, as Ariel tells them, are ministers of Fate, from whom there is no escape but in "heart sorrow and a clean life ensuing." Alonzo is overwhelmed by this discovery that the universe is not a dead thing:

> O, it is monstrous, monstrous!
> Methought the billows spoke and told me of it,
> The winds did sing it to me, and the thunder,
> That deep and dreadful organ-pipe, pronounced
> The name of Prosper; it did bass my trespass.
> Therefore my son i' the ooze is bedded, and
> I 'll seek him deeper than e'er plummet sounded.

The solution of this play, however, is found in their "heart sorrow" and their forgiveness by

Prospero, who has attained not only to mastery of the elements but to mastery over himself. His most famous speech dismisses the whole material world :

> These our actors,
> As I foretold you, were all spirits, and
> Are melted into air, into thin air,
> And, like the baseless fabric of this vision,
> The cloud-capped towers, the gorgeous palaces,
> The solemn temples, the great globe itself,
> Yea, all which it inherit, shall dissolve,
> And, like this unsubstantial pageant faded,
> Leave not a rack behind. We are such stuff
> As dreams are made on, and our little life
> Is rounded with a sleep.

Those are the last words, perhaps, of Shakespeare to the world. But the essence of the play is concentrated in Ariel's music, an air so bewitching that we can well believe it to have been overheard in Elfinland :

> Come unto these yellow sands
> And there take hands.
> Curtsied when you have and kist,
> The wild waves whist,
> Foot it featly here and there,
> And sweet sprites the burthen bear. . . .

No lyric of the sea can be compared with the next fragment of that song for the sheer magic of colour and sound that are compressed into its short lines. It has all the lucid lights and shadows of the world below the sea, and a spell beyond even this, a haunting suggestion that we are at the back of things, watching the changes in the crucible of the universe, watching the secret of the annual resurrection of the Spring, the transformation of dust into flowers, of fishes into birds, of apes into men, of men into angels, in the twinkling of an eye, at the turning of a tide, like a change from the minor to the major key in a solemn music. Here, though we cannot seize it and hold it, is something abiding in the universal ebb and flow of things. And the miraculous part of it is that Shakespeare conveys all this by hardly more than the note of a bell—the stop at the end of the third line, which gives so wizard-like a swell to the music of the fourth, and so full a cadence through the fifth and sixth. The juxtaposition of the two heavy syllables at the end of the fifth line delays the music, as if, indeed, some mysterious tides were at the turn ; and the two adjectives which close this brief masterpiece of song seem in their context to be proof that one master-thief, at any rate, has broken down all the bars of mortality, and returned to us with a melody from the spiritual world :

> Full fathom five thy father lies ;
> Of his bones are coral made ;
> Those are pearls that were his eyes.
> Nothing of him that doth fade
> But doth suffer a sea-change
> Into something rich and strange.

SWINBURNE'S TRAGEDIES

At a time when the "reaction" against Swinburne is in full swing, it may not be inopportune to consider an aspect of his work which has been forgotten by too many of his readers. It is as characteristic of the greater part of his lyrical work as of his tragedies, but it can be analysed and weighed more easily in the latter.

It is a curious fact that—with one or two pre-eminent exceptions—the most ardent appreciation of Swinburne has usually come from the decadent, or from those who mistook his faults for his merits. A study of his life and writings, published some years ago, lauds one of his volumes in wildly imitative Swinburnese, thus :

> The volcanic exuberance of its metres and rhymes is not more astounding than its sustained ebullience of amorous imagination, its metrical music and beautiful verbiage than its frenzied erotomania.

It is not without difficulty that one gradually gathers, during the perusal of this "study," that all the words and phrases quoted above are intended to be complimentary. But they undoubtedly are ; and the writer goes on to admire the poems as "dreams of an exasperated imagination," and their "loves" as the "loves" of one "brooding in his study over the *fancied deliria* of beauty and lust and blood." He admires Swinburne intensely for "consciously" painting (though Swinburne emphatically states he had no such intent) in his Scottish trilogy the picture of a "vicious, fascinating, and infamous woman," not so much as a portrait but as a thing to be admired. All subjects are legitimate to the artist. It is legitimate to paint an Iago; but it is not legitimate to bow down in worship before the infamy, whose every blot and stain the great poet may expose to the candour of the sun. Swinburne did not intend to make Mary Stuart "infamous": he intended to fight for her in song as his fathers fought for her in the field. We have had quite enough of the sham æstheticism which has been attempting to play the amateur Borgia in the English literature of recent years, an æstheticism which has made one of our greatest poets its special pandar, and has no more right to do so than a man would have to issue an edition of *Othello* with a scrofulous frontispiece. There never was a healthier, keener, harder, brighter, more English and open-air muse than this of Swinburne's tragedies. Here is a typical speech of *Mary Stuart*:

> If I should never more back steed alive,
> But now had ridden hither this fair day
> The last road I must ever ride on earth,
> Yet would I praise it, saying of all days gone
> And all roads ridden in sight of stars and sun
> Since first I sprang to saddle, here at last
> I had found no joyless end. These ways are smooth,
> And all this land's face merry; yet I find
> The ways are therefore not so good to ride,
> And all the land's face therefore less worth love,
> Being smoother for a palfrey's maiden face
> And merrier than our moors for outlook; nay,
> I lie to say so; there the wind and sun
> Make madder mirth by midsummer, and fill
> With broader breath and lustier length of light
> The heartier hours that clothe for even and dawn
> Our bosom-belted, billowy-blossoming hills
> Whose hearts break out in laughter like the sea
> For miles of heaving heather.

Whatever may be the spirit of *Poems and Ballads*, that passage is one of the most characteristic of the tragedies ; and this brings us to another point. The consensus of recent opinion seems to be that Swinburne's dramas are hardly worthy of serious consideration ; but, on the whole, it is quite as mistaken as the opinion that Tennyson held in his boyhood with regard to Shakespeare. The beauty of a lyric like " O mistress mine, where are you roaming ? " makes a more instant appeal to the casual reader than the larger beauty of *Macbeth* ; and similarly it is possible that the five hundred closely printed pages of *Bothwell* may, in the eye of indolent readers, have weighty disadvantages as compared with the *Laus Veneris*. But those five hundred pages are written in the same lyrical blank verse as *Phædra* in *Poems and Ballads* ; in the same flawless blank verse as *Atalanta* ; and, quite apart from their dramatic value, those tragedies often rise to a lyrical sublimity that is quite their own. Their songs, in French and English, have a dramatic undercurrent of meaning in the moment of their outbreak, in addition to their lyrical beauty. When Mary Stuart, for instance, walks beneath the window of Darnley on the eve of his murder, and sings the exquisite French song that Rizzio had sung to her in an earlier scene, immediately before his assassination by Darnley and his friends, the setting gives it an extraordinary dramatic force. But apart even from considerations like these, the blank verse alone, as in the passage quoted above, has often a lyrical value which places it with the best work of Swinburne. The curiously external and superficial nature of most of the criticisms which take the opposite view leads one to suppose that the chief objection to the five hundred pages of *Bothwell* is the laziness of readers who would probably be unable to lay their hands on their hearts and affirm that they can read or have read *Paradise Lost* itself in more than a very perfunctory fashion. It is an age of selections and little books; but it may safely be said that Swinburne's tragedies are not of an age or twain. They will last as long as the language, though the audience may be few.

Another accusation brought against them, and against *Bothwell* in particular, is that of "verbiage" in the uncomplimentary sense. Now it is true that John Knox sometimes makes a speech of many pages, and Mary Stuart is hardly less eloquent. But it is also true that the thunder-fraught climax and close of *Chastelard*, the crowning tragic utterance, is compressed into the last two lines of the play; two lines that would hardly appeal perhaps to a public nursed on blood and sensational pageants and carpenters' dramas; but nevertheless two of the most truly tragic lines in literature. When the execution of Chastelard is over—it takes place off the stage—the play is closed by the entry of an usher, crying:

> Make way there for the Lord of Bothwell, room,—
> Place for my Lord of Bothwell next the queen.

Similarly in *Bothwell*, amidst many speeches of all lengths, there are some, of very great importance, which consist of a single syllable. When Queen Mary speaks to George Douglas, for instance, on the eve of her flight from Scotland:

> Douglas, I have not won a word of you;
> What would you do to have me tarry?
> *George Douglas.* Die.

That is all; and it is quite as typical of Swinburne's method as his longer speeches are. He is often very much longer than other poets. He is often very much more concise than other poets. The fact that the former characteristic is necessarily the more obvious must not prevent recognition of the latter. Nor is it true to say—as it is so often said with parrot-like insistence—that he is carried away on the wings of his music. There never was a poet who was so consciously the master of an art as Swinburne. His metrical gift is not essentially the gift of music in words. The two things are quite distinct. Music in blank verse depends very largely on the chime and change of the vowel-sounds and the balancing of one against the other in harmony. Tennyson is very fond of balancing the two sounds of the vowel *o*, as in *more* and *moan*, against each other, as in the line,

> *So all* day long the noise of battle *rolled*.

Hundreds of lines could be quoted from Tennyson illustrating his exquisite play on those two vowel-sounds alone ; and the music of Milton has a similar basis. But Swinburne is *not* the musician he is so often accused of being. If one wished to parody his blank verse, one would write something like this :

> Nor should I not distrust thee nor mislike
> Who did not creep nor spring not in the dark.

His lines are often full of sibilants and hiss like snakes : they are curiously monosyllabic, and sometimes they suggest a sort of elemental language. They are welded inextricably into a perfect and artistic unity ; but they are *welded*. That is the only word to describe them. Of all their thousands, there is not one line in which any flaw could be discovered, not one line which errs from the laws of his art ; but they are the work of a master of metre rather than the work of a master of music. In this he is almost exactly the opposite of Shelley, whose lines are often "careless ordered," yet always, or almost always, music incarnate. Swinburne, in his dramas especially, gives one the idea of a man who grips his subject so hard as to break it up into its component parts. The intensity of his passion melts and resolves the world into its elements, and this is what the critics have mistaken for "verbiage." When Mary Stuart, for instance, wonders whether she can feel any maternal love for her child by Darnley, his grip of the thing he is describing is so intense that it becomes resolved into its elements, thus :

> I will yet see, before I take my leave,
> If there be such a nature in our blood
> As can command and change the spiritual springs
> And motions of our thought, advance or check
> The pulse of purpose in the soul that moves
> Our longings and our loathings to their end
> By mere control and force unreasonable
> Of motiveless compulsion ; if such blind
> And sensual chances of the stirring veins
> That feed the heart of child or mother may
> Divert and dull the mind's design, or turn
> The conscience and the current of the will
> From its full course and action.

That is how Swinburne breaks up the simple question of Cowper :

> Can a woman's tender care
> Cease towards the child she bare ?

And though the simpler method has led to the higher results (and Swinburne himself has used it on occasion), it must be remembered that the method of that blank verse passage is that of Shakespeare in some of his greatest passages.

In considering these poems as dramas, *Chastelard*, the first of the Scottish trilogy, must be regarded as the most successful. It is flawless both as a poem and as a play. The concentrated dramatic suggestiveness of almost every sentence is extraordinary. In the first act a terrible little hint is thrown out as Chastelard stoops to examine the new breast-clasp of the Queen, a present from the French King. It has a crowned Venus worked upon it.

> *Queen.* The legend is writ small :
> Still one makes out this—*Cave*—if you look.
> *Chastelard.* I see the Venus well enough, God wot,
> But nothing of the legend.

And there are some passages of great dramatic effect, where, on the eve of Chastelard's execution, Queen Mary comes to visit her victim and lover in his prison, and he speaks to her in words that she remembers and recalls in *Bothwell* :

> It may be, long time after I am dead,
> For all you are, you may see bitter days ;
> God may forget you or be wroth with you ;
> Then shall you lack a little help of me
> And I shall feel your sorrow touching you ;
> A happy sorrow, though I may not touch ;
> I that would fain be turned to flesh again,
> Fain get back life to give up life for you,
> To shed my blood for help, that long ago
> You shed and were not holpen ; and your heart
> Will ache for help and comfort, yea, for love,
> And find less love than mine. . . .
> But I for all my love shall have no might
> To help you more. . . .
> You will not have to grieve ;
> For, being in such poor eyes so beautiful,
> It must needs be as God is more than I
> So much more love He hath of you than mine ;
> *Yea, God shall not be bitter with my love,*
> *Seeing she is so sweet.*

Then as the Queen, with a shudder of foreboding, declares that she is sure she shall die somehow sadly, he answers with what must surely be some of the most terrible lines of dramatic irony in the language :

You, die like me?
Stretch your throat out that I may kiss all round
Where mine shall be cut through; suppose my mouth
The axe-edge to bite so sweet a throat in twain
With bitter iron; should not it turn soft
As lip is soft to lip?

The play ends, as I noted above, with the dramatic crying of the herald, "Place for my Lord of Bothwell," and the first two acts of the second part of the trilogy are occupied with the growth of Bothwell's mastery over the Queen. Perhaps the most marvellous feature of these two acts is the character-study of Darnley, his vanity, his cowardice, his boyishly boastful simplicity. The scene in which he "talks down to" the subtle-souled Queen, after the success of his plot to murder her friend Rizzio, is a masterpiece of art; and the way in which he is gradually snared in her toils till even he feels the approaching shadow of death is second to nothing in our literature since the Elizabethans. He feels it first as a mere chilly touch when he takes her hand in a patronizing manner and leads her out of her captivity through the underground passage and place of tombs; but his blind foreboding is gradually worked up by a hint here and a hint there till he is almost mad with terror. The very type of a dramatic situation is presented to us when he lies ill in a chamber over the loaded vault that is to send him howling up to the heavens; a loaded expectancy whereof he knows nothing, except that the Queen has passed below singing the French song that Rizzio sang on the eve of his murder. The shadowy hints that touch and elude him lead to a cumulative and pitiful outcry of abject and utter fear as he lies there and tries to read the Psalmist—that other David—with his servant.

Darnley. Dost thou feel to-night
Thy living blood and spirit at ease in thee?
Taylor. Surely, my lord.

Darnley. I would thy lord did too.
This is a bitter writing where he saith
How in his prayer he mourns and hath his heart
Disquieted within him ; and again
The fear of death is fallen upon him, see . . . .
. . . Wouldst thou think
She set this ring at parting on my hand
And to my lips her lips ? And then she spake
Words of that last year's slaughter. O God, God,
I know not if it be not of Thy will,
My heart begins to pass into her heart, . . .
Mine eye to read within her eye, and find
Therein a deadlier scripture. . . .
Is there no hand or heart on earth to help ?
Mother ! my mother ! hast thou heart nor hand
To save thy son, to take me hence away,
Far off and hide me ? . . .
Taylor. I pray you, comfort your own heart, my lord ;
Your passion drives your manhood out of you.
Darnley. I know it doth ; I am hare-hearted, for
The hunters are upon me. There—and there—
I hear them questing. I shall die, man, die,
And never see the sun more. . . .
Taylor. Sir, for God's love——
Darnley. I say I hear their feet— . . .
How do men die ? but I so trapped alive,
Oh, I shall die a dog's death and no man's !
Mary, by Christ whose mother's was your name,
Slay me not ! God, turn off from me that heart—
Out of her hands, God, God, deliver me !

So ends the second act of *Bothwell* ; and, in passing, it may be noted that this great master never strives after the " mighty line," though he has written some of the mightiest. There is here no din of gong and cymbal, no libretto-like opportunity for pageant. His lines are not independent of one another. All is continuity, " the long, slow slope and vast curves of the gradual violin." In short, his work is organic literature.

It is impossible, of course, and unnecessary, to

examine these tragedies in detail here. They will form the subject-matter of many essays and studies in years and centuries to come. At the beginning of this essay I spoke of Swinburne's consistent exaltation of thought. Paradoxical as it may seem to his following of amateur Borgias, and whatever his detractors may say, that is his chief characteristic, an extraordinary moral elevation. His lines appear sometimes to have been passed through white-hot purgatorial furnaces. Their passion has the chastity of a burning fire. All that is of the earth earthy has been burnt out like dross. *Marino Faliero*, the finest of his later plays, is a splendid instance of this. In adopting the subject and the very title which Byron used a century ago, Swinburne entirely justified himself. His play, compared with Byron's, is as a star to a blood-pudding. I am not speaking here of Byron's slip-shod verse. It is true that his play is packed with lines like those that open the fifth act:

> There now rests, after such conviction, of
> Their manifold and manifest offences,

while the fabric of Swinburne's verse is like the ideal Venice of his Doge's dreams, a city washed white of blood:

> Clean, splendid, sweet for sea and sun to kiss
> Till earth adore and heaven applaud her.

But Swinburne's tragedy has exaltation, moral and intellectual, that was beyond the reach of Byron on that particular occasion. Byron's *Marino Faliero*, for instance, makes the following dying speech:

> Then, in the last gasp of thine agony,
> Amid thy many murders, think of *mine*!
> Thou den of drunkards with the blood of princes!
> Gehenna of the waters! Thou sea Sodom!
> Thus I devote thee to the infernal gods!
> Thee and thy serpent seed!

From which we gather that the Doge was a sort of regal pupil in mind and tongue of the modern cabman. Swinburne's *Marino Faliero* has a far different utterance, reminding one of the last words of Socrates, in their tone and accent, quite apart from the classical radiance of the style. The old Doge is speaking to his young wife and son :

> Live thou, and love thy Venice, boy,
> Not more than I, but wiselier : serve her not
> For thanksgiving of men, nor fear, nor heed,
> Nor let it gnaw thine heart to win for wage
> Ingratitude : let them take heed and fear
> Who pay thee with unthankfulness, but thou,
> Seeing not for these thou fightest, but for them
> That have been and that shall be, sons and sires,
> Dead and unborn, men truer of heart than these,
> Be constant, and be satisfied to serve,
> And crave no more of any. Fare thee well.
> And thou, my wife and child, all loves in one,
> Sweet life, sweet heart, fare ever well, and be
> Blest of God's holier hand with happier love
> Than here bids blessing on thee. Hark, the guard
> Draws hither : noon is full : and where I go
> Ye may not follow. Be not faint of heart :
> I go not as a base man goes to death,
> But great of hope : God cannot will that here
> Some day shall spring not freedom : nor perchance
> May we, long dead, not know it, who died of love
> For dreams that were and truths that were not. Come :
> Bring me but toward the landing whence my soul
> Sets sail, and bid God speed her forth to sea.

The sea ! That is the first word, the first symbol and the last with Swinburne. It sets an infinite horizon round his work. Every great poet is a "Pilgrim of Eternity" ; and through his fiery negation of the lesser gods Swinburne has always postulated an unknown and unrealized glory of Godhead. It matters very little whether he calls it the Word with St. John, the Act with Faust, or Freedom with

Mazzini; for in the words of his own dedication to *Marino Faliero*:

> Our words and works, our thoughts and songs turn thither,
> Toward one great end, as waves that press or roll,
> Though waves be spent and ebb like hopes that wither
> These shall subside not ere they find the goal.
> We know it, who yet with unforgetful soul
> See shine and smile, where none may smite or strive,
> Above us, higher than clouds and winds can drive,
> The soul beloved beyond all souls alive.

SOME CAMBRIDGE POETS AND POETRY

THE predominance of Cambridge in English poetry is undisputed and unexplained. A flippant theory ascribes it to a reaction against the tyranny of mathematics, an extension of the principle that poets " learn in suffering what they teach in song."

To touch the fringe of so vast a subject as the literary associations of Cambridge would require a considerable volume. Here I can indulge in only a few unmethodical notes on the great men of letters who have walked as undergraduates by the banks of the Cam. For a Cambridge man to assert the pre-eminence of any particular college in respect of the richness of its literary associations would be an indiscretion few would attempt to commit, but to an impartial Oxonian this is a matter of the greatest interest.

Three colleges are close competitors for this honour —St. John's, Trinity, and Pembroke. The claim of the last might well rest alone on its association with the poet's poet, Edmund Spenser. In a very special sense Spenser is a Cambridge poet. It was there that he fell under the influence of the Platonism which is reflected in most of his work. The Cambridge of his time stood for Platonism and Puritanism, and Spenser was deeply influenced by both of these movements. It was at Cambridge that Spenser met Gabriel Harvey, who was the means of introducing him to the brilliant circle over which Sir Philip Sidney presided. Pembroke can also boast of Crashaw and Mason, and pride itself on having given a refuge to

Thomas Gray when he was driven from Peterhouse by the horseplay of the undergraduates.

St. John's has a long and brilliant roll of honour. In the drama it is represented by "Rare Ben"; in translation and scholarship by Fairfax and Bentley; in lyric and light verse by Herrick and Prior; and to the Romantic Triumph it gave William Wordsworth.

If we consider literature generally, it is impossible to refuse the palm to Trinity. There is no branch of science or literature in which it has not sent forth a master-mind. From Trinity came Francis Bacon, the supreme English example of "pure intellect," so often praised for a philosophical greatness he never really attained, and so constantly undervalued as the model historian he undoubtedly is. From Trinity also came Cowley, the last of the "metaphysicals," and one of the great pioneers of modern English prose. The same college was the *alma mater* of Dryden, the founder of the classical school of English poetry and the first great name in English criticism. It has Isaac Newton, through whom science began, once more, with the great imaginative poets, "to see all things in one." But the fame of Trinity reached its highest at the beginning of the last century, when Byron was succeeded by Tennyson and Thackeray and all the illustrious friends associated with these names—Fitzgerald, Spedding, Arthur Hallam, to name only a few.

With Christ's are associated the names of Milton and "Lycidas." It was also the college of Charles Darwin, and is pleasantly fragrant with the tobacco of Calverley. Corpus Christi boasts of Marlowe and Fletcher. The literary glories of Jesus College are the strangely assorted couple, Cranmer and Coleridge, whence the latter departed to enlist in the dragoons. At King's, Phineas Fletcher, Edmund Waller, and Horace Walpole were followed, *longo intervallo*, by J. K. Stephen, wittiest of University versifiers.

Clare has no poetic fame, but in Tillotson it gave us one of the early masters of English prose. Emmanuel claims Sir William Temple; Gonville and Caius, Jeremy Taylor; at Magdalene repose the jealously guarded secrets of Mr. Samuel Pepys; and Queen's figures proudly in the history of the New Learning by its association with the name of Erasmus. The roll-call is capable of indefinite extension.

The claim of Cambridge to be the nursery of our poets is established if we remember but the names of Spenser, Milton, Dryden, Byron, Wordsworth, and Tennyson. The list includes the majority of the brightest stars in the firmament of English poetry.

It is impossible to treat the whole field of our subject as if it were on one plane or had any unity. The recognized Olympian poets have in many cases been at daggers drawn with their universities. Milton had the unique distinction of being the last undergraduate to receive corporal punishment from the maternal hands of Cambridge; and perhaps that is a reasonable excuse for the elephantine humour of his two elegies on old Hobson, the university carrier. Was there ever a more ponderous forestalment of Tom Hood than those mighty lines ending with the Apocalyptic jest—"his wain was his increase"? Shelley, despite his expulsion from Oxford, maintained a more discreet silence on the subject. Tennyson wrote an angry sonnet about Cambridge. William Morris inveighed against Oxford dons. Swinburne attacked the fame of Calverley in prose, while Byron abused the dons of Cambridge to this effect in verse:

> The sons of science these, who, thus repaid,
> Linger in ease in Granta's sluggish shade;
> Where on Cam's sedgy bank supine they lie
> Unknown, unhonoured live, unwept for, die.
> Dull as the pictures which adorn their halls,
> They think all learning fix'd within their walls;

In manners rude, in foolish forms precise,
All modern arts affecting to despise;
Yet prizing Bentley's, Brunk's, or Porson's note,
More than the verse on which the critic wrote.

Wordsworth, in one of his greatest sonnets and also in the *Prelude*—probably as a man who never came into conflict with the authorities—was able to devote himself to the beauty and high associations of the place itself.

On the whole, Cambridge might be said to have justified its existence, if it had done no more than inspire those fourteen immortal lines of Wordsworth on King's College Chapel:

Tax not the royal Saint with vain expense,
With ill-match'd aims the Architect who planned
(Albeit labouring for a scanty band
Of white-robed Scholars only) this immense
And glorious work of fine intelligence!
—Give all thou canst: high Heaven rejects the lore
Of nicely calculated less or more:—
So deemed the man who fashion'd for the sense
These lofty pillars, spread that branching roof
Self-poised, and scoop'd into ten thousand cells
Where light and shade repose, where music dwells
Lingering—and wandering on as loth to die;
Like thoughts whose very sweetness yieldeth proof
That they were born for immortality.

It is said that Swinburne left Oxford without a degree owing to his refusing to recognize the existence of the Divinity examination. But that this did not prevent his recognition of the natural beauties of the place or preclude his life-long friendship with Jowett is now almost as well known as the fact that University College has erected a statue to Shelley. But Swinburne has given us no poetry on the subject.

Perhaps Matthew Arnold is the only real Oxford

poet, therefore, in the sense of this essay—that is to say, the only voice of Oxford itself; and it is difficult to say whether he or Tennyson has the better of it as an academic interpreter. Tennyson's little cameo, entitled *A Character*, was studied from the life at Cambridge, probably from a don :

> He spake of beauty ! that the dull
> Saw no divinity in grass,
> Life in dead stones, or spirit in air ;
> Then looking as 'twere in a glass,
> He smoothed his chin and sleek'd his hair,
> And said the earth was beautiful.

However, Tennyson, who went down without a degree, recovered sufficiently from his early spleen to give us " dawn-golden " pictures of Cambridge and its real life.

The Princess has much of the Cambridge atmosphere ; while *In Memoriam* is—from its subject—necessarily a Cambridge elegy :

> I past beside the reverend walls
> In which of old I wore the gown ;
> I roved at random through the town,
> And saw the tumult of the halls ;
>
> And heard once more in college fanes
> The storm their high-built organs make,
> And thunder-music, rolling, shake
> The prophet blazoned on the panes ;
>
> And caught once more the distant shout,
> The measured pulse of racing oars
> Among the willows ; paced the shores
> And many a bridge, and all about
>
> The same gray flats again, and felt
> The same, but not the same ; and last
> Up that long walk of limes I past
> To see the rooms in which he dwelt.

Another name was on the door :
  I lingered ; all within was noise
  Of songs, and clapping hands, and boys
That crashed the glass and beat the floor ;

Where once we held debate . . .

With Tennyson's extraordinary power of summing up and expressing his age, certainly it is all given to us there—the whole of Cambridge.

When we come to what may be called the *Punch* tradition, where the gay spirit predominates and only for short swallow-flights dips its wings in tears and skims away—Cambridge is first again. C. S. C. and J. K. S. and R. C. L. and O. S. remain triumphant over all comers. Their Cambridge writings have formed a little independent literature, filled with the atmosphere, the joys and sorrows of an independent world, a sort of little modern Greece, where athleticism has something that belonged to the Olympic games, and humour something of the classic, because philosophical, sparkle. As a background to the picture of this world, I cannot do better than quote Mr. Shuckburgh's admirable No. 63 of the *Tatler* in Cambridge. He is describing how a Cambridge undergraduate has just received a very desolate and heart-rending poem from one of his friends about some unhappy love-affair :

I thought this a little more serious than most of my Friend's complaints, because it had somewhat less Love in it. I therefore went on my Way to see him. I found him lying on his sofa, by his Open Window, smoking a Pipe and reading a novel ; the room was full of Violets and other Flowers ; the Window looked out into a Pleasant Garden, and through it a most deliciously soft and fragrant Spring Breeze was gently blowing ; his Face wore that fresh, sleek and glossy Appearance which a Man's face does in the Prime of Youth and Health, when he is smoking his First Pipe after Breakfast, and has not left his Tub more than Half an Hour. By his side stood a Pewter filled with that delicious Drink compounded of Beer and Gingerbeer. He looked the Picture of Indolence and Comfort. After regarding him for a few Minutes in Silence, while filling my own Pipe, I remarked with my usual easy wit: "Then I suppose Sin and Time have stopped their shooting Match?"

It is difficult to say why that has a Greek atmosphere; but it is really more Greek than *Atalanta in Calydon*—not, despite the violets or the youth's nickname (which was Narcissus), in the details, but in the whole sunny atmosphere it is Greek and pagan essentially. If Plato wrote nowadays he would abound in passages of that kind. It is not an attempt to reproduce the old: it is merely itself—and therefore all the more purely Greek. Calverley's *Ode to Tobacco* has the same classic charm, a charm heightened by the limpid purity of his style:

Sweet when the morn is grey:
Sweet when they 've cleared away
Lunch; and at close of day,
  Possibly sweetest.

Epigrams, too, have here, in the literature of Cambridge, exactly the old spontaneity and vitality. Porson, who was Professor of Greek at Cambridge, and William Lort Mansel, Master of Trinity and afterwards Bishop of Bristol, were the terrors of the University. Some of their epigrams are almost as unfit for modern print as the frankest of classical achievements. J. K. S., however, is always quotable, as here to *One that Smokes*:

Spare us the hint of slightest desecration,
  Spotless preserve us an untainted shrine;
Not for thy sake, oh goddess of creation,
  Nor for thy sake, oh woman, but for mine.

I quote this, not as a specially brilliant example, but merely as an obvious heir of all the classical ages. Spontaneous, tossed off between two cigarettes, as no doubt it was, it is a mere gesture of a man essentially at one with Greece and Rome, and not less so because he is at one with modern England.

Sir Owen Seaman recognized the paganism of the university world (though for him it is a Horatian paganism) when he entitled one of his most charming volumes *Horace at Cambridge* ; and perhaps one of the finest and purest examples of what I may call the Roman spirit in its modern aspect is that memorial poem by the Cambridge oarsman, R. C. Lehmann, to Hugh Benjamin Cotton, of Magdalen College, Oxford, who died in 1895. I quote from the volume entitled *Anni Fugaces* :

> So, here in Magdalen, hail again,
> Beneath the Tower, or in the Hall,
> Or through the Cloisters, where a rain
> Of red leaves flutters from the wall,
> Or where in old and happy days
> The Barges echoed with your praise. . . .

And yet again, two years later :

> For summer has not yielded yet ;
> Still in stray gleams her tresses glow.
> But, ah ! with tears her face is wet,
> She lingers, but she turns to go !
> And on the air her whisper dies—
> " Farewell, damp earth and chilly skies ! "
>
> So let her pass ; the shadows fall ;
> I set the ruddy fire alight ;
> Its glamour flickers through the hall,
> A sober silence holds the night.
> And as I sit, dim shapes of air
> Appear and fade about my chair. . . .
>
> Two years are gone, your welcome voice
> Makes music still to dull my pain.
> You smile and bid my heart rejoice,
> Your friendship cheers me yet again.
> I call you, and unchanged you stand,
> As first you stood and clasped my hand.

And thus, recalled at will, you prove
  That Death is naught and Fate is blind.
Life's brightness in your eyes, you move
  Through the clear chambers of my mind.
This Nature grants, since death controls
Our breath, but not the world of souls. . . .

And you, O friend of former days,
  Be with me, make my purpose strong ;
Still through the world's encircling maze
  Help you my faltering steps along.
The last flames flicker, fade and die,—
Good-night, dear friend, but not Good-bye.

The Horatian tradition of English light verse during the last half-century has been of great critical value to English literature. In its regard for form it has helped to maintain the standards of good writing through a chaotic period ; and it would not be surprising if the future anthologist should find some of the best verse of that period in certain pages of *Punch*, where that classic tradition has been developed. It is almost entirely a Cambridge tradition (though one of its best recent exponents, Mr. Knox, is of Oxford, and there has been more than a little serious work in poetry by Mrs. Eden and D. M. S., of a higher order of craftsmanship than is to be found in many contemporary anthologies). Cambridge, in a sense, has absorbed them all. Major Kendall (" Dum-Dum " of *Punch*) is to be counted among her cavaliers perhaps, rather than among her sons ; but though he rides away, he is also hers. He often displays a craftsmanship and a technical finish that are a delight to the eye and ear. In some of his mock-serious odes —the *Elegy on a Rhinoceros*, for instance, or the delicious address to his own sense of humour, beginning

Come not, as thou wast ever wont to come,
  Making a scandal of thy saving grace,

there is more sense of style, more of the real pleasure

of craftsmanship, more beauty even (though it is achieved with a jest), than in nine-tenths of the current volumes of "serious" poetry. Many of his odes in *A Fool's Paradise* are object-lessons in the art of verse.

The poets that have arisen in Cambridge during the last two decades would require another essay; but, to name no others, among living writers, Mr. J. C. Squire, in such work as *The Birds* and *A Far Place*, has made a contribution to English poetry of a very high order:

Whispering, faint, the garden under the hillside . . .
  Under the stars . . . Is it true that we lived there long?
Was it certainly so? Did ever we know that dwelling,
  Breathe that night, and hear in the night that song?

For my present purpose this record must close with a Cambridge writer of an earlier generation, a writer who has always remained independent of any group or school, and in the variety of his work has been somewhat too big for the kind of criticism that runs in grooves. Mr. Barry Pain, who was one of the early contributors to the *Granta*, has written for the third part of a century now. He has written for our modern world as the Elizabethans wrote for their own, with a large mastery over laughter and tears. Sometimes he has flung out a book as lightly as a jest, for the crowd to read as it once read Nash; and sometimes he has quietly slipped a masterpiece into the memory of the few. Some of these latter books are worthy of the author of *Every Man in His Humour*; for, while he has always remained an artist, he has always—unlike the majority of artists—expressed in his work a life that is bigger than art or literature, and so continually escapes the mere man of letters. His work, of course, has inequalities; but this quiet strength in him has been recognized by one or two of the subtlest artists of our time, including poets and critics so entirely different in other respects as W. E. Henley and Alice Meynell. His *Exiles of Faloo* is a novel ; but it has something of the quality of the greatest satirists, who are also the most human.

He has long been among the established masters of the short story in English. His *Stories in Grey* and *Here and Hereafter* contain some of the few examples that we can show to France as worthy of her own masters. But in his *Army of the Dead* he contributed to English literature one of the few poems of the war that can be read now that the war is over. In many ways it was the best poem written during the war, for it caught and held, even then, a point of view that requires not the slightest alteration to-day.

I dreamed that overhead
I saw in twilight gray,
The Army of the Dead
Marching upon its way,
So still and passionless,
With faces so serene,
That scarcely could one guess,
Such men in war had been.

No mark of hurt they bore,
Nor smoke, nor bloody stain,
Nor suffered any more
Famine, fatigue or pain ;
Nor any lust of hate
Now lingered in their eyes—
Who have fulfilled their fate
Have lost all enmities.

A new and greater pride
So quenched the pride of race
That foes marched side by side,
Who once fought face to face.

That ghostly army's plan
Knows but one race, one rod.
All nations there are man,
And the one King is God.

No longer on their ears
The bugle's summons falls ;
Beyond these tangled spheres
The Archangel's trumpet calls ;
And by that trumpet led,
Far up the exalted sky,
The Army of the Dead
Goes by, and still goes by.

THE NATURE POET OF THE EIGHTEENTH CENTURY

THE most curious phenomenon in the literature of a century that had almost forgotten Nature was its great attempt to return, or remember, in the person of James Thomson. This bard, " more fat than bard beseems," wandering about his garden and, with hands thrust deep in his pockets, eating the sunny side of his peaches as they hung upon the wall, has a human interest all his own. As poetry his works have little meaning for the present age ; and for those who try to judge historical figures out of their historical setting the praise bestowed upon him by so many notable critics must always be puzzling. There is always a note of humour in the introduction of the sophisticated to Nature, even though the sophistication be no more elaborate than that of the literary artificialities of the eighteenth century. But if one were making an anthology of unconscious humour in poetry, surely nothing more diverting could be found anywhere than that early piece of " psychological " investigation into the mind of Damon in Thomson's *Summer*. It will be remembered that young Damon sat where the rambling dale runs out into pleasing solitudes. He was " pensive," of course, and pierced moreover with love's " delightful pangs." And lo ! his Musidora—such was the lady's euphonious name—sought that same cool retreat :

> Robed in loose array, she came to bathe
> Her fervent limbs in the refreshing stream.
> *What shall he do ?* In sweet confusion lost,
> And dubious flutterings, he awhile remained.

A pure ingenuous elegance of soul,
A delicate refinement known to few,
Perplexed his breast and urged him to retire ;
But love forbade. Ye prudes in virtue, say,
Say ye, severest, What would you have done ?

This is a kind of unconscious humour that is not lacking in a certain degree even in *Paradise Lost*, and certainly is very much present in Thomson's contemporaries, as in Riccaltoun, whose poem, *A Winter's Day*, helped to inspire Thomson. It opens thus :

Now gloomy soul ! *Look out—now comes thy turn.*

Perhaps this is to be unduly flippant, and indeed the temptation is a strong one when we consider the difficulty of reconciling such passages with any self-respecting modern ideal of poetry. Yet—and now we must turn to the standpoint of the literary student —Thomson has great merits, and he deserves his cosy little nook half-way up Parnassus. The first of these merits is his broad sincerity and truth. Musidora's limbs were, no doubt, really "fervent." Whether the word is happy artistically is another matter. Swinburne could use the word and make it sound at once classical and English. When Thomson uses it, we somehow feel that we must mentally translate it. But if we are content to accept his own convention, we begin to enjoy the process, with something of the same pleasure as that which Stevenson cunningly and consciously provoked when he put the story of *The Master of Ballantrae* into the pedantic but truthful mouth of Ephraim Mackellar. There is hardly a descriptive passage in Thomson which is not capable of giving the reader some degree of that pleasure which comes from recognition of one's own fleeting thoughts or observations, however slight, permanently recorded by the mind of another. In speaking of the sculptures of Greece, for instance, he makes remarks which are better suited to a book on anatomy than to a poem, yet there certainly is a pleasure to be derived from his quaintly truthful observations :

> The well-known Hero, who delivered Greece,
> His ample chest, all tempested with force
> Unconquerable reared. She saw the head,
> Breathing the hero, small, of Grecian size,
> *Scarce more extensive than the sinewy neck* ;
> The spreading shoulders, muscular and broad ;
> The whole a mass of swelling sinews, touched
> Into harmonious shape.

There is something finer in his description of the two gladiators, a description which may be compared —greatly to its own disadvantage, of course—with that of Byron ; yet it is not impossible that something of the retributory thunder in the atmosphere of the later and greater work was gathered from Thomson's heavy cloud of incumbent words :

> Rushed impetuous forth
> The gladiator : pitiless his look,
> And each keen sinew braced, the storm of war,
> Ruffling, o'er all his nervous body frowns.
> The dying other from the gloom she drew ;
> Supported on his shortened arm he leans
> Prone, agonizing ; with incumbent fate
> Heavy declines his head ; yet dark beneath
> The suffering feature sullen vengeance lours,
> Shame, indignation, unaccomplished rage,
> And still the cheated eye expects his fall.

The debt of other poets to Thomson, and among them notably Gray, is obvious enough. *The Castle of Indolence* was very certainly not without influence on Keats, and even on Tennyson—in *The Lotos-Eaters* :

Full in the passage of the vale above
A sable, silent, solemn forest stood,
Where naught but shadowy forms was seen to move,
As Idless fancied in her dreaming mood;
And up the hills, on either side, a wood
Of blackening pines, aye waving to and fro,
Sent forth a sleepy horror through the blood;
And where this valley winded out, below,
The murmuring main was heard, and scarcely heard, to flow.

A pleasing land of drowsy-head it was,
Of dreams that wave before the half-shut eye;
And of gay castles in the clouds that pass,
For ever flushing round a summer sky.

The philosophical musings which follow undoubtedly suggested much in Tennyson's far finer poem. Man is portrayed by Thomson as pushing the load of life uphill; but when he thinks that he has almost gained the summit,

Down thunders back the stone with mighty sweep.

It is the most vain of vanities, in other words,

To toil for what you here untoiling may obtain;

or, in Tennyson's exquisite words, to be

For ever climbing up the climbing wave.

Other passages in Thomson's diffuse and badly constructed poem had some influence on *The Palace of Art* and the opening of *The Vision of Sin*.

But, after all, Thomson's finest work is to be found in *The Seasons*. His chief merits are those of keen observation, his alertness to sights and sounds and fragrances, to atmospheric effects, and especially to colours: and it was in *The Seasons* that he was best able to exercise his gifts. We get nothing, it is true, of that deeper vision which is the first essential of great art ; but we do get the broad sincerity and truth of draughtsmanship manifested in such lines as :

> The yellow wall-flower, stained with iron-brown,

or these (for after all, it is to the super-added human interest we must return if we are to read Thomson, and we must not part with our good eighteenth-century poet of Nature, our truthful old Ephraim Mackellar, without a smile) :

> But chief to heedless flies the window proves
> A constant death ; where, gloomily retired,
> The villain spider lives, cunning and fierce,
> Mixture abhorred ! Amid a mangled heap
> Of carcasses, in eager watch he sits,
> O'erlooking all his waving snares around.
> Near the dire cell the dreadless wanderer oft
> Passes ; as oft the ruffian shows his front.
> The prey at last ensnared, he dreadful darts,
> With rapid glide, along the leaning line ;
> And, fixing in the wretch his cruel fangs,
> Strikes backward, grimly pleased ; the fluttering wing,
> And shriller sound, declare extreme distress
> And ask the helping hospitable hand.

Hard indeed would be the heart of the critic who would deny to the amiable old peach-eating poet of that passage his easily won nook half-way up the slopes of Parnassus ! And did he not—probably after swallowing a peach-stone —arise on the tip of his toes and sing the most famous of all English lyrics, *Rule, Britannia* ? That is, at any rate, as satisfactory an account of the authorship of our national war-cry as any other.

WORDSWORTH

When Aristotle, the founder of all our modern science, gave to poetry a higher place than to any of the more "practical arts," he did so on the ground that poetry was the most philosophic form of writing. Poetry, in fact, all through the ages has helped to keep open one of the two chief gates to knowledge—that inner gate which, since Bacon declared the inductive reason to be "the true method," the modern world has been inclined to close. But, though science would perish without the inductive method, Bacon made one very great mistake when he suggested that by "ascending" from fact to fact we at length "arrived" at the greatest generalization of all. Science never does, and never can "arrive" at that, for the distance is infinite; and all the agnosticism of modern science is based on its realization of this one truth. But, inasmuch as we ourselves are part of this inscrutable universe, by opening within ourselves our own private wicket-gate into the Reality, of which we ourselves are part, it is possible for us to attain to certain forms of knowledge beyond the reach of the inductive reason. All great art does this in its inspired moments. All great art reaches, in a flash, something of that universal knowledge which Plato, by his own method, endeavoured to draw through the gate of the individual soul.

All this has an obvious bearing on Wordsworth's great description of the function of poetry. He corroborated the Greek critic, and said that the object of poetry was truth, "truth which is its own testimony," as in all great works of art it always is.

Those who are qualified to do so recognize it at once as "inevitable." It arises often from certain intuitions, and deductions which have the quality of intuitions; and so, throughout Wordsworth's own work, its greatest moments arise from

> High instincts before which our mortal nature
> Did tremble like a guilty thing surprised;
> Those first affections,
> Those shadowy recollections
> Which, be they what they may,
> Are yet the fountain-light of all our day,
> Are yet the master-light of all our seeing.

It is not necessary to accept the Platonic metaphysics to recognize the truth of this. For the intellect, that which seems to come last in nature and in the order of time, comes before everything.

But it is this master-light which, I believe, we are in danger of losing in modern poetry and the arts generally. The inductive method has surrounded us with deserted altars; and the temple of the Muses themselves has been more directly affected than we realized in the last century. We have to-day many writers who understand the senses and the passions; and few who seem to have any experience of what Wordsworth called those "first affections"; fewer yet who have any glimpses of spiritual vision. It is difficult to speak of these things, for in speaking of them we run the risk of losing them. But even that risk is better than apathy. The art and poetry that abandon those vital inner fountains can have no real or enduring life. Often we find them attempting to achieve their end by moving from insignificant fact to fact, with a false realism, and sometimes choosing their facts for a false sensationalism, to procure a violent and immediate effect of no permanent value and with no ultimate meaning. This is not to say that great poetry disregards the particular fact. It is passionately concerned with the particular fact, and presents it all the more vividly because it perceives it in its universal relations. Poetry stoops upon the particular fact like an eagle from its universal heaven.

We shall never build the temple of true knowledge until we recognize that science herself, so far from "ascending" from fact to fact, has constantly descended, from the greater to the less, in direct opposition to one of her own first principles. "Quite correctly," as Professor Haeckel would have put it, we trace mankind back, through the descending ages, through a more and more primitive history, back to the protoplasm; and in every branch of knowledge we follow the same diminishing road. It is of the utmost importance to this age that it should realize the truth of this generalization. Science gropes from fact to fact, and discovers "laws" in regions that the spirit of man transcends. Science may even cut the stones of the temple. But it is only the other method, the method of poetry, that can set them truly, and build the walls to music. It is only in poetry that "the glory of the sum of things" can be flashed along the chords. Poetry is "the impassioned expression which is in the countenance of all science," because that countenance is turned, in the moments of poetry, not towards that descending path, but in the opposite direction.

"The Divine," said Hegel, "is the centre of all the representations of Art; and great poetry may be likened to a statue whose pedestal is upon the dark earth, but her face, emerging from the shadows into a loftier air, is turned towards that divine centre, and reflects the glory of God." It was this that Wordsworth meant when he said that "poetry is the breath and finer spirit of all knowledge: the impassioned expression which is in the countenance of all science."

> Time may restore us in his course
> Goethe's sage mind and Byron's force ;
> But where shall Europe's latter hour
> Again find Wordsworth's healing power ?

Europe will find it when it rediscovers its own deepest need—something in which it can believe, a fundamental faith. It is useless to rave about "progress" while our pessimists bury all things in universal darkness and point all our aspirations to an insignificant tomb. "In poetry, where it is worthy of its high destinies, our race will come to find an ever surer and surer stay," and it can only have been with the faith of Wordsworth in his mind that Matthew Arnold sent that lightning-flash of the truth through the stagnant fogs of the decaying creeds. But when Matthew Arnold declared that the strongest part of our religion to-day was its unconscious poetry, he was uttering only a small part of a truth that in an older fashion had been stated most completely and lucidly by Wordsworth, in a passage that throws more light on the nature and meaning of art and poetry than any other in the whole range of criticism. If we set it aside lightly at the present day, or state it in lower terms, we do so not only at our own peril, but at the peril of all art, all literature, and all that holds mankind together. I mean, of course, the great passage in which he shows how a man should value what he sees chiefly as "an imperfect shadowing forth of what he is incapable of seeing": matters that are too weighty for the mind to support without resting a great part of the burden on words and symbols, in a process where much is represented in little.

For Wordsworth was the prophet to us all of the abiding in the transitory. No poet has ever been the prophet "of things as they are," but all the greater poets have held to that greater and essential conservatism by which the stars are preserved from wrong, that universal conservatism upon which even the "sacred right of insurrection" depends. "If there be no God, we must make one," said the French revolutionists; but Wordsworth's intellectual balance—which made him the most salutary power that had appeared in English literature since Milton—was devoted, from first to last, to saving thought from these false and cynical pretences. He did not choose the middle way of middling souls. He comprehended and embraced these trivial contradictions in a wider unity.

His freedom must have its charter and its laws, or it was no freedom; and it is in this union of law and liberty that his poetry, at its greatest, possesses a healing power for our perplexed world, and at certain sublime moments descends upon us like a benediction. There are moments when the universal spirit seems to be speaking through his lips, with the very sound and motion of its rhythmic tides and wheeling stars; moments when his poetry suddenly ceases to be the work of man, and besieges us with the secret meaning of the sunset and the sea:

> The holy time is quiet as a nun
> Breathless with adoration. The broad sun
> Is sinking down in his tranquillity.
> The gentleness of heaven is on the sea,
> Listen! the mighty Being is awake,
> And doth with his eternal motion make
> A sound like thunder, everlastingly.

It is by such work as this that Wordsworth earned his place among the greatest poets of the world. Even the mind of so austere an agnostic as Lord Morley was touched with devotion in the presence of this majestic spirit. He speaks of Wordsworth's secret of bringing the infinite into common life, of his power thereby to touch "the depth and not the tumult of the soul," and to give us quietness, strength, steadfastness, and purpose, whether to do or to endure. All such art, he says, is great and noble. "And the creator of it will always hold, as Wordsworth holds, a sovereign title to the reverence and gratitude of mankind."

This confession from Lord Morley is hardly less interesting than the confession made by John Stuart Mill in his autobiography of the "permanent happiness" that Wordsworth brought to him. And these two confessions confirm the statement of Matthew Arnold that "in poetry, where it is worthy of its high destinies, our race as time goes on will come to find a surer and ever surer stay."

They show how poetry could touch the modern intellect with spiritual consolation and could sustain it at a time when the creeds were dissolving. They show how it could bring what Lord Morley called the "infinite" even into the otherwise intellectual lives of distinguished agnostics.

And Wordsworth accomplished this by what may be called his passionate repose in the one great certainty of his life. The visible universe was to him a perpetual shadowing forth of the invisible; and it was his mission, as it was that of Dante, wherever God touched him through Nature, to record it in his poetry for his fellow-men. The most glorious heights of his poetry are precisely those in which this is most manifest, moments when he was actually able

> To express what then I saw, to add the gleam,
> The light that never was on sea or land,
> The consecration, and the poet's dream.

Lord Morley, despite his belief in the "infinite" which he says Wordsworth "introduces" into common life, was inclined to be sceptical as to the existence of system and ordered philosophy in Wordsworth. We shall regret this the less when we have carefully considered the meaning of those phrases "system" and "ordered philosophy" in their relation to the "infinite" on the one hand, and to our own small lives on the other. But it is quite certain that Wordsworth wrote these words :

> Not without hope we suffer and we mourn,

and their sober sincerity was based on certain very definite and consistent beliefs.

It was not the hope of the modern agnostic who, after many revolutions, looks forward to a time when the sanitation of our cities will be somewhat more satisfactory than it is at present ; and, soothed by that blessed vision, can contemplate with equanimity the final extinction, at a distant but quite definite period, of the entire human race. If it were for this that we were to "progress," Wordsworth would have expressed no more hope than Mr. Thomas Hardy. But he did not believe that the dust could choke the highest that we know, and obliterate all that the human spirit has builded. One sure certain day, if this vision be true, we shall reach this final demonstration that the horse is drawn by the cart. But, even if this be a "system," we can afford to be sceptical about it so long as we are able to catch even one intuitive glimpse of the nobler world that Wordsworth knew, a world that in the very nature of things must be utterly beyond the scope of all our systems.

> Our birth is but a sleep and a forgetting:
> The soul that rises with us, our life's star,
> Hath had elsewhere its setting,
> And cometh from afar :
> Not in entire forgetfulness,
> And not in utter nakedness,
> But trailing clouds of glory do we come
> From God who is our home. . . .

We may dismiss this as Platonic metaphysics; but, if we are to dismiss every one of the greatest passages in poetry as idle, if we are to dismiss the increasing power of their spiritual witness through two thousand years as illusory, we are placing criticism in a very strange position. It is very easy to dismiss these things one at a time, as if the real greatness of poetry were to be found somewhere else; but we cannot dismiss them all together without self-stultification. Wordsworth himself was quite ready to admit his lack of "system"; he was ready, with a profounder humility and sincerity, to base his faith upon

> those obstinate questionings
> Of sense and outward things,
> Fallings from us, vanishings;
> Blank misgivings of a Creature
> Moving about in worlds not realized,
> High instincts before which our mortal nature
> Did tremble like a guilty thing surprised: . . .
> Hence in a season of calm weather,
> Though inland far we be,
> Our souls have sight of that immortal sea
> Which brought us hither,
> Can in a moment travel thither,
> And see the children sport upon the shore,
> And hear the mighty waters rolling evermore.

"We may dismiss Wordsworth's metaphysics, we may dismiss Wordsworth's theology," said Lord Morley; and it would be less easy to disagree with him if it were not in those very passages where Wordsworth "introduces the infinite" that Lord Morley finds his greatest poetry—passages which every critic accepts as his greatest. Take, for instance, those exquisite lines on the skylark, lines even more beautiful, because more profound, than any in the more famous ode of Shelley:

> Leave to the nightingale her shady wood:
> A privacy of glorious light is thine;
> Whence thou dost pour upon the world a flood
> Of harmony, with instinct more divine:
> Type of the wise, who soar, but never roam;
> True to the kindred points of heaven and home.

We cannot dismiss that heaven without dissolving the whole structure of the poem into thin air.

It is useless to say, as Lord Morley does, that Wordsworth's claim to greatness rests on the sincerity with which he idealizes the vast universe around us.

That, indeed, is a very vague statement where Wordsworth was both lucid and profound. How shall we idealize the universe, we poor pessimists, without hope or faith, who see so clearly—as Lord Morley points out—that the universe is a cruel and blind thing? Shall we "introduce the infinite"? And if we do, even with a small *i*, shall we be guilty of "theology" or "metaphysics"? Perhaps, after all, it would save our latter-day pessimists from a good deal of intellectual fog if they went straight back to the first four words of Genesis, and used a word that, while it commits them to little more than the "infinite," has yet a content that has been hallowed into significance by time, and even though it be anthropomorphic, at least raises to the *n*th the highest that we know, instead of dissolving the universe into something less than ourselves.

But Wordsworth looked before, as well as after. Lord Morley flatly contradicts the poet's gentle assertion that "one impulse from a vernal wood may teach us more of man, of moral evil and of good, than all the sages can." Well—perhaps a little attention to the order of Wordsworth's thoughts, or even to the words criticized in such poems as *Tintern Abbey*, may help us here. He says, to begin with, "*may* teach us." Secondly, he was himself a living example of what thousands of other lives have proved, that

> Nature never did betray the heart that loved her,

and may even have something to teach it. Those, therefore, who have in the very slightest degree experienced a truth which is as old as human life may flatly contradict the critic's contradiction. Thirdly, we may point out that Wordsworth's lines were not simply about "a vernal wood"; they were about the impulse received by a human heart. There is an interaction here as delicate as that between heaven and earth in the poem on the skylark. And if further elucidation be necessary, we may add those wonderful lines which are among the very greatest in English poetry, lines that emphasize once more the fact that we receive from Nature what we give:

> Thanks to the human heart by which we live,
> Thanks to its tenderness, its hopes and fears,
> To me the meanest flower that blows can give
> Thoughts that do often lie too deep for tears.

We have also to remember that for Wordsworth this world was the shadowing forth of the Infinite Being, and the image of the sea returns to us, a motion and a spirit that impels all thinking things, even through the "vernal woods"; so that in the smallest leaf or spray there might be said to be a real Presence.

The mighty import of this sublime poetry defies analysis. Wordsworth himself in many an exquisite strain of music seems to lament his own inability to hold in sight for ever the gleam of those visionary waters:

> Many a tempting isle,
> With groves that never were imagined, lay
> 'Mid seas how steadfast! Objects all for the eye
> Of silent rapture; but we felt the while
> We should forget them; they are of the sky,
> And from our earthly memory fade away.

But this does not destroy the exquisite balance of his soul between the great extremes of the universe ; between the ebb and flow of light and darkness. And if one had to choose one only guide through the perplexities of life to the unseen goal, what friendship, what consolation, what enduring faith we should find in walking with this one poet towards the sunset and the immortal sea :

> What ? You are stepping Westward ? Yea,
> 'Twould be a wildish destiny
> If we, who thus together roam
> In a strange land, and far from home,
> Were, in this place, the guests of chance.
> Yet who would stop or fear to advance,
> Though home or shelter he had none,
> With such a sky to lead him on ?

ACCEPTANCES

THE great enlargement of the fields of human thought during the last century has had one serious consequence which, though commonly disregarded at the moment, may yet be a disastrous one, in the view of posterity, for much of our modern literature. Art shows signs of forgetting its "length," and life is now not only brief, but very broad also, and astonishingly quick in movement and growth. The age has outgrown its literary garments; not so much in poetry, as has been suggested—for poetry has always and necessarily dealt broadly with a more permanent subject-matter—but it has outgrown its literature in a hundred other directions. If the robe is drawn up to cover the shoulders, the knees are left bare. If we consider the feet, the head and the heart suffer. The old completeness of view, the old single-hearted synthesis which saw the complex world in its essential unity, saw it steadily and saw it whole, man as a soul and body, life and death as a march to immortality, and the universe as a miracle with a single meaning, all that white light of vision has been broken up into a thousand prismatic and shifting reflections. We are in danger of losing the white light, not because it is no longer there, but because the age has grown so vast that we cannot co-ordinate its multifarious and multicoloured rays. Analysis has gone so far that we are in danger of intellectual disintegration. It is time to make some synthesis, or we shall find ourselves wandering through a world without meaning. We are already in such a position that our eagerness to accept new and often doubtful gains makes us drop our old certainties out of both hands. There is a tendency all over the world—more dangerous, because more persistent than ever before in the history of mankind—to grasp at little shadows and lose the great substance.

In every age there has always been a tendency to belittle the work of immediate forerunners. Progress may depend to a certain extent on these reactions and narrow rejections, though they be only a transitional stage to a wider view and a larger acceptance. But quite apart from the, perhaps, natural desire to seize the torch from the hands of our predecessors, and to belabour them about the head with it, there is a tendency to throw away the torch altogether and to go on our way tossing up coloured crackers ; to throw the torch of Wordsworth into the gutter and proceed with a meaningless splutter of epigrammatic squibs, whose charm is in the unexpectedness of such explosions as even their holders cannot foretell or direct ; or to throw away the torch of Turner and dance down to posterity in a blaze of post-impressionist Bengal lights. Certainly we want our new little discoveries ; but we do not want to kick away the whole world from under our feet as soon as our fingers have touched the new toy. There are certain possessions of ours, certain heirlooms that we must accept from the past, or perish. Our reactions and our rushes after novelty did not matter very much so long as we accepted these. There are, perhaps, not very many, but there are certainly some essential and traditional acceptances which are the first postulates of our civilization, the basic elements of life, thought, art, literature, and religion for all time. These basic elements, these postulates, a large part of our recent literature has been in the habit of accepting tacitly for the purpose of making books which could not otherwise be made at all, and, at the same time, rejecting them and forgetting them in its rush after novelties which, unless they could be brought into harmony with those primary postulates, it was the business of literature to wave aside as chimerical and false. By this simultaneous acceptance and rejection certain modern works of superficial brilliancy are turned into complex and complete examples of logical fallacy. The disease may be encountered in its simplest form away from the intellectual and artistic fields altogether. There are various pseudo-sciences and pseudo-religions, "New Thoughts" and "Higher Thoughts," and other solemn quackeries which have made astonishing headway among the more gullible sections of the community. Some of these quaint religions base themselves on a singular acceptance of a few detached phrases from the New Testament. Their apostles, having heard that "faith can move mountains," cry "Eureka," shut their ears and will hear no more. Everything else in the book that might qualify, interpret, or add to that knowledge, they are content—or determined—to reject or ignore. They have hit upon that sentence, and—let the sun blacken and the moon be blood—they will base upon that one sentence a fantastic, lop-sided, jerry-built modern creed which is to replace all the great synthetic labour of the centuries, and to improve upon all the logical and spiritual fabric of Christianity. And in what does it end?

Having swept away all that nobler fabric, they will substitute for the old belief in the immortality of the soul a half-hysterical notion that by some kind of mechanical self-hypnotism you may cure a cold, or that by making your mind a blank and by staring fixedly at a printed form of words you may escape what is to them, not the change, but the annihilation, of death. To such materialism does their "new spirituality" lead them, and to such an absurd tangle of self-contradiction; and these cases are only symptomatic of a widespread evil, arising almost always from a rejection of the truth laboriously acquired in bygone centuries, and the insistence on a small fragment of the truth.

We do not want to be fettered by the past; but we may be very sure that we cannot each make the world over again for himself, and that there is no possible progress in cutting ourselves adrift from the past, any more than there would be in losing our individual memory. "If there be no God, we must make one," said the French revolutionists; and so extraordinary in its effects is the modern vagueness, the modern loss of memory, of tradition, with regard to the fundamental principles which were once safely left to the keeping of a great historical religion, so completely have the masses of men broken free from its broad and profound philosophical system, that our intellectuals may well ask themselves if they have gained anything whatever, even in their own limited intellectual field, by dropping the substance of that system. Certainly there is need, and urgent need, of something to take its place; if not a natural development of it, at least a religion based in some way upon those essentials which we must, perforce, accept from the past; and, when we have made this great synthetic philosophy of life and death, joy, and—be it remembered—pain and suffering, in all their aspects, it will, after all our striving, be indistinguishable from the highest form of the religion we have lost. But it will take us very much longer to achieve than if we had been content to accept and develop the good we already had. The question becomes a little more serious when it is clear that our individual intellectuals have failed to do the work of natural development, failed to make their greater synthesis, not because they were too big for their age, but because their age was too big for them;

not because they had made new discoveries, but because they were unable to bring the new into relation with the old, unable to deal with the multiplicity of things, overwhelmed with details, drowned in analysis. Over and over again we find them speaking of "institutions" and "forms" as things utterly contemptible to the free soul. What their "free soul" may be they do not tell us, but they certainly forget that the universe itself is an institution and a matter of form. It is becoming clearer every day now that in the latter half of the nineteenth century our men of science, from Darwin downwards, were simply doing in an intellectual way what the New Thought sects are trying to do in an unintellectual way. One has only to discover Darwin's attitude towards beauty, music, and literature, to realize what tremendous substances he had dropped because his hands were full of beetles. He was like a man who should explain a great musical symphony (quite accurately so far as he went) by tracing the cat-gut and wood of the instruments to their sources, and forget both the significance of the music and the mind of the Composer. The men of science were not exactly clutching at shadows—though Shakespeare's summary of their universe as the insubstantial stuff of dreams still holds good in the last analysis. They were, however, clutching at small particular laws which were, and are, of immediate value, but are insignificant as scraps of paper tossed into a stormy sea, when compared with the religion of Dante or Milton for example, from the point of view of philosophy and in the light they throw upon the universe as a whole, spiritual and material, on the meaning of existence, and on our relations to God and our fellow-men.

We do not destroy science because Darwin made a striking contribution to it; for science readjusts herself with very little trouble, and still claims and includes Darwin as her son. But religion is a science that includes all other sciences. It gives us an incomparably greater synthesis than any that the secular sciences can make, and it is no more stationary than they. It moves more slowly because it is greater, and its essentials do not change. Yet, even now, we may catch up the cry of Galileo and say with profounder truth, "*It moves!*" But we must take a larger view of the heavens even than Galileo. Science may be the moon of truth; but Christianity is the whole universe of suns and stars, all-embracing, and though apparently so still, sweeping through the illimitable spaces, without and within us, on its own triumphant way. Darwin had hardly published his *Origin of Species* before his work was assimilated in the vast system of Christianity, brought into relation with it, into unity with it, not as evolution now, but as redemption. A few years hence his originality will be as fully incorporated, swallowed up in religion, as the astronomical originality of Galileo. But it is religion that will be able to cry, "*It moves!*" For religion accepts, accepts, accepts. It demands greater tests than those of secular science, but when they have been made it makes the synthesis. Its strength is this—that its fundamental acceptances are simply those that are necessary to all men in one form or another; that its last entrenchment is, indeed, an unshakable rock; that the first four words of its Book are these: *In the beginning, God.* Whatever else there may be to accept, winged men in Mars, or elephants with silver tusks in Martaban, it has only to bring them into relation with that. There is no possibility of religion dropping that substance, any more than there would be of a botanist denying the existence of the earth because he had found a perambulating flower upon it. In the same way Christianity has accepted the fact that there are pain and suffering upon the earth, and she has made her synthesis, taken pain and suffering to the heart of the Eternal and bidden Him, too, to bear them, with a sterner clarity of logic than any defiant Prometheus. Our individual habit at the present day, and especially in literature, is to seize on a novel presentment of the problem and jump at an evasion of the one little difficulty with cries of "Give us a religion of pure beauty and joy." We drop the substance, the reality, both of our own immediate world and of the Eternal, by forgetting to make any synthesis at all. We lose sight of our first acceptance amidst the multitude of details, and abandon our last entrenchment to the cynic and the pessimist.

Whole volumes that stand high on the present-day roll of fame are vitiated by this self-annihilating habit. Turn the pages of almost any of our modern pessimistic writers, poets, and novelists, and it is almost safe to say that the more nearly they approach the great problem the more certain are they to destroy the value of their work by a fault which is as inartistic as it is illogical, for artistic form is impossible without logic, and harmony—if not rhyme—impossible without reason. Harmony, in fact, is itself a subtle kind of orderly logic, the golden mathematics of beauty. Again and again, however, in writers of great distinction at the present day, one finds that not only are the great primary and universal acceptances of mankind throughout the growth of Christendom dropped at the sight of a particular detail which it was rather their business to bring into relation with those acceptances, but one even finds them dropping their own acceptances. I know not how many of them use the name of God when it serves their dramatic or emotional moment, and forget that sudden acceptance on the next page; but I do know that there are far more startling and more serious logical somersaults in the literature of the present day than was possible in any former century, before we became wealthy enough to forget our wealth and dream that we are paupers. See what play we have made with the pain and suffering of the world. How we will affirm, nay, almost accept the strong assurance of our fathers, that our life has, at any rate, a meaning, and that if death clashes with that meaning, then death is not the end. How we will affirm (on political grounds) that human life is sacred, and in the very next chapter how we will drop that substantial acceptance because there has been an earthquake, and how we will promptly wail to the stars that we are certainly trapped in an ungoverned and meaningless world, and that it is a mockery to speak of the love and justice of God. Yet, long ago, Pascal was able to bring all these things into harmonious relation with one another, simply by accepting all the factors and going deep enough. Christianity, from the beginning, has made a synthesis at least wide enough, deep enough, and logical enough to justify the God who sends His rain upon the just and the unjust, the creative, self-sacrificing God who dies into immortality with the meanest of His mortal creatures. All that we can do is to deny explicitly or implicitly the first and most important and only essential factor of the problem—*In the beginning, God.* The listeners to a symphony at least wait to hear how the musician brings his warring notes, his necessary discords, to their harmonious solution ; and Christianity has, at least, been logical enough to say, for instance, that death is not the end. We cry that we are agnostics, that we do not know—then assume that we do actually know it to be the end, in exactly the fashion of the pseudo-philosophers described above ; and, on the strength of that quite unjustified and illogical assumption, we declare the world to be meaningless, and the Power behind it—whose existence we probably deny on the next page—to be a hideous, grinning Mockery and a blood-stained Jester.

It is not enough that in the next chapter, at the sight

of a sunset, or of some triumphant human accomplishment, we should say something else. Or if it be enough for us, we may be very sure that it will not be enough for posterity, which will compare our self-contradictions with the harmonious work produced under the great synthetic system of a logical, even if human and incomplete, religion and philosophy. It is not a question of varying moods, which are legitimate and necessary enough in the literature of any age. It is the far more serious question of the intellectual integrity, and even of the logical and artistic form of our work. At one moment we write as visionary prophets of the absolute beauty, and in the next paragraph we are prostrate pessimists before a grinning skull. At one moment Stevenson tells us that the artist is a mere butterfly of pleasure. At another he describes the height of art as a stately music! "Enter God!" and "Ah! but you know until a man can write that 'Enter God' he has achieved no art, none!" We all accept Stevenson nowadays as one of the most lovable writers of his century; but I wonder which of his statements we are to accept, and if we accept the latter—which had deep feeling in it—why we are to accept it only for the moment? If we are to accept the first part of *Pulvis et Umbra* and its assumptions of complete agnosticism, how are we to allow him the force of those final "God forbids," which imply such tremendous assumptions?—unless words have no meaning at all, and then, of course, we must abandon the quest. Surely we need a synthesis, a white light again. Our optimists are shutting their eyes to the suffering of the world, and bidding us worship Apollo and Aphrodite. Our pessimists are shutting their eyes to the joy of the world and bidding us abuse an eyeless Blunderer. Our materialists deny us room for the soul, and then write a lyrical love-chapter in which—unless words are quite meaningless—they see the angels of God ascending and descending. Our idealists declare the glory of God, and then refuse His kingdom in heaven, earth, or the waters under the earth. With the exception of the very few works in prose which were produced in some accord with Christianity, almost the only prose creative work of recent years which is of a harmonious and logical form throughout is to be found among books that avoid the "solemn music" altogether, books like *Treasure Island*, where the author possesses himself, is at unity with himself, and runs no risk of floundering in deep waters. But surely this is to a certain extent a condemnation. For we do, and must, accept that test of the stately music. Without it there is no art, no great art at any rate. It is necessary for us to have once more that unifying view of life the lack of which—as the greater Caird wrote—"has made knowledge a thing for specialists who have lost the sense of totality, the sense of the value of their particular studies in relation to the whole; it has made action feeble and wayward by depriving men of the conviction that there is any great critical aim to be achieved by it."

Our work in this twentieth century will be to find that dominating critical position, to see that we are ruled from the centre, not from the circumference. Mere individualism means the disintegration of modern civilization. We must find some principle of unity, and to find it we must make certain fundamental acceptances of a judgment that is more than private judgment.

"To find and maintain this central critical position," says one of the most brilliant of the younger thinkers in Germany, "is the whole salvation of man, and all social work is without foundation if it be not inspired and directed from thence."

It cannot be found by cutting ourselves adrift from all the past, or by individualistic anarchy. One of the truths that we acknowledge and ought to accept, but forget and drop in our rush after new gains, or are too impatient to consider simultaneously with our new wealth and in relation to it, is the all too certain fact that great social and religious systems develop and move more slowly than the minds of individuals. They wait for the weak; and sometimes, I imagine, they wait for the strong, who have a little more mind to make up than the hasty innovator. But that will be as true of all great systems in the year 2000 as it is to-day, and it certainly is not a reason either for destroying them, together with all other fixed standards and ideals, in favour of general anarchy, or for turning the stony stare of British philosophy upon them. It is rather a reason for accepting them, accepting their long results of good, and—as we progress—developing them with patience. Civilization cannot survive without law; there is no law possible without certain fundamental acceptances; there is no law possible in the self-contradictory schemes which, if a large part of our recent literature and drama means anything, it certainly does suggest that we want. We want a government, a religion, beauty, love, and the laws of love, "whose service is perfect freedom." But we are in the greatest peril of forgetting once more that licence is not liberty. There is no freedom without certain submissions. Not even the traffic on the roads could progress without submission to law. Nothing is more admirable than the right spirit of generous rebellion against wrong. But at the present day it is necessary to be sure that we are not deceived by the mere name of "rebellion." The lonely idealists, the lonely rebels, at the present day, are not to be found among the crowds of self-styled "rebels" who drift before every wind of fashion; but they are to be found, sometimes, defending lost causes against an intellectual mob that is incapable of understanding its own deeper loss.

SOME CHARACTERISTICS OF MODERN LITERATURE

DESPITE the vagueness of the title which I have given to this essay, its aim is perhaps unusually definite. I believe that the time has come, in art and literature, as in every other department of life, when we must take our bearings ; when we must try to discover, if possible, the direction in which we are moving, and—still more important—the direction in which we ought to be moving. We ought to make up our minds about certain fundamental principles, and say definitely whether we really want or do not want some of the new ideas which—to speak quite plainly—the police are engaged in suppressing and many critics of art and literature encouraging. It is time, in short, to wake out of our Laodicean slumbers, and decide whether we are on the side of development and construction, or on that of destruction and a return to barbarism. The intellectual world is suffering to-day from a lack of any profound belief. It has lost its religion, and it has lost that central position from which it could once see life steadily and see it whole, under the eternal aspect. Rules and conventions, being no longer related to any central certainty, have degenerated into mere social codes which are subject to every whim of fashion. The ruling passion, with old and young, is the desire to be in the "movement," no matter where it may be leading ; and still more, the fear of being thought to be "out of the movement." It is a matter for curious reflection that these blind followers of the blind are doing precisely what they quite erroneously think was done by the nineteenth century. They are slavishly following conventions, and forgetting (simply because their conventions are new) that there are realities, and eternal realities; standards, and eternal standards; foundations, and everlasting foundations.

One of the results of the great enlargement of the field of human thought during the last century was the increasing tendency among modern writers to lose sight of these realities, and to lose their hold on any central and unifying principle; to treat all kinds of complex matters as if they were quite simple, and, where a hundred factors were involved, to treat a problem as if it involved the consideration of only two or three. It was a century of specialization, and each group of specialists strayed farther and farther from the common intellectual centre where they could once all meet. The result in art and letters has been a growing decentralization (or in the most exact sense of the word a growing "eccentricity") which may be disastrous. There are signs of it already on every side. On every side the same fight is being waged in art and letters as is being waged politically in Russia, a fight not between old fogeyism and bright young rebellion, but an abnormal struggle between sanity and downright insanity; between the constructive forces that move by law and the destructive forces that, consciously or unconsciously, aim at destroying real values, at obliterating all the finer shades and tones in language and in thought, and at exalting incompetence.

There is an enormous difference between some of the destructive movements of to-day and the progressive revolutions of the past. Up till about thirty years ago revolutions in art and letters had a way of adding something of value to what we already possessed. The new revolutions merely take away. They say, for instance, to the painter: "It is unnecessary for you to know how to draw." (The value of that statement, of course, can be estimated by the multitude that it admits into the fold.)

In poetry your new revolutionist invents no new forms—that would involve a difficulty, and he searches always for the easier way. He very often uses the old forms made easier. He says, sometimes, you should abandon metrical form altogether, and he believes apparently that the regularly recurrent rhythms of the tides, the stars, the human heart, and of almost every true poet from Homer to the present day, were an invention of Queen Victoria. His own contribution is what he calls "free verse," and, as Mr. Chesterton said recently, "you might as well call sleeping in a ditch 'free architecture.'" The movement is backward from the highly and delicately organized to the indifferent homogeneousness of the lifeless—halting on the way, of course, at various stages of primitive brutality.

But there is a more serious aspect of the matter than this. All over the English-speaking world this hunt for the easier way in technique has been accompanied by a lowering of the standards in every direction. The quality of the thought and the emotion has been incredibly cheapened, and the absence of any fixed and central principles has led to an appalling lack of discrimination. Literary judgments in many cases have become purely arbitrary. Sometimes they are merely a matter of the coterie to which an author belongs, and they are marked by an intolerance, a dogmatism, and an ignorance for which there is no parallel in our literature. The desire to break the continuity of our tradition has been fought by three or four outstanding critics. It has been met by Mr. Edmund Gosse, with the weapon of an irony as delicate as that of Anatole France. Critics of a later generation like Mr. Clutton Brock, Mr. J. C. Squire, and Mr. Robert

Lynd have also steadily sought to maintain a just balance between the old and the new. In the *London Mercury* some months ago there was an article by Mr. Clutton Brock which should be read in every educational institution of the English-speaking world. But the tendency of the moment, backed by a hundred influences, some of them political, some of them apparently originating in Central Africa, and others in the cinematograph studios of Los Angeles, is to submerge all the finer shades of thought, all the subtler tones of beauty, in the general flood of half-educated mediocrity, tyrannously ruled by little literary Soviets, the members of which are able to spread their views in slackly edited journals. Instead of endeavouring to comprehend all that is of value in our literature, these writers are continually endeavouring to eliminate everything but the particular result which they themselves desire to achieve.

The modern revolutionary, who merely uses the old forms made easier, does not usually know enough about them to recognize the really new and more difficult development. I say development because the really new is always a development. Your modern will congratulate himself on his freedom from the restrictions of Dryden, Gray, Wordsworth, Tennyson, and Swinburne, without considering whether he has subjected himself to any compensating law, or evoked the beauty that can only arise out of a difficult medium, rebellious to the hand and brain. But if our new revolutionary is confronted with a really new development, a new lyrical measure, for instance, springing out of the unspent and unageing fountains of our national poetry, with a throng of new harmonies, outer and inner, his faculties are about as much use as a basket of new-born kittens. He devotes himself then to the task of misrepresentation, by one of the ancient methods described by

Coleridge in the *Biographia Literaria*, or—and in this he must be admitted to be comparatively new—by sheer bluff and the parrot-like use of a meaningless catchword. Forgetting how Coleridge proclaimed it before him, he will proclaim that all poetry must now specialize in the making of "images," and he will turn a sublimely blind eye upon the fact that all the great poets from Homer to the present day have filled their work with "images," and that they had the advantage of including other things too.

Another "modern" will specialize in great "bleak" thoughts, of an immensely "noble" and impressive character, about the austere futility of human life and the august fatuousness of the universe. Such thoughts are easily discovered if one is a thought-hunter; and they are certainly no newer, at their best, than Lucretius. But, instantly, every other kind of writing becomes "shallow" or trivial. The note of joy and human affection is sneered out of existence by vicariously "bleak" critics. A steady disparagement of the intellectual capacity, and even the sincerity, of those who disagree with the great and noble conclusions aforesaid, begins to flow through the literary columns; and all the literature produced by those who have something to say and something to believe in is dismissed as "rhetorical." Tennyson, of course, is condemned for writing even those vivid and biting lines in *Locksley Hall*, so very much more realistic than any living poet has ever dared to pen—the lines about "the crowded couch of incest in the warrens of the poor"—because that is "rhetoric," and "rhetoric" is a word that your "moderns," with a social passion, will apply to any poet of greater power and broader outlook than their own, even when he is fighting their battles. They forget that there is not only the false rhetoric of the second-rate politician or decadent poet, but also a true rhetoric which throughout the ages has formed part of the highest poetry; that the Greeks of Homer often spoke rhetorically, and that this is no more incompatible with poetry than that they also spoke grammatically. They forget that Rome lives in the rhetoric of the *Æneid*; that the best of the speeches in *Paradise Lost* are rhetoric; and that a very large proportion of the great familiar passages in Shakespeare can be called rhetoric. Some of them—in *Henry V.* for instance—are even (Oh, hideous intellectual crime!) "patriotic rhetoric"; while in *Julius Cæsar* there is a blaze of rhetorical poetry that ought to make some of our fluttering and fastidious "moderns" shrink like startled fawns. The greatest of his sonnets—like some of the greatest of Wordsworth—are rhetoric. Even in Shelley—and in *Adonais*—the spirit of poetry and the rhetorical form are often inseparable. The *Ode to the West Wind*, from its opening apostrophe to its final rhetorical question, might be printed in a text-book on rhetoric, as a classical example of the art of pleading. When men are in earnest about anything, it is sometimes quite natural for them to plead; and in such a case it would be bad art to let them do anything else. But facts mean nothing to the parrot, and the parrot-cry "rhetoric" is used simply as an offensive weapon, or to bluff an innocent public into the idea that now, at long last, a coterie has discovered "images," and that everything else is superseded. The sheep who follow the coterie become, as Mr. Gosse said recently, "obsessed with an almost crazy fear of rhetoric," and they might almost as well be afraid of syntax. Indeed, in American anthologies, published by reputable houses, this movement, initiated in England, has even gone so far as the announcement that such and such a work cannot be true poetry, because it is so ultra-conservative as to be grammatical. The demand is for "radical" poets. The word has no political significance in America. It means only poets who can substitute "like" for "as" (in accordance with the captions of the cinematograph), poets who can blunt the fine edge of the language and obliterate the delicate shades and tones, poets who can break down their heritage and use their hob-nailed boots on the memories of their own most illustrious dead. It may be admitted that Longfellow is not a great poet—not nearly so great a poet as the Emerson of the *Threnody*—but there is not a single writer among the so-called "radicals" in America who could write anything comparable for a single moment with Longfellow's introductory sonnets to Dante, or a lyric like that which once fascinated W. E. Henley:

> I remember the black wharfs and the slips
> And the sea-tides tossing free,
> And Spanish sailors with bearded lips,
> And the beauty and mystery of the ships,
> And the magic of the sea.
> And the voice of that wayward song
> Is singing and saying still:
> "A boy's will is the wind's will,
> And the thoughts of youth are long, long thoughts."

This may not be poetry of the highest order; but which of the "radicals" could even approach it, and by what right are dozens of incompetent and dishonest critics confusing all real values and trying to teach the new generation to despise its simple beauty? There is, of course, no direct connection between the intellectual snobbery that sniffs at Longfellow and the grimmer assault that has been made elsewhere upon what the Bolshevists call the "literature of the bourgeoisie"; but the spirit behind these movements is the same, and it is an evil spirit—a spirit of destructive hatred. I have seen the exponents of both movements talking on platforms to men and women engaged in education, and the exponents of both movements are of the same type. They usually have a grudge against civilization, and nearly always an intense hatred of their own country. They are all great enemies of "institutions"; and, in many cases, they forget that the universe itself is an institution, and bump their heads not only against the laws of civilization, but also against the laws of Nature. Worst of all, they are frequently praised, almost passionately, by that fine old institution, *The Spectator*. That able editors should exalt this fraternity to the intellectual heights is to play the old game of sacrificing truth's allies to the enemy; and it is time that some revaluations were made in the contemporary intellectual world.

The almost malignant desire to depreciate the writers of a former generation who, like Tennyson in his landscape work, made technical rivalry difficult, has been accompanied by obvious and amazing ignorance with regard to the quality of his thought in his greatest work and its relation to the thought of his own age. The work of this great poet has been spoken of again and again with the contempt of complete ignorance, and occasionally of malicious perversity. An intellectual world as "sincere" as ours in its desire to set art and literature above every kind of propaganda (except that of its own political or personal prejudices) should be able to realize that the landscape work of Tennyson can be enjoyed for its own sake. When a leading "intellectual" dismisses Tennyson and Longfellow together as if they were of equal calibre, it is as if he were to put Gainsborough and Landseer on the same level. It is simply suggesting the thing that is not, and there is no excuse for it. I have even read an attack upon the "shallow thought" of Tennyson in which he was accused of not having faced the fact that Nature was "red in tooth and claw," the writer being beautifully unconscious of the authorship of a phrase which has become one of the chief weapons in the armoury of the modern specialist in pessimism. Even the morality of Tennyson has been impugned as unworthy of the young generation, who were—quite ridiculously—said to be in revolt against it; and, at the same time, in the columns of English journals something happened which is quite without precedent in the history of any civilized people. I have the documentary evidence to prove what I now assert, and I think the time has come for some plain speaking.

In a recent number of the *Quarterly Review* there was a review—an exceedingly able review—of a recently published novel, which I say without hesitation is the foulest that has ever found its way into print. Much of it is obscure, through sheer disorder of the syntax. My attention was first called to it by a column and a half in a leading journal, where it was said to be eagerly awaited by "select literary circles." I call the reader's particular attention to that phrase. The writer said that "its very obscenity is somehow beautiful," and "if this is not high art, what is?" A weekly journal followed with eight columns, in which the book was compared with Goethe's *Faust*. The critic who wrote this particular article is one of the most brilliantly gifted of the new generation. I do not make this comment to depreciate those gifts. I make it because I am conscious of them, and of the importance to our literature that gifts of this quality should be used to elucidate and not to confuse values in the minds of his readers. I am concerned, not with personalities, but with truth. I want to say as emphatically as I can that I am making, not an attack, but a plea for some of those honest simplicities of thought and art which the cynical mood of the hour is obscuring to our national peril. A leading novelist proclaimed the author of the book in question to be a "genius." Writer after writer took up the word, until the name of the author and "genius" seemed to be almost inseparable. Even those who shrank from this book acclaimed an earlier work by the same author as that of a "genius," quite unmistakably. (I am quite ready to deal with this matter separately, if necessary; for I have read the book, and it is contemptible in every respect.) The *Quarterly Review* is fully justified in printing its exposure of the critics who praised the more insane product, but even the *Quarterly* is unable to tell the whole truth about it. The technical quality of the writing is beneath contempt. An artist at least endeavours to select significant details, but this author simply puts everything in, chaotically. No word or thought conceivable in the gutters of Dublin or the New York Bowery is omitted. There is no criminal court in this country which would not brand the book as inexpressibly degraded; and yet only a short time ago, in a leading newspaper, I saw its author referred to as one of our masters. Weighing every word, I say that, whether we know it or not, this is nothing less than a national disgrace; a disgusting blot upon our national heritage; and it is all the more disgusting in that it took place at a time when some of the noblest work of the last century—work with human faults, but, as in the case of Tennyson, work that may outlive England as Vergil has outlived Rome—work of this quality was being depreciated and treated with a silly and ignorant contempt. One critic, in a leading journal recently, said "we resent" the fine defence of Tennyson recently made by Dean Inge. I have not noticed any resentment of this far more serious matter, which absolutely confirms that defence; for the author of this book in more than one passage echoes the fatuous depreciation of Tennyson.

I have cited the extreme case of this book, because it is a complete reduction to absurdity of what I have called the literary anarchy of the hour. The book was exalted as a work of "genius" by a system of mild condemnation—for, of course, it was "condemned"—just as others have been damned by faint praise. It ought to have been simply consigned to a sewer. Intellectual Bolshevism has brought us to a point where work of this kind is, even if condemned, regarded as work of "genius," while we may wait indefinitely before we find the leading reviews dealing properly with some of our best contemporary fiction. Let me make it quite clear that I cite this extreme case only because there are a thousand gradations of shadow before this blackest depth is reached ; and it is most imperative that attention should be called through this particular example to the thousands of other cases which are merely of the same tendency ; and to the gross incompetence or cynicism of certain sections of metropolitan "criticism." The book itself is utterly worthless and beneath consideration ; and it is too corrupt to have more than a brief and surreptitious existence. But what concerns us all, and most urgently demands consideration, is the appalling fact that a very large section of our metropolitan criticism—the section which is called "intellectual" and is most vocal—should have treated the works of this author as works of genius simultaneously with the condemnation of some of our noblest literature. A leading French critic said, "With this book Ireland makes a sensational re-entry into the high literature of Europe." And some of those metropolitan journals which are responsible for the formation of opinion in this country and allow their literary columns to advocate what they editorially condemn, accepted the statement with the characteristic respect which these literary rebels against authority will pay to every authority on earth except that of truth and right. The result is deadly to literature, for it confuses all real values in the minds of the new generation. It is not the young ; it is not the new generation in revolt that is responsible for this confusion. The confusion is produced by the cynical, sophisticated, middle-aged or elderly pseudo-intellectual, sitting in London and stimulating his jaded senses with the abnormal and the corrupt. They tell the young that these things are the hall-mark of genius, and the young are bewildered.

Genius ! What do these men know of genius ?—the clear water of the spring at the door, the water stirred by the wing of the angel, the Spirit moving where it listeth, and speaking, not through the lips of those whom the sophisticated would choose, but through the lips of the child, and the lover, and the poet. I open the pages of one of the poets whom they delight to dishonour as having no word for our own time, and I read :

> The year 's at the Spring,
> The day 's at the Morn,
> Morning 's at seven,
> The hillside 's dew-pearled,
> The lark 's on the wing,
> The snail 's on the thorn.
> God 's in His heaven,
> All 's right with the world.

That is genius ! The power, in eight lines, to reintegrate a disordered world, by relating all its scattered and fragmentary tones to the central and eternal harmony.

A good deal of scorn has been poured upon the last two lines of this poem and the intellect of its author by those who have forgotten or never known that it had any context, and that it occurs immediately after one of the most vivid murder scenes in poetry. Browning deliberately paints the world in its blackest and most evil disorder before he gives you that exquisite moment in which he reintegrates it and shows you once more " the glory of the sum of things."

That basis of the universe in an ultimate harmony is the first postulate of all thought, all science, all art, all literature. Without it there is nothing left to us that has the slightest meaning. And, indeed, a large part of our modern literature does seem to have reached that final stage of negation. It has reduced the world to dust and ashes and left it there. It has turned from the world in its completeness ; turned from the world that contained the souls of Shakespeare and Beethoven, and insisted on pointing us to the dust and ashes in which it says that these and our whole universe must end. It has turned from the things which we *do* know about the greatness of human life (for if we have any inward life at all we have experienced them), those great factors which can only be referred to something greater than themselves, some divine Power at the heart of the universe, and has declared that all these things are illusion ; while, in the name of realism, it has occupied itself with the dust of which we know nothing, except that, under the scrutiny of science, it does indeed become an insubstantial pageant.

Some of the most notable figures in contemporary literature have been telling us or basing all their work on the assumption that the world is an accident ; and it has been made one of the tests of a man's power in art and literature that he should be able to state a negative and despairing philosophy in a new and startling way, without the slightest regard to its truth, or to anything but its value as a means of impressing careless readers with the intellectual greatness of the author. For such writers as these, the secret of great poetry, the poetry in which Matthew Arnold could affirm that our race would come to find a surer and surer stay, would seem to be lost. And what is that secret ?

Perhaps the truest and most comprehensive description of the nature of poetry (and by poetry I mean the essential substance of all the arts) was made by Wordsworth, in some sentences that sound curiously remote from the present day, and yet are worthy of the closest attention, even from the charmingly sophisticated young lady who conducts the poetry columns of that wildly anarchistic and rebellious journal, *The Spectator*. "The religious man," he wrote, "values what he sees, chiefly as an imperfect shadowing forth of what he is incapable of seeing. The concerns of religion refer to indefinite objects, and are too weighty for the mind to support them without resting a great part of the burden on words and symbols, by a process where much is represented in little, and the Infinite Being accommodates Himself to a finite capacity. In all this may be perceived the affinity between poetry and religion."

All creative art, in other words, is consciously or unconsciously symbolical, and the mistake that has been made by modern realism lies not in its insistence upon "images" of superficial details and appearances, but in merely reporting them without regard to their significance as shadows of the eternal reality, or the possibility of using them as images of that beauty which is also truth. This is the sole aim of all the true poets and of every imaginative artist. Their songs and tales are, in their most tragic and in their lightest vein, touched with a gleam from a world beyond our own. For what is tragedy ? It is not a declaration of universal futility, a description of the painful things that may happen to an Accident from Nowhere or the annihilation of a meaningless toad under a nonsensical harrow. It is perhaps a farewell to everything in the world that we know, but it is at the same time a welcome to the heavenly powers. All great tragedy surveys the world under the eternal aspect ; and though it may be able to affirm nothing of the world beyond, it is in its very agony a postulation of that world. If you turn to the poets in their lighter vein you will find that Wordsworth's theory still holds true. When Toby Belch and Andrew Aguecheek call on the Fool to give them a song in *Twelfth Night*, he suddenly lifts above their half-witted and half-drunken mirth one of the most exquisite of all the brief songs of youth and love in the whole range of literature :

> O mistress mine, where are you roaming ?
> O, stay and hear, your true love 's coming
> That can sing both high and low.
> Trip no further, pretty sweeting.
> Journeys end in lovers' meeting,
> Every wise man's son doth know.

And in those lines there is a deep undertone of music which conveys far more than the superficial meaning. It is an instance of how the poet, as well as the musician, can take three sounds and make of them, not a fourth sound, but a star. He is dealing not only with terrestrial journeys, but with the journey to that land beyond our horizons, the land where all roads meet. It has a profound metaphysical meaning, though it is touched in as lightly by the hand of the master as a butterfly settles on a flower. The meaning is conveyed by the music ; and it is not to be estimated as one estimates the content of a sentence in a scientific text-book. But it is just this undertone of music that differentiates this poem from the mere drawing-room ballad, and exalts it to the realms of great art. It is just this undertone of music that the destructive minds in modern literature have never been able to create, to understand, or even to hear. When he speaks of the "true love that can sing both high and low," there is a suggestion of that music which George Meredith heard rolling through the universe from the heights to the depths, and from devils to angels; and the distance from which we hear it, the lightness of touch with which it is rendered, does not prevent our recognition of it. Though it is hardly more definite or less clear than a glance of the eye, it is in its own way an appeal to

> That Light whose smile kindles the Universe,
> That Beauty in which all things work and move.

Coming nearer to our own period, it would be easy to show how the theory of Wordsworth holds good for poet after poet. It has nothing to do with any didactic system. Wordsworth himself exemplified it nowhere better than when he first struck the note of that neo-paganism which developed later into the religion of beauty of Swinburne and his contemporaries:

> So might I, standing on this pleasant lea,
> Have glimpses that would make me less forlorn,
> Have sight of Proteus rising from the sea,
> Or hear old Triton blow his wreathèd horn.

The fire was caught from the hands of Wordsworth by that greatest literary artist of the nineteenth century whose name, until quite recently, it was hardly permissible to mention in certain intellectual circles. I mean, of course, Tennyson. Mr. Kipling once wrote in answer to a line of praise from Tennyson: "When the private in the ranks is praised by his general he does not presume to thank him, but he fights the better the next day." Mr. Kipling's early letter to Tennyson should, I think, be inscribed on the title-page of that complete study of modern poetry for which we are waiting. The new gospel of to-day, of course, is "intellectual arrogance." But self-conceit is a poor substitute even for youthful hero-worship, and a still poorer substitute for the gratitude and affection which filled the eyes of Southey in the presence of his never-failing friends—the mighty dead. There were many among the new intolerants who were bewildered by Mr. Saintsbury's recent inclusion of Tennyson among the twelve greatest writers of the world ; but their bewilderment has no remedy unless they are prepared to read, with proper care, a certain poem called *In Memoriam*. It is probably the greatest elegy in any language, not because this or that authority says so, but demonstrably.

It is the greatest because there is no other to compare with it in range of thought, or in the exquisite delicacy and quiet strength of its craftsmanship. But its thought must be examined in its proper historical relationship, and strength must not be confused with crudity or the mere absence of light and shade.

Most important of all, there is no other to compare with it in the unfailing pulse of that profound music which flows from the source of all great poetry. In eight lines he can give you a pageant of the process through which this planet has passed ; he can give it with the scientific precision of a Huxley and the profound music of a Lucretius. The simplicity of the words in those eight lines (they are almost all of one syllable) has doubtless misled many of our moderns into thinking that their moving tide is asleep :

> There rolls the deep, where grew the tree.
>   O earth, what changes hast thou seen !
>   There, where the long street roars, hath been
> The stillness of the central sea.
>
> The hills are shadows, and they flow
>   From form to form, and nothing stands.
>   They pass like clouds, the solid lands.
> Like clouds they shape themselves and go.

We may not all be able to affirm our clear vision of the goal to which Tennyson affirmed that universal pageant to be moving—but all the true poets, from the greatest to the least, have allowed us to see their music flowing in the same direction. Brooks and rivers, they all flow onward to that one immortal sea. Stevenson allows you to see it, even in his *Child's Garden of Verses*—a perfect example of how the poet can use small things to shadow forth greater things.

You find him carrying out his theory even in verses so purely literary as those which he addresses to the Muse :

> Resign the rhapsody, the dream
>   To men of larger reach ;
> Be ours the quest of a plain theme,
>   The piety of speech.
>
> As monkish scribes from morning break
>   Toiled till the close of light,
> Nor thought a day too long to make
>   One line or letter bright.
>
> Till last, when round the house we hear
>   The evensong of birds,
> One corner of blue heaven appears
>   In our clear well of words.

That glimpse of the sky is all that is needed to corroborate the theory of Wordsworth, and I do not for a moment mean to suggest that poetry and art have any direct didactic function to exercise. We find the same piety of speech directed to the same end in work which at first sight might seem to be primarily concerned with the revival of an interesting literary form, as, for instance, Mr. Edmund Gosse's *Ballade of Dead Cities*, where the same suggestion of an infinite horizon touches the forgotten walls and towers with the light of poetry.

Another modern poet has shown us how even our modern machinery lends itself to the uses of poetry, how indeed it may be treated as a kind of microcosmic symbol of the universal processes. As in *M'Andrew's Hymn*—

They 're all awa! True beat, full power, the clangin' chorus goes
Clear to the tunnel where they sit, my purrin' dynamoes.
Interdependence absolute, foreseen, ordained, decreed,
To work, ye 'll note, at any tilt an' every rate of speed.
Fra' skylight-lift to furnace-bars, backed, bolted, braced an' stayed,
An' singin' like the Mornin' Stars for joy that they are made.

It would be possible to give many examples from the best of contemporary poetry to show that all art at its finest passes beyond the material facts of this world and lays up its treasure elsewhere. There are, of course, forms of art which are purely decorative and at the same time fully justify their existence, but even these, in their rhythms and harmonies, are a part of and blend imperceptibly into the larger music of art and the universe.

In summing up, it can be said with perfect truth that never in the history of the world was there a time so fraught with danger to the great heritage that we have received from the past. Our literature shares that peril. We see the signs of an ignorant charlatanry, often—as one of its exponents has confessed—deliberately ungrammatical, taking upon itself to dismiss not only all former metrical English poetry, but the metrical poetry of all the ages, on the ground that those who cannot spell or master the elementary technique of their art have nevertheless attained to a subtler truth of expression. Again and again it is affirmed by superficial critics, whose tastes seem to have been formed by the cinematograph, that the crude language of a drunkard in a pothouse is a more vital and subtle means of expression ("red-blooded" is, I believe, the phrase) than the English language as used by the masters, with their exquisitely delicate shades of meaning and their infinitely subtle and precise tones and semi-tones. In America this movement has gone further than in England; but its initial impulse was given by weary critics in search of a new sensation on this side of the water, and they are frequently hailed as masters in our own literary columns. One of the leaders of this school in America recently published, says a great American journal, the following typical "poem":

> My shirt is a token and a symbol
> more than a lover for sun and rain
> my shirt is a signal
> and a teller of souls.
>
> I can take off my shirt and tear it,
> and so make a ripping razzly noise,
> and the people will say,
>
> "Look at him tear his shirt."
> I can keep my shirt on
> I can stick around and sing like a little bird
> and look 'em all in the eye and never be fazed.
> I can keep my shirt on.

"These men," said John Burroughs, one of the finest of modern American writers, in commenting on this "poem," "claim to get their charter from Whitman. I do not think he would be interested enough to feel contempt for them. These men are the 'Reds' of literature. They would reverse or destroy all the recognized rules and standards upon which literature is founded."

I am quoting, of course, an extreme case here, but the author of this work is frequently spoken of with immense reverence by poets and critics who ought to know better, and, incredible as it sounds, educational institutions (for whom John Burroughs is as out of date as Emerson) have given this work their benediction. There is little danger of work of this kind imposing itself upon the larger public. The danger is not so direct as that. The danger—and it is a very real one—arises from the fact that a very large part of the metropolitan criticism in both England and America has grown weary and cynical, and likes to amuse itself by waving aside its proper task and confusing the minds of the new generation by suggesting that to be new and unlike anything that has ever gone before is the sole worthy aim of any artist. It is only in time of rigid order that the destructive mind is really useful, and even then it is only useful as a means to an end—the construction of something better. The destructive mind can only exist when it is in a very small minority. As soon as it is in the majority the civilization by which it is produced comes to an end. At the present moment the destructive mind in literature is popular, fashionable. It is the conventional thing to be a rebel, and the rebels are patronized by the reactionary Press. In fact, the whole ground has shifted under our feet during the last ten years; and unless we realize that a revision of values is necessary, with some attention to the changes in the meaning of our former literary labels, there will be nothing but chaos in literary criticism for the next few years. We want all the new ideas, and especially all the new achievements, that the new age can give us; but one can hardly be regarded as a reactionary, even by the *Spectator*, if one asserts that our great new cities will not be built any the more quickly if we devote our energies to the destruction of Westminster Abbey. The predominance of the destructive mind in what I have called certain sections of metropolitan criticism is closely connected with that loss of the central position, that loss of a belief in the fundamental harmony of things of which I spoke earlier. It has become the fashion to estimate a man's power in art and literature by his ability to suggest the utter futility of human effort and the ultimate meaninglessness of the universe. There is, of course, a shallow optimism ; but I do not know that it is any more common than a shallow pessimism. I do not know that it is any easier to be optimistic at the present day than to be pessimistic. Those who take the view that, ultimately, nothing matters, are of little value in any department of life, and certainly they cannot produce the greatest art. If the universe is meaningless, so must be the art produced by it. There is, of course, a profound pessimism ; but its depths are not sounded by the discovery that there is a skeleton an inch beneath the skin of man. There is a profound pessimism in the Book of Ecclesiastes, but the greatest word of that Book is not in the proclamation that all is vanity, but in the moment where the writer is caught up into the universal harmony, and calls upon youth not to revolt but to remember, and does so in the recurrent rhythms of poetry : "Or ever the silver cord be loosed, or the golden bowl be broken, or the pitcher be broken at the fountain, or the wheel broken at the cistern."

We are sometimes told that those of us who profoundly disagree with the philosophy of futility must not venture to criticize or state our reasons for disagreeing with the eminent intellects who proclaim it ; but, if the appeal to authority is to hold good in this curiously self-contradictory era of rebellion, I for one am quite ready to make my appeal to the highest name of all in literature. Those who affirm that, because beauty fades and youth perishes, we are all the puppets of a meaningless power, were answered in anticipation, three hundred years ago, by the greatest of all dramatic poets, speaking, not through one of his characters, but through his own lips and from his own ever-living soul, and affirming that above all our tempests there is an ever-fixèd mark, a star "whose worth 's unknown, although his height be taken."

> Love 's not Time's fool, though rosy lips and cheeks
> Within his bending sickle's compass come;
> Love alters not with his brief hours and weeks,
> But bears it out even to the edge of doom.
> If this be error and upon me proved,
> I never writ, nor no man ever loved.

We talk of giving the new generation its opportunity, and our cynics are laying upon its shoulders the heaviest and dreariest burden the young have ever been called upon to bear. We are giving them only one-half of the message of their profoundest pessimist, the half that can choke their souls with dust. We are telling them that dust ends all; we call on great contemporary names in literature to emphasize it and to silence the reply of their own hearts, and they are not always able to summon up that vast cloud of witnesses which in all ages has pointed the human spirit to a realm beyond these voices. The editors of journals concerned with literature are making the most stupendous mistake if they think that the little metropolitan coteries who have been substituting cleverness for feeling, and sophisticated brutality for the simplicities of our fathers, in any way represent the great majority of the public, or even that part of it which reads literature. The claims of some of the new rebels to be representative of the modern spirit appear to be based on the extreme smallness of the sales of their books; but this does not prevent a disastrous confusion of values if editors of journals do not realize this and are not alive to their responsibilities. One of the great difficulties is that the critics who ought to be safeguarding the best of our literature are the very men in whom familiarity with it has induced weariness and a desire for anything that will tickle or scorch their jaded palates. But this is not what their audiences may justly require of them. The new generation is being confused from above and misled even by "educational" introductions to literature. It is quite ridiculous to suggest that the young men of this generation are themselves in revolt against the masterpieces of literature of former generations. I have had the opportunity of addressing audiences of many thousands of students in the colleges of the New World, and I have seen them again and again kindling to the work of poets like Wordsworth, Browning, and Tennyson, when they are given the faintest chance of appreciating it. Not one young man in ten thousand, among those capable of appreciating literature, will revolt against even the familiar poem that found, in the "first affections" of youth, the "master-light of all our seeing."

But our metropolitan journals have been dinning into their ears that there is no knowledge or device in the past that can help them, and no real hope in the future to which they are going. I know of nothing sadder than the sight of the young trying to conceal the intellectual wounds that the elderly cynics have inflicted upon them; for the quiet sadness of many of the more thoughtful of the younger generation arises from that bitterest and most desolate feeling of the human heart—"They have taken away my Master, and I know not where they have laid Him."